The ET-Human Link

Other books by Dana Redfield:

Nonfiction:
   Summoned: Encounters with Alien Intelligence

Fiction:
   Ezekiel's Chariot
   Lucy Blue and the Daughters of Light
   Jonah

The ET-Human Link

Dana Redfield

HAMPTON ROADS
PUBLISHING COMPANY, INC.

for the evolving human spirit

Cover design by Rosie Smith/Bartered Graphics
Cover art by PhotoDisc

For information write:
Hampton Roads Publishing Company, Inc.
1125 Stoney Ridge Road
Charlottesville, VA 22902

804-296-2772
fax: 804-296-5096
e-mail: hrpc@hrpub.com
www.hrpub.com

If you are unable to order this book from your local
bookseller, you may order directly from the publisher.
Call 1-800-766-8009, toll-free.
Library of Congress Catalog Card Number: 00-111927
ISBN 1-57174-205-0
10 9 8 7 6 5 4 3 2 1
Printed on acid-free paper in Canada

Dedication:

For my dad, Nolan Morse, salt of the Earth, and
Mother, the sea-wind at my sails.
You could not go with me on my journey . . .
so much greater your love for supporting me at
every stumble, and catching me up at every fall.
And Michelle, love most pure, gift of God,
given back to me . . . of your own will you came,
like a fountain for my desert heart.
And my siblings . . . Sue, Paul, Mike, Tim, Steve,
and Phillip . . . I am so proud of you all.

Contents

Once Upon a Time . . .

Extraterrestrial soul in a human body . . . how does it feel? Skin doesn't fit quite right, a couple of toes are skewed; these arms, no flap power; these feet, tripping over things on a ground too far from eyes too small; this mouth, set with too many teeth—alien dentistry conspiracy? Surely a cosmic mistake—this body curvaceously created to give birth in an age of too many who cannot feed nor clothe nor heal themselves of diseases of body and mind gone crazy from too many lies in the spellbound hives weighing down the limbs and branches swaying in the arid winds of intellectual debate over what is real. Lightning strikes, splitting the old trunk, opening the way for a Light Tree rising up out of the mists of consciousness, crackling with creative potential.

Seriously, one who has experienced contact and interactions with "Other Folk" believed to be extraterrestrials can only question the stories of our origins taught by human beings who seem no better informed in lost memories and lack of experience. This book is as much about who we listen to, and why, as it is an exploration of the question of "dual reference."

One day, exasperated with all this business, I blurted, "Who are these aliens really?" (Thinking about the forty-eleven Other

Kind described by experiencers worldwide, stirred my skeptic's mind to doubt that the ones we encounter are quite the cosmic fellows thought to be ETs.) In response to my vocal blurt, a "thought-gram" impressed instantly: *When you answer the question, "what is a human being," you will have answered the question, "what is an alien?"*

The koan smoothed the wrinkle in my mind for a moment; pause to remember that we are all one. Yes, but the Grand Notion does not relieve us of the challenge to know ourselves in this wonder world with the many kinds of people on the ground waking up to the presence of the multi-kinds of sky people gathered to help us birth a new kind of human being; or to kill the child in an embattled story that seems to replay like a needle spinning in a groove on an ever-revolving record. We are one like the stars in the Heaven burst into glitter to dance the Eternal Jig.

I use the term ET to mean the Other Folk, whether space age dandies bedecked in *Star Trek* garb, the rogue alien gooks of abduction, feathered friends of biblical yore, or balls of blue or gold light. Our perceptions are as varied as the wildflowers of a hundred fields. "Celestial ancestors" best fits my perception of the ones with whom I have conversed and interacted, the best my mind can fathom, based on my experience to date. The UFO presence—whether Galactic Federation or menacing fetal geek archetypes dancing in a consciousness about to descend the chimney—is still in the realm of mystery.

In any case, UFOs are a little about aliens, and a lot about human beings.

The question of extraterrestrial origins is really a question about human nature and origins, a multi-dimensional question about consciousness, evolution, reincarnation, communication, will, spirit, and love. Beyond this is the question: Why have so many of us been activated and schooled in a new realm of consciousness? Perhaps after a long journey in this garden of evolution, we are rounding an arc, soon to experience a new threshold some call the "shift," some call a new world, or a new age, and others describe as movement into a fourth or even fifth dimension of reality. I was told by my Source that the change would be "unprecedented," never before experienced by human beings. Preparations are elaborate and complex, involving the whole of humankind.

How does it feel . . . feelings were an issue in the contract to write *Summoned: Encounters with Alien Intelligences*. Readers may recall that *Summoned* began with a "feeling story" that was originally a letter to my editor (and chairman of the board) Frank DeMarco. When initially Frank asked how I felt about the ET-UFO business in my life, I stuttered and stammered, as if the word "feeling" were foreign to my ears. So I wrote him a letter, a story about hay. . . .

Muse, music, and art are the natural realms of expressing feelings, but here I was challenged to write with feeling about embattled and forbidden knowledge. If it weren't so personal, I would be forgiven for diving into foxholes to hunker down alongside the erudite, offering up wordy doxologies to the gods of intellect. However, I was a child of the message, "infused" at birth, "encoded" and coaxed to show the ruffles of my ET underwear. Hello, I am an ET-human voyager. What planet are you from? The ghost of delirious hope taps me on the shoulder to remind with a thrill that I am life's child in a belonging story in the Book of Becoming.

Prior to initiation in the "UFO catalyst" in May 1994, there was nothing in my life that indicated involvement with extraterrestrials. Nothing except for the appearance of implants in my hands in 1986; except for the contact in 1989, resuming in 1993; except for missing times in childhood; except for years of suspicious dreams about ETs and UFOs; except for a string of subtle mind links and "metafractals" all along the way, hinting that I was a stranger to myself. (A metafractal is a physical event linked to a metaphorical meaning.)

The ET-Human Link is a deeper look at my life and experiences, old and new; and, in this book are communications I thought were too controversial in the writing of *Summoned*. Or maybe I just didn't feel safe exposing so much of myself and the intimacies of my involvement in the UFO presence. But autobiography is only the backdrop for the quest to find the missing links. I examine "whole being" links, and reach into history's treasure trove for ancient legends to compare to ET communications and bold new scientific theories about connections between DNA and consciousness. And, of course, I can't write a book without an irreverent story. What is truth without humor? Jonah Blows It. . . . is a story that explores the nature of human will (chapter 6). As well, I explore other perennial biblical lore that I feel pertains to the UFO presence today.

There is life, and there are the stories about life; what is believed and perceived, according to individual experience, education, level of intelligence and awareness, and the particular ways in which each interprets what is seen, heard, touched, tasted, and smelled. The possibility of senses beyond these five is disputed by people who do not experience them, as is true in the case of alien spaceships appearing in our skies.

When life shows us something different from our story about life, it is the story that must change. . . .

Soon after we exploded the atomic bomb, alien spaceships whirled into our skies, perhaps through a hole ripped open by the explosion. It would seem a story hole, too, for all the tales that have ensued in the wake of the first reports of Kenneth Arnold's sightings of nine "flying saucers"; the Roswell, New Mexico, incident; and, the UFOs that buzzed the White House in 1952. The story expanded with accounts of alien abduction, beginning with Antonio Villas-Boas, Barney and Betty Hill, Betty Andreasson-Luca and Whitley Strieber, whose book *Communion* etched the face of the "grey" in collective consciousness. Soon, it seemed, the sky over everywhere was perforated with holes, through which descended the rogue aliens of abduction. Bewildered citizens of Earth began to report being snatched up to gaze at faces shockingly humanlike—but not quite—to participate in dramas that mimicked the most sacred and intimate of human acts, our most awesome creative power, the miraculous making of babies; a story perceived by many to have resulted in the literal births of alien-human hybrids. Maybe there are "hybrids" among us; maybe some of us are voyagers from the stars; maybe Mark Twain had it right: "I believe that our Heavenly Father invented man because He was disappointed in the monkey" (Bernard DeVoto, *Mark Twain's America* 1997).

There were provocative references in my long dream resume of the existence of highly intelligent children, dubbed, in my journals, "smart babies"; and when regressed to explore a missing time event in childhood, I observed non-human babies in fluid-filled containers. But early in my contact experience, I was invited to consider the "birth story" in a different light. Page 125, *Summoned*:

> We would not need to appear in ships and shine cone lights down if you were familiar with these altered states. But you are children in this respect, so we enact dramas. Do you not create dramas for your children, with bright toys and people in costumes? Your Santa Claus, clowns, puppets, all are used to teach your children about this reality. And we do the same.

> (Me: But your games scare people.)
> Yes, because there is need to accelerate. A person is challenged to hurry, catch up, see quickly . . . as you work to "bring Heaven to Earth," so to speak. Is not birth traumatic? You are in the throes of labor pains.

The birth of the "wonder child," and the "golden children" are metaphors imparted as symbols for the new human becoming (chapter 16). But please remember, I am only one person with one story of experience, and my "memories" and communication link are as questionable as anyone's. Wisdom waits for more to be revealed before final conclusion. It is in the whole of our messages and experiences that truth is glimpsed.

"We are the message," I said at the International UFO Congress in Mesquite, Nevada, in August 1999. We are the message, and we are the evidence. It seems almost a conspiracy that investigators would chase the dream of getting their hands on the nuts and bolts and smoking guns of the UFO, while we, the living evidences of the presence, were gestating in the miracle wombs of change. Abductees are like children plucked off the jungle gyms on the hard ground of the left-brain, to be born again in cradles suspended on a bough between left and right hemispheres. As we toddled, disoriented in a world that ignored us for the dazzle of new technologies, muse-babble was our language. But now we are beginning to find our voices. . . .

Deep into the book in a conversation with "Rowah," I was reminded of a little story I had written about a golden scroll. I had thought it not quite right for this book, but the words of Rowah caused me to reconsider. Writing the whole book was like this, one surprise unfolding out of another. But should I be surprised? When was life *not* surprising?

If this story makes no sense in context to the UFO enigma, wait . . . read on. By the end of the book, maybe it will (discussion in chapter 16). In any case, the tinkering of angels, a Scotsman, and a bit of alchemy prefaced examination of the missing links. . . .

The Golden Scroll

Once upon a time, there was born on planet Earth a child of her ancestors, and the ones who made them all. For this story, we will call her Evangeline. Willowy and tall for her age, Evangeline was ten years old. Her hair was long, and wavy, and auburn; her eyes were sparkling green; and, Evangeline wore the clean, drab frocks of a peasant girl. She lived with her parents and three older brothers on a small farm in a hamlet near the Isle of Forgetfulness where reigned a king and queen who ruled over everyone in the whole world, so far as Evangeline knew. Surrounding the castle was a moat, the watery abode of a green-headed dragon that hissed fire when peasants were foolish enough to broach the shores of the Moat of Memory.

Life on the farm was simple and hard. There was work to be done in the potato fields, fish and greens to gather from the sea, berries to pluck in the forest; and, the cooking, sewing, mending, repairing, gardening, and maintenance of the small thatch-roofed cottage that perched on a grassy knoll, wherein the MacDonalds lived at the edge of the hamlet, in clear sight of the great greystone castle on the Isle of Forgetfulness.

The many spires on the castle seemed to Evangeline so high, surely they must puncture the sky, which was at once Earth's ceiling, and the blue carpet upon which God trod. Maybe all those spires pushing up through God's carpet annoyed Him sometimes, causing Him to lose patience and make storms that provoked the waters of the sea to erupt in great angry waves, slapping the land and flooding the potato fields. Someday, would God become so angry He would plunge his long arm down and smash the castle into the sea? Evangeline imagined the grey stones broken into huge chunks to bob upon the sea like impossible boats. She knew it was a silly story in her mind. Castles were forever, and potato fields were like peasants: so fragile you had to treat them with tender care if they were to survive the storms and plagues of even short life spans. Sometimes Evangeline felt so tired, she wondered if she would live to be twenty-three, the age at which her Aunt Maida had died while giving birth to Cousin Donnelly.

But for all her worries and weariness, Evangeline possessed a sunny temperament. Frequently she stole away to the woods to read a small weathered book of verses, bequeathed her by Aunt Maida. Sometimes her brother Caleb would lend her his zither, which she would take into the woods, to strum the strings and sing to the birds and other small forest creatures that sometimes approached her, eyes glowing with curiosity . . . or so Evangeline imagined.

One day a velvety-brown doe stepped into the clearing, eyes sparkling like pools of liquid amber. Evangeline was so enraptured she dropped the zither. The deer gracefully loped away. There were creatures more awesome than human beings, Evangeline knew then. But the appearance of the lovely deer was only prelude to an event so extraordinary it would change Evangeline's life forever.

One day, as she was resting against the trunk of a mighty oak tree reading her book of verses, she felt a sensation of warmth, which made no sense, for it was a cool, foggy day. Much more startling than a doe stepping into the clearing, now the silver-pearly light around Evangeline began to glow a color of gold so rich and dazzling, she thought it might be God's breath. Later she would wonder how she could sit there calmly, as the angel appeared in the sparkling golden light. He was dressed in white and his countenance was so radiant, Evangeline could barely distinguish his features. His voice was as melodic as chimes, and as deep as rolling thunder. Evangeline felt his words like vibrations flooding her whole body.

In his melodic, thundering voice, the angel commissioned her to deliver a shimmering golden scroll to the king and queen who lived in the castle on the Isle of Forgetfulness. He then read the words on the scroll, an announcement heralding the birth of golden children on Earth. Evangeline would never read the words on the scroll herself, but she would remember the message clearly. Everyone was invited to serve as midwives to the golden children, who were the meek of ancient legends prophesied to become the stewards of Earth. All-merciful, all-compassionate God was extending the invitation to everyone—even peasants—to attend the birth of the golden children. When and where these golden children would be born, and who their mothers would be, was not stated, but Evangeline felt sure the miraculous births would happen soon.

The angel did not have to tell Evangeline her mission would be a difficult challenge. Peasants were never allowed on the Isle of Forgetfulness; much less did any ever gain entrance to the castle. But in his soothing, chiming, thundering voice, the angel said he would accompany her on her journey. He would be invisible to her eyes, but she would feel his presence as a soft warm glow in her heart.

He then rolled up the scroll and slipped it into a fine oblong leather sheath. Under no circumstances was she to remove the scroll from the sheath. The instruction was simple; she was to take the sheath containing the golden scroll to the castle and offer it to the king and queen.

Presently Evangeline fell into a deep sleep, and when she awakened, there was the leather sheath on the ground.

As the fates and hardships of the lives of peasants would have it, Evangeline was a woman of twenty-four, married to Terrence, and mother to Gregory and Dulsie, before she approached the king and queen. It was her husband, Terrence, who thought of a way to cross the Moat of Memory. A herbalist with a little knowledge of alchemy, Terrence had a dream that inspired him to concoct a potion of the quality of perfume. The fumes had no effect on humans, but Terrace was ninety-nine percent certain it would work to cause the dragon to fall into a deep slumber.

One night, by the silvery light of the moon, Terrence and Evangeline stole down to the banks of the Moat of Memory, and Terrence released the fumes from a special glass jar. They returned to the cottage, and, early the next morning, they hurried down to the moat. Floating on the water was the dragon, his pasty yellow belly exposed to the sun. Terrence threw a big stone at the dragon, and it did not flinch. Tucking the sheath under her arm and putting out of her mind the thought that the dragon might awaken before her errand was done, Evangeline climbed astride her husband's shoulders. It was then that she felt a warm glow in her heart, and remembered the words of the angel. He was somewhere near; she could feel him.

A robust man, six-foot-four, Terrence moved into the water, only his head and neck showing as he bore his wife across the Moat of Memory to the opposite shore. For reasons we can only guess, no villagers saw the two crossing the moat, and the silence around the castle was such that Terrence and Evangeline wondered if the potion had caused everyone to fall asleep. But as they clambered, soaking wet, up the grassy slope, four husky guards appeared. Their swords were sheathed, however, for they could see the two were just foolish peasants.

As the story comes down to us, we do not know the details of how Evangeline managed court with the king and the queen; we only know that she did, and was shocked to discover that under all their fine robes and other adornments, they were as plain-looking as ordinary peasants, with faces as weathered, not by work in the fields, but by the worries that etch the faces of royalty.

Standing before the king and queen that day, her hair in a tangle of wet curls, and shivering in her damp clothes, Evangeline was breathless as the king took from her hand the sheath with the golden scroll inside. From her throne, the queen leaned close to the king as he opened one end of the sheath, and shook out . . . not a golden scroll but a dingy piece of paper, as common as a butcher uses to wrap meat!

As he read the words aloud, the king's eyes bugged out with royal annoyance.

"Free my people," he said in a sneering tone.

Evangeline could hardly believe her ears. She nearly fainted. Terrence must have quickly escorted her out of the royal chambers; but like the details of how they entered the castle, we do not know how Evangeline escaped with her life, only that she did.

Soon after the event, on a snowy night when the wind was whistling around the cottage, and the fire was ablaze and softly roaring, Evangeline told Gregory and Dulsie about the golden scroll given to her by an angel.

"'Twas pure gold, I swear, saw it with me own true eyes!" Evangeline cast a helpless look at her husband. Reclined in the wool-stuffed chair, Terrence was smoking a pipe.

"But when I took the scroll to the king and queen," Evangeline continued, "it was no more than a dingy parchment, showing like old woman McAfferty's petticoat unwashed for forty days! And the words upon it were not the words of me angel!"

Gregory gasped, and Dulsie's hands flew to her mouth. "What were the words?" Gregory asked.

"Free my people!" Evangeline shot another look of consternation at her husband.

Terrence removed the pipe from his mouth, and leaned forward, his ruddy face aglow in the firelight. "Oh, the words were true, and the golden scroll, too," Terrence said mysteriously. "It was a trick of light . . ." He snapped his fingers. "The king and queen, they think themselves as rulers o'er the kingdom they see, and all the peasants, their slaves, and the wee folk, too; that's how blind they are. 'Twas not a *command* to free the people, don't you see? For do angels come with swords to make it true?"

Evangeline and the children shook their doubtful heads.

"'Twas a *tinkering*," said Terrence. "An invite to the birth of these golden children, in the only words the royal arses could hear for the brambles in their ears!"

The children laughed; Evangeline smiled curiously at her husband.

"Why, right there . . ." Terrence pointed a finger at Dulsie. "And there . . ." He patted his son's shoulder. "Ye are the golden children . . . in the seed ye will bring like the pollens of the flowers."

"Could it be so simple?" Evangeline smiled at her children, then said to her husband, "Why then such mad theater?"

"That the story would be remembered!" said Terrence.

Evangeline tossed her auburn locks. "'Twould have been a story dear without the king and queen, and nearly off with our heads!"

"Ah, my sweet Evangeline," said Terrence, cupping her face, as the children watched, wonderstruck at their father's mysterious wisdom.

"Don't you see? The world is all a mix of royals and paupers, and those that much lust for the one, and not the other . . . never seeing the wonders that be; the very golden faces shining everywhere with the secret that will not keep, as sure as babes will be born to be making more. 'Twas not the words nor the scroll; nor even the angel that bore the message. Ah, it was a merry tinkering, a twisting of words, inviting the royals to remember that people *are* free!"

"Free to grow potatoes and feed ourselves, I see!" Evangeline said, her cheeks flushing scarlet.

"Free to give birth to golden children," was Terrence's gentle reply. Stroking his crinkled beard, he gazed at the fire. "'Twas a miracle crossing the Moat of Memory, even by the scents of alchemy," he said thoughtfully. "And dangerous to embark upon the Isle of Forgetfulness, for we could have fallen under the spell."

"Spell!" Evangeline said.

"Would they live there imprisoned in that stone dungeon if they remembered the golden rule?" said Terrence.

"Now a priest!" Evangeline declared.

"A priest, a pauper, a peasant, a principle . . . it is the golden truth. How else are children born?"

"In a womb, I recall!"

"'Tis the truth," Terrence said, leaning back in his chair with a smile, as if he had neatly solved the mystery.

Evangeline would have cutted him, but she was stopped by the glow she saw in her children's eyes, the magic shining there, the story tinkering in their minds, no doubt to be embellished in the telling to their children, and to the grandchildren to come . . . all born of wombs . . . until . . .

"Ah . . ." Evangeline said, her gaze fixed on the gently falling snow out the window. "It is a story to keep in the heart until the day the Isle of Forgetfulness falls into the sea, and all remember . . . "

"The story . . ." Terrence finished.

Ah, the innocence, the trust, the faith; that's what I like about these simple folks. Has it not been true of humans throughout history? And for what do we keep the faith and remember the stories? For the love of humanity, whatever our curious and mixed origins.

Mitakuye oyasin . . . we are all related.[1]

---

[1] Lakota expression

Acknowledgments

The list grows longer every year. The acknowledgments in *Summoned: Encounters with Alien Intelligences* still stand as salute to the heart of humanity, increased now by new and renewed friends: Jim Veitl, Carla L. Rueckert, James McCarty, Roman Vodacek, Nancy Dorman, Jan Schmidgall, Donna Kenworthy, Chuck Mascarenez, Richard Frager, Kathleen Dusek, Janice Patrick, Dave and Derrick Dunsmoor, Connie Isele, Garrett Carlson, Larry Schmitt, Ann Dekker, Connie Mills, Jose and Barbara of the Back of the Beyond, Gary Anthony, Mary Rodwell and friends of the Australian Close Encounter Resource Network.

Thanks all for your friendship and support . . . love made visible.

Rebecca Williamson, thank you for expert editing, and the special care you gave to me, and this book. And Frank DeMarco, mentor, my timeless friend, thanks again. Thank you, everyone at Hampton Roads. . . . Robert Friedman and the rest of the family . . . too many now to name all.

And thanks, Rowah and El for helping me to write this book in the sparkles of the Creator cast before us.

Foreword

by Jenny Randles

One of the strangest things that ever happened to me was the time that I woke up in the middle of the night and I was not inside my body. Instead I was floating in midair looking down upon my sleeping self in a manner that was stunning in the audacity with which it challenged all that, at nineteen, I knew to be true. As if injected with a heavy shot of terror the incident was over. Catapulted back into my body I sat bolt upright breathing heavily, staring into the darkness, much too afraid to go back to sleep. I knew absolutely that this had been real. But I did not have the faintest clue what it was that had just happened to me.

At the time, my life was in catastrophic turmoil. I was at university studying geology, and yet nothing I was being taught made the least sense of this. Emotionally, I was in a flap as I had given up a university place two hundred miles away in Edinburgh, where I was going to be an astronomer, in order not to be half a country away from my boyfriend. And the night when this incredible event took place, I was preparing for the funeral of my grandmother. She had died suddenly in front of me whilst talking to invisible people that were clearly real to her, taking with her the last link with my spiritual home in the Pennine Hills from which I had been forcefully uprooted as a child.

This extraordinary phenomenon—an out-of-body experience as I now know it to be—hit me like a brick. I was told that it was a nightmare. I was told I was having a nervous breakdown. I was told it was just one of those things. Everyone I spoke to had a different way of dealing with it, but every one was a dismissal, a way to not have to think about the implications. I was never told what I wanted to hear: a reasonable answer to what had really taken place. All I knew was that something profound certainly had. When faced with the impossible, there are three ways of looking at life and reality. How you interpret this book may well depend upon which one of these visions drives your quest for personal truth and happiness.

Many today, sadly, follow a very somber course in which they see a bleak path laid out before them paved with chance, random acts that govern creation and leave human beings with no destiny or higher purpose. It is bereft of meaning, inspiration, and hope. But it is, I have been told by well-meaning materialists, not a bad perspective because it is an honest one. We should accept the limitations of the cosmos because they are the truths that we have uncovered by the exercise of our intellect; and inch by inch they have distanced us from the superstitions and the wishful thinking that have inspired endless wars and self-delusion.

For me this is a leaden view of life that, of course, I do appreciate may ultimately prove "true." But, equally, it may not be. And because it may be in error, I feel we lose far more than we can gain by existing on this basis. Far better, surely, to live with optimism that there is more to us than dust and death, although tempered by realism in knowing that there may not be.

For if you die in hope that there is a greater purpose and the truth is that there is not you will hardly be in a position to regret your error. On the other hand, if you deny such a thing until your final day you will awaken to the deeper truth seriously underprepared.

However, perhaps the biggest problem that rationalism faces is in responsibly encountering the wealth of experience shared by literally millions of people across the world and throughout history. Real life experiences—such as my own, and the many you will meet within this book—simply defy any way of perceiving the universe that disavows past lives, out-of-body experience, or alien contact.

These weird experiences are too often anathema; so much so that many rationalists descend to the level of condemning not just the phenomena but the witnesses. The worst failing of far too many skeptics is not to say "I doubt" (because that is always healthy) but to say "it cannot be possible," since defining the boundaries of reality assumes an arrogance that does not become our humble status. Even worse, many skeptics, when they fail to find rational answers that hold together very long, presume a simple resolution. As there can be no reality to such mysteries that defy their worldview, the only thing left is that the witness is making them up. That last refuge is to label whatever is left unsolved as hoax.

Yes, at times, people do make stories up. Certainly, we should not believe everything we are told. But all of my background working day to day with weird phenomena says that hoaxing is relatively uncommon. The vast majority of people who say they have had an incredible experience have indeed had an incredible experience. The only thing in doubt is what this incredible experience means. This leads into the second way of looking at life—the scientific perspective. It is often wrongly assumed that this is the same as the rationalist way. In fact, they are very different. The true scientist is a broad thinker. He or she can see the whole picture, think the unthinkable, and posit ideas that are well outside the structure of known reality. This is how Einstein understood relativity—by asking questions that appeared to have absurd answers, such as: Can we make light slow down and stop, and, if we do, then what would we see? Scientists collect evidence without making presumptions about it. They categorize and organize and wonder what it all might mean, but do not answer questions before they ask them. They seek patterns and suggest theories that might cohere, then design experiments that will allow them to determine which theory works best in the face of the newly acquired data.

To the scientific viewpoint, evidence is king. If that evidence contradicts a cherished concept, then it is the concept that is considered open to question, not the evidence. However, rationalism has a tendency to snipe away at the scientific thinkers with siren songs that lure them from the mysterious towards the mundane.

It is wise that the true scientist remembers the maxim that not everything can be reduced to experiments and data. Whilst scientists may be able to dissect atoms and comprehend the meaning of chemical equations, they cannot dictate why they love their spouses. Whilst their machines can show the subatomic structure or the vast reaches of deepest space, they cannot reveal one's inner thoughts or explain the visions that our minds may conjure.

The bane of scientists is to believe that they are omnipotent, that all things can fall to the steady march of reason. It is right that we should try. It is proper that we be aware that we can often fail, and that, indeed, it may be that in some ways we always must. Which takes us into the third way of looking at the universe: the idea that part of it is ineffable and permanently beyond our comprehension. This has several guises, such as the religious concept that something unseen and all-knowing guides our lives, or the spiritual one that conceives of human beings as both material body and immaterial spirit. But the key is the realization that there are experiences and phenomena that are simply not knowable by any normal means.

By this perspective, of course, understanding things such as out-of-body experiences or otherworldly contacts becomes less strenuous. You do not need to reduce them to equations. You do not need to force their repetition in the lab. You do not need to hold your hands up in despair and say, well these things just have to be fabrications. You can accept that they are just true, and move on from there to define what they teach us about reality. It might be argued that the paranormal is a battleground in which the armies of rationalism fight the champions of spirituality with science struggling vainly to act as referee. But this confrontational stance is needlessly destructive. For in truth there are things to be gained from each of these views on life.

From rationalism, we can learn the need to presume nothing and always question our observations. From science, we can learn the value of designing and testing theories that seek brave new ways forward. And from a spiritual viewpoint, we can recognize that there may indeed be hidden dimensions that reveal the ultimate truths that might otherwise escape our more obvious methods.

I have been fortunate, in some respects, to have had to deal with each of these ideologies: to train as a science teacher; to be taught to be a rationalist by many tutors; and yet to face the spiritual reality brought about by my own experiences that defied these worldviews.

These things, of which my out-of-body encounter was but one, were never extraordinary or profound in the sense of the phenomena that Dana Redfield has to relate. But they were enough for me to know that all the calculations and dismissive language that were ranged against them were insufficient to explain reasonably what they might mean.

Perhaps you do have to go through the lightning to understand the power within. And perhaps you can only go through the lightning if you are willing to walk out in stormy weather and face the consequences. Either way we are all changed by the events that befall us, and should treat them as a learning experience and a challenge to be overcome.

Unhappily, too many consider them a trauma to be fled. Often we fear whatever we fail to understand. Sadly, we do not understand what we fail to study. As such, it is easy to say no, to say that such a thing simply cannot be. But it is braver to say hang on—what if it this is actually true?

These are some of the things you will need when embracing the ideas and the experiences contained within this book. If you are skeptical, then that is fair enough, provided you are willing to give room to the possibility that your skepticism may be misplaced. If you are a believer, try not to merely accept what you read as being true, but to question other possibilities and consider other meanings. If you have had strange experiences for yourself, then appreciate the courage it takes to reveal them and face the rebukes that will surely follow. But also take heart from the knowledge that these things are not absurd or rare as you might have been led to believe. In fact, they are widespread and remarkably consistent.

What you will read in these pages may, or may not, amaze you. But this is one story in a world that is teeming with the strange and the mysterious. Ignore the implications, and you are walking through life with one eye closed.

Jenny Randles
Buxton, England

Trained in geology and physics, author Jenny Randles was director of investigations for the British UFO Research Association from 1981 to 1984. She has written forty-six books, including: *Sixth Sense, Science and the UFOs, Spontaneous Human Combustion, Time Travel, The Truth Behind the MIB, The Afterlife, The Paranormal Sourcebook*, and *The Complete Book of Aliens and Abductions*.

In addition, Randles is a consultant to the J. Allen Hynek Center for UFO studies in the U.S., and she has written many articles, and done extensive media work, creating documentaries for radio and TV, such as "Britain's Secret UFO Files," plus consultation on the production of two books based on the ITV series, *Strange but True?* (1993-1997).

Jenny Randles' most recently published book is titled *Time Storms*. Editions of her books have sold to twenty-seven countries with one and a quarter million copies in print.

Part I:
Intimate Revelations

To paraphrase an old Chinese saying, mystics understand the roots of the *Tao*, but not its branches; scientists understand its branches, but not its roots. Science does not need mysticism and mysticism does not need science, but men and women need both.

—Fritjof Capra
The Tao of Physics (1987)

CHAPTER ONE:

The Voice of Mystery

It is curious to observe that even scientifically trained researchers who accept the idea of multiple universes, or the few ufologists who understand the idea that space-time could be folded to allow almost instantaneous travel from one point in our universe to another, still cling emotionally to the notion that any nonhuman form of consciousness is necessarily from outer space.

—Jacques Vallee
Revelations: Alien Contact and Human Deception (1991)

In the beginning were the letters, then the numbers, then the communications began. In the beginning, I called them guides, and resisted the idea they were extraterrestrials. They knew me intimately. When they called me Little Sister, I did not blink, did not think, *why are they calling me that?* Maybe it was just a term of endearment.

First contact, in 1989, was brief, with a group intelligence who said they didn't have bodies like us, and had no names. I had read a book that mentioned an "invisible college," which had rung a bell inside me. So during meditation, I asked about it. Was this invisible college real? A "voice-thought" responded, calling me Little Sister, informing me that I would have a dream that night that would answer my question. Nothing like this had ever happened before. I knew it wasn't my own thoughts, not a "higher self," not God . . . who/what was this?

That night, I dreamt of being in a huge auditorium, packed with people. We were engaged in meditation, and other spiritual practices. The next day in meditation, I asked for them, and amazing me again, they responded. I pressed for a name. "Big Brother?" (I was Little Sister . . . figures.) Next, they suggested "Mountain," then "Tree," until I got exasperated with their jokes.

"Come on, give me a name that will impress me and tell me something about you."

"Clio."

After the conversation, I looked up the word. Clio is the muse of history. I was impressed because I had been studying ancient history. Who *were* these guys?

The contact with Clio was short-lived. After a few conversations of a spiritual nature, I asked them a question about my husband's work status and what they said turned out to be true. Then I asked them if my husband would pass a ham radio test. Oh, yes! And Tom would receive the call letters he wanted. But he didn't pass the test. When I asked Clio why they had lied, they said, "Don't use us for trivial matters." Knowing they lied, I could not trust them, and ceased the contact. Later I understood the lesson. Who, in the flesh, can we trust one hundred percent to always speak the truth? And yet we tend to expect the truth from telepathic or channeled sources. Contact with unseen intelligences is not an advantage. It's a responsibility. We are responsible to exercise discernment. Many have been made fools by passing on bogus channeled information. While at the time I was miffed by Clio's trick, later I was grateful I was forewarned not to trust everything that came over the transom.

The record in my journals (details in *Summoned*) showed a significant number of UFO-related dreams and "nocturnal events," from 1985 to 1989. When Clio inserted themselves into my consciousness, I was not of a mind to consider my dreams or the occasional light and sound phenomena as signs of involvement with ETs, this despite the evidences of implants in my hands in 1986. But later I would wonder about a dream that occurred a few months before the contact with Clio. I dreamt I met with Nordic kinds of ETs who were standing outdoors in a countryscape beside a disc-shaped silver spaceship. They commissioned me to write a book for them, and I agreed. My "dream self" knew the beings, but awake, no way did I think that such a meeting had actually occurred. In those days, my view of out-of-body travel, and various other adventures in consciousness, was detached and intellectual. I thought such things were possible, but if I were engaged in something like this during the night, wouldn't I *know?* You know when you know, and it is a kindness not to know too much, quicker than can be readily assimilated and integrated into the "daylight consciousness." The "veils" were thick in those days, serving as a protective shield. These were the days of education in preparation for more to come.

Four years after contact with Clio, communications began again, now with several different intelligences. Feeling a taboo against it, I didn't ask for names this time. As with Clio, the communications were telepathic—immediate and two-way. I recorded the conversations as they happened, never expecting to share them with the public. If I had thought that, I doubt the conversations would have been as light and as intimate. When I did consider sharing some of the information, it was always in terms of a novel.

From the fall of 1993, I was in contact almost daily, until the phenomenal events began in May 1994, nine months later. Contact didn't cease then, but it would never again be quite so relaxed; it was more formal, then taking on the characteristic of messages. Then came downloads of "encoded" information.

The advent of the phenomena that breached my physical domain (the "UFO catalyst") was cause for emotional and spiritual crisis. I felt betrayed by the intelligences with whom I had communicated. Why didn't they prepare me? They did. I would come to understand that it was part of the challenge to exercise my own mind to expand consciousness of these events and their mysterious purposes. As I moved through the catalyst, I suffered disruptions in relationships and residences. I was confronted with ridicule from the public, and suspicion in my personal relationships. The public didn't care, and my loved ones wanted me to "change back." Stop all this nonsense. But I couldn't. And then I didn't want to. I wanted to solve the mystery. How could such a thing happen to a person, and the public not care? This was the greatest mystery.

On the emotional level, I felt like a victim at first, but on the spiritual level, deep in my soul bones there was a sense that I was cooperating in a purpose. This faith carried me through the mental, emotional, and physical trials. The "dual identity" feeling was with me constantly then.

The dreams, the phenomena: all were expressing in the "language and signs" of alien abduction. And yet I couldn't "buy" the alien invasion story, the one that cast me as a breeder of hybrids, or a "plant" in some kind of conspiracy to overtake the world. Symbology for that was present in some dreams, leaked into some of the conversations, and presented during hypnotic regressions; but I had something others did not: nine months of contact preceding all this business, when the telepathic communications were intimate, and a different story was recorded in my journals, one that I understood in the feeling-remembering-recognizing way. I survived the phenomenal catalyst by keeping the faith of those early communications, remembering that I was connected to "old friends," who never left me, though sometimes I certainly felt they should have rescued me from my troubles. But they did send flower holograms, and sang to me in tones.

Over the years, from the dreams of extraterrestrials, to the communications, through the catalyst, and afterward, I was always of two minds, one skeptical, logical, and analytical—the "daylight mind," which tenaciously clings to taught knowledge; the other, the part that "just knows" things, but has no words to communicate the knowing until I wrestle with angels to give voice to the mystery.

It began innocently enough in August 1993, as an excitement building up in me, as I prepared to host a writers' workshop for a Seth Conference in Colorado. I wouldn't be talking about writing in conventional ways; instead, the focus would be on the magic of communication, which I had stumbled upon like a crystal rose left on the path by fairies.

As was stated in *Summoned*, it began when I noticed certain correlates of letters in names and words that were meaningful to people in personal ways. For instance, the letters MO were strung like pearls on an unseen string around my life. My birth name was Moore, I was adopted by Morse, I was living in Moab on Moenkopi Street, and my best friend's name was Montgomery. These were hints of something profound that seemed to overlay our lives like an invisible template.

As I prepared my presentation for the conference, my mind was galvanized by the mystery. I hoped to show aspiring writers something of the enchanted forest of communication beyond the concrete city of language. I was seeing something of the blueprint and inner architecture of communication, a mechanics of meaning hidden within the outward structures, like seeing, in a wooden rocking chair, the tree from which it emerged.

And so in a fire of excitement like nothing I had ever felt before, I whipped together charts and posters and handouts, marked up with the formulae and hieroglyphics of my discovery.

I was a child discovering a new face in the mirror, a soul behind the silver shining through.

By October, the presentation was a vague memory of kindergarten stuff, as I sat at my kitchen table, day and night, a student in the invisible college of communication.

It was both me bringing up into the light of consciousness memories, it seemed, of a long forgotten science of language, and angel energies attending, as if hovering over my shoulder, instructing, guiding, inspiring. The rightness, the passion, the ecstasy I was feeling made it seem that I was born to do this work, with everything else quickly receding into a pale memory of a life spent stumbling in the shadows of the sparkling world I was penetrating at my kitchen table.

The essence of the light was discovered in the letters of our alphabet, their very lines hiding mysteries of designs and energies unseen by eyes trained to recognize only the outermost meanings taught and recorded in dictionaries and thesauruses.

I was rediscovering the music of language and her minstrels were talking to me. But the form of the genius came not as melodies on the page, but rather as a hidden design glimpsed in the numbers behind the letters. These were discovered by analyzing the geometric shapes of the letters and how each related to the others, revealing an esoteric mathematical design that I sensed underlay every created thing on Earth. I had studied quantum physics, and the geometry of fractals was speaking to me. Like Benoit Mandlebrot, who discovered the mirror world of fractals, I was seeing its glimmer in language, the art forms of the letters generating pictures in the conscious mind that translated to meanings in the subconscious beyond the reach of the intellect.

As a cloud cannot be captured and studied under the lens of a microscope, it was impossible to record on paper everything I was seeing in the door of light between two worlds. The complex letter and number formulae were but chicken scratchings on the ground compared to the vision in my mind. The complexity evolved into drawings that captured the essence of concepts too large to be contained in words. Sometimes I felt a force moving my hand to draw at a level of artistry beyond my normal abilities.

It all made for a suspicion in the minds of observers that I had cracked my beam and had gone over the edge. But I knew it was not so; I discovered I was not alone in knowing about the hidden design in language. A friend recognized in my work a similarity to *kabbalah*, an ancient esoterica practiced by Jewish mystics. Ordering a couple of books on the subject, I confirmed that, indeed, my work resembled that of Jewish mystics. And some of the stories emerging from my work with letters and numbers were Jewish in tone and flavor, persuading me to believe that the ease and familiarity that had attended me at the table was suggestive that I had done this work before in a past life.

In one book about kabbalah is a picture of a Jewish mystic bent over a table at work. Though it is only a painting, I knew that man intimately: his soul, the passion that drove him, my own fire. It seemed my soul was Jewish, but behind and above that was this "other" beginning to penetrate my consciousness—the extraterrestrial element, like a breeze sighing through the branches of a new Tree of Life.

Tangential to my work with letters and numbers, contact with alien intelligences had begun. It was as if the energy of the work with the alphabet and numbers spilled so much light into my mind, it seemed to brighten out to a mystical landscape beyond the borders of my normal consciousness. And this, too, was familiar, and more intimate even than I had felt from the guidance working over my shoulder at the kitchen table. Now there were "voice-thoughts" speaking by the energy of telepathy, and the communications were so natural and intimate, I was swept up in the conversations without a thought of ramifications in my everyday human life.

The information conveyed to me in the beginning struck deep chords of familiarity, as if the purpose of the work with letters and numbers had been to scramble the circuits in my daylight mind to widen channels for contact with higher dimensions. I was quickly shifting into a "wave mode" of communication, finding in it an immediacy of understanding that seemed to bypass the intellect and speak directly to my soul. Unaware that this shift in communication was affecting my speech and writing patterns, for a long time I could not understand why people couldn't "hear" me, while, in contrast, I felt I was experiencing leaps in insight. If I was to be scribe and messenger, reality was showing me the opposite: glazed eyes, conversations cut short, complaints people didn't know what I was talking about, or hints that I was sounding awfully high and mighty, like some Mother Superior who thought she knew the woof and warp of Wisdom.

While I suffered this bewilderment, unable to understand what exactly I was doing to alienate people, I had a need to talk about events that were occurring on the periphery of contact; but not yet events that made me suspect I was more than a person engaged in communications with "old friends." For instance the dream that was so vivid it seemed like a visitation, the appearance of "Los Angelos," who also seemed an old friend, someone I had dreamt about before. Except there was no facade of chumminess that night. The widow-peaked visitor conveyed a sense of extreme devotion and serious purpose. His face haunted me for weeks.

Behind and above the enthusiasm I felt for having rediscovered an ancient art-science, which had initiated communication with the Others, I knew this was not all for my edification and entertainment. In the background, there was a lumbering purpose yet to show. I could feel it, and it made me uneasy. I needed to talk it all out with *human* old friends, but I had slipped into a mid-zone between two worlds, a place that would eventually be cause for a degree of isolation never before experienced . . . extremely difficult for someone who thought her talent was in communication.

I was unaware that I had crossed a line over which I would be unable to cross back. Life would never be the same. There would be no going back to the comfortable slumber of consciousness that was uninformed of this tangential world into which I had stumbled like a child discovering a magic ring in the sand and stepping inside it with all the trust of a newborn thrust into this foreign world we call reality. Earth is a world foreign to a newborn, and I was that again, a neophyte plunged through some magical hidden womb and secret birth channel, like the center of the spiral on a snail's shell, seemingly an inert thing, but hiding a vortex as active as a whirlpool.

This was hardly the common story in the literature of alien abduction. I was well read on the subject, I thought, and nothing in my experience pointed to abduction.

Except, in 1986 there was the appearance of triangle-shaped lesions, showing blood, on my hands, and a small spherical ball protruding beneath the top skin of my left hand: a small drama I had neatly forgotten.

Though the marks and the ball suggested implants, my rational mind could not accept it, in the same way so many scientists cannot accept the UFO presence, despite volumes of documentation of sightings, and testimonies of encounters with nonhuman beings. I reasoned it out. It was ludicrous to think that a spaceship had hovered over my house, swooping me up to implant the devices with no signs whatsoever that I had left my bed. This was my intellect protecting me from evidence of intrusion. My emotions could not cope with the notion of intrusion from an unseen *inner cosmos*. But there was undeniable physical evidence that I had been messed with. I glossed it all over with humor and a small vaudeville of recording the incident in my journal, drawing pictures, engaging my husband as photographer of the peculiarities, and displaying the marks and the protrusion to my chiropractor. I was not inclined to anything as radical as MRI (magnetic resonance imaging) or even X-rays, for that would have been to admit I believed the ball was more than a calcium deposit, coincidentally appearing at the same time the triangular marks startled my attention.

Soon afterward, I was compelled to study quantum physics, ancient history, mythology, and genetics, not connecting the compulsion with the discovery of the evidences of implantation. It was as if my mind dropped a shade in order to forget the suspicious marks and the ball as I pursued these new subjects; as if this were a logical next step on the path of a novelist and artist. I was a virtual illiterate in the world of mathematics, and sciences beyond anthropology and archaeology had never interested me. But quickly I found in quantum physics a language that spoke to the mystic in me. Though I had no grasp of the math, reading about quantum physics was like feeding my brain ice cream sundaes.

This study would later serve as stabilization as I was jostled through the UFO catalyst; for in quantum physics was explanation of how we could move through walls and windows to enter ships that plausibly could fold through space/time dimensions, rendering irrelevant concerns about the limits of travel faster than the speed of light. Super strings, multi-dimensions, and time warp tunnels were still controversial theories, but I had done my homework. With a little learning, I could not be intimidated by people who claimed it was scientifically unlikely, or impossible, that extraterrestrials could be visiting us. The resistance to our reports of contact and encounters was not based in sound thinking, but in fear of the unknown. Scientists were just not ready to study experience as a viable doorway to knowledge.

Communication, dated November 4, 1993:

> The true mysteries will remain veiled until such time that you
> create new structures[2] to receive this data. In the meantime, we can

---

[2] "Create new structures": I believe this means something that is occurring in fields of consciousness. Example: A book is more than pages bound between covers, and the content is more than multiple lines of words. That is one kind of structure, but the ideas and feelings expressed by the words form another kind of structure in consciousness. We do not see it with our eyes, but the energy structure of a book exists, as unique in pattern and form as the designs the words make on the flat pages.

point and describe and express, *reminding* you of the drama unfolding, so people will more smoothly transit in preparation to transform *aspects* of this dimension . . . pushing through the gates, so to speak, in preparation for a new journey in a strange land. As you know, all *new* lands are strange at first, as this (one) is to a baby, as to this dimension and all of its players.

(Me: Does this dimension cease to be?)

No! It is uplifted! Transformed! A dimension being a word to describe a particular experience that you have "mapped" and therefore came to believe was an actual place/space . . . whereas no place/space is fixed, all is undulating . . . and from "time to time," some very big waves rise, causing quite a commotion. . . .

CHAPTER TWO:

The Atlantis Link

. . . [I]n 1552, Francisco Lopen de Gomara, Cortez's secretary, wrote that native Americans said they had come from the lost island of Aztlan, which he believed was Plato's lost continent of Atlantis. After 1589, with the publication of Acosta's theory of a land-bridge, the Atlantis theory fell out of favour. . . .

—Rand and Rose Flem-Ath,
When the Sky Fell: In Search of Atlantis (1995)

Life as a child was gathering pop bottles to exchange for penny candy; it was walking barefoot to the swimming pool, and downtown on Saturdays to check out four more books. It was going to church, and musical comedies at the theater once a week, and going rabbit hunting with Dad, or to see an oil well, or a picnic in the mountains, roasting marshmallows, coming home swollen up from allergies, to find a tick to coax out of the skin with a lit match. Life was paper dolls, Kool-Aid stands, and hopscotch, playing the violin, singing, acting, roller- and ice-skating (but never did we play gun-down-your-classmates).

There were no overt signs of alien abduction in childhood. Except for the missing times.

And there was nothing from which to weave a story about Atlantis.

Vigorous and healthy, I was raised in the Mormon religion, much protected from the world, a reader, a poet, and a classical violinist, eldest of seven children. Eight years old, I washed the family dishes for ten cents a day, until I had earned twenty-eight dollars to pay for my first violin. I was interested in astronomy, the Mayans and the Hopis; and, at a young age, my mind was focused on the future of humankind, but not to paint a picture of an adultlike youth. I was the typical teenaged trial for my parents; I lived the peculiar rebelliousness of youth that seeks distinction, though never outside the boundaries of convention. I would not begin to know myself as a true individual until my thirties, after making a mess of my life, creating obstacles on the path that were extremely difficult to overcome. I was by no means an extraordinary child . . . except in hidden potentials, which can be said of anyone. We seem at once to discover and create ourselves.

Of course, I was taught the prophecies of my religion about the millennium, but there was another story in me, like an underground river, one I am sure would have alarmed the elders of the church, had it been a story I could have put into words.

When I was twenty, two years after I left the church, my mother loaned me a book about Edgar Cayce, an American prophet. She had begun to explore metaphysics, and we both wondered about reincarnation.

The first time I read the name Atlantis, a charge went through my body, practically setting my hair afire. *Atlantis*! I knew that name. And without anything like a firm belief in reincarnation, I "just knew" I had lived there, a feeling that would never leave me, although I would continue to debate the reality of reincarnation for years to come.

The story of Atlantis was totally different from what I had been taught in church, yet it sounded like the most sensible thing I'd ever heard; for at the age of twenty, I had begun to feel I was a stranger on Earth. Maybe I was Atlantian! Energetically attached to the name Atlantis was a "gathering" impulse. The gathering impulse was strong . . . I felt there were others like me, and I felt compelled to find them . . . a "feeling story" that would haunt me for years.

I looked for books on Atlantis, finding only one by Ignatius Donnelly, written in the late 1800s. The story in me wasn't in Donnelly's book; nonetheless, I was stirred, discovering that even Plato knew about Atlantis. This was in 1964; by the 70s, Atlantis was a hot topic.

We are all programmed from the cradle and on into our lives by our parents, human guardians, teachers, religion, and culture. While I was duly programmed at church, at home I was allowed my own thoughts and a freedom of expression in art, music, and imagination, which made for a distinctive personality, and unbeknownst to me, an independent spirit. But at the age of eighteen, that I could so easily walk away from my childhood religion shocked me, for I had been a devoted church member, believing my destiny was to be a mother in Zion who would marry a man in the priesthood and give birth to at least six children. There was no other future for a Mormon girl, unless she was so homely no man would marry her, or she was otherwise unable to fulfill a role as wife and mother. But in the Mormon religion there is provision for all saints who keep the faith. The men in Mormon Heaven can have multiple wives, and by the time they arrive there, presumably they will be of such pristine moral character, they will not hesitate to snatch to their bosoms the women who were wanting on Earth.

I was snatched up, but I doubt by anyone of the Mormon faith. I was snatched early, it appears, before I was five years old. And maybe before this lifetime.

Maybe I was noticed for my vitality. Mother said I took my first steps at seven months, and shook my crib all over the room. As a toddler, I had to be watched carefully; turn your back, I was running down the street, off to seek my destiny. One day when I was three years old, I got away and Mom found me at the bus stop, wailing. "It won't catch!" I cried. I had seen children getting on the bus, and had heard them talking about "catching" it.

At the age of two, I learned the alphabet from my grandmother, who was my prime caretaker while my mother worked. Doubtless, my love for letters began then. At age three, I was drawing paperdolls—with triangle bodies.

Maybe the triangle was an imprint associated with my "imaginary childhood playmate," Rowah, and the missing time events at ages four and five. But this and other associations were not made until I investigated my history, searching for signs of the genesis of my involvement with the ones who breached my physical domain in 1994, taking me up, causing me to believe I was an abductee.

The full story of Rowah, the missing time events, and the hypnotic regression to explore this dynamic are in *Summoned*. A brief review . . .

Naturally, experiencers are suspicious of "imaginary" childhood playmates as perhaps disguises for alien involvement. When I probed for information about Rowah in hypnotic regression, I saw him in two ways: as a shape-shifter—he appeared to be a monkey-man, leaping around, making me laugh; and second, he was a tall, stately extraterrestrial of the Nordic kind, except his eyes and hair were leonine. The scene that left a strong imprint on my mind was of him sitting with one knee up, the other flat on the ground, as he pointed across time and events—impossible to describe what I saw. With his right hand resting gently on my back, Rowah told me my life would be hard, and I was to "remember the silver." I wrote a fable for *Summoned*, to capture the essence of what I thought the "silver" represented. It's a story, not about ETs, but of the current quickening of consciousness I see happening worldwide; a lifting of a condition of spellboundedness, a forging of communication portals to reconnect with celestial ancestors, of remembering who we are, and a purpose soon to be performed.

But the "silver" may as well refer to the implantation event on a ship with a mercurial silver seam on the ceiling, which I described as a portal through which the ship enfolded into another dimension. The beings on the ship resembled Rowah and Los Angelos, stern-looking fellows in white body suits and having black widow-peaked skullcaps, or hair.

Readers of *Summoned* may recall I made an association between the domed ship and the human brain, divided into two hemispheres by a fissure that could be symbolized by the silver mercurial seam on the ceiling of the vehicle, which captured my attention. In chapter 14, I will expound on other "metafractals" linking events in actual life with metaphors, in reference to the notion that UFO events may be dramas staged in realms foreign to human consciousness.

Over the years of dreams about extraterrestrial activity, with occasional lights and sounds accompanying, and the appearance of implantation in 1986, I worried I might be an abductee. But I had good reasons to dismiss the idea, mainly because *there was no missing time in my life*. But there was. And it wasn't even hidden. For years I had joked about being kicked out of kindergarten, due to times I had come home late from school, supposedly because I had been visiting schoolmates in their homes. I wasn't actually kicked out of kindergarten, but was withdrawn because it was the only way my parents knew to put a stop to the errant "visits."

But I had no memory of visiting human children after school, so, at the beginning of my investigation in 1994, I pressed my mother for details. The subject was immediately embroiled in emotional resistance to the idea that these events might point to involvement with extraterrestrials. Mother recoiled at the suggestion, and yet she could provide no details to argue against it. Simply, I was missing after school, sometimes for hours, and my parents did not know my where-abouts. The last episode: I came home, four hours late, from a dirt road, looking exhausted and bedraggled. My parents tried stern warnings, spankings, and deprivations to stop the behavior, but nothing worked except withdrawing me from school.

But Mother admitted that I was also missing occasionally when I was four, before I began kindergarten. We lived in Vernal, Utah, which was, and still is, a hot spot for UFO sightings and cattle mutilations, making plausible the possibility that there is truth in what I viewed in the regression. But it is not cut-and-dried for me; I don't consider what I view in trance states to be the last words in any case, whether probing for hidden memories in this life, or past lives. I am still pondering the possible metaphorical or symbolic significance of all such events viewed in trance.

So far as evidence goes, there were actually "missing times" (or holes in my memory), which I was investigating, because in my adult life, there were actually encounters and contact with alien intelligences. If not for the contact and encounters, I would never have thought the missing times in childhood might have been for the purpose of meetings with ETs. Previously, the thought had never occurred; even having read Budd Hopkins's book, *Missing Time*. I was too focused on all the ways I was *not* like the cases discussed by Hopkins.

Some people place a lot of weight on their feelings about such things. After two unsuccessful tries at hypnotic regression, confronted by a strong taboo against "telling my mother," I felt relief in finally seeing something about the missing time mystery. On the third try, when I broke through the barrier, I was baffled at how I could have kept separate these two compartments in my life, if indeed what I "remembered" was true. In the scene viewed, I seemed at home with the tall, spindly beings, saying matter-of-factly that I belonged with them. If, at my real home, I dropped hints, as child abductees are known to do, it is long submerged in my mother's memory. How did I feel about viewing my young self in the company of alien beings familiar to the child? I felt it was essentially true, but still I wonder if it was precisely as "remembered."

Arriving home in Utah, after viewing Rowah in my inner mind's-eye during the hypnotic regression, there were tears and an intense yearning to see him again. Something like this happened recently. I was drawn to order a video made by experiencers in Australia (details in the afterword). A drawing by an experiencer named Jane was particularly familiar. When Jane's rendering of a "lion man" came on the screen, the tears flowed. Even though the drawing was not exactly like Rowah, I felt the same intense grief, like one might feel for a loved one who has died.

The "memories" of the five-year-old felt real enough, but I can't fully accept that I was going into the woods in the afternoon after school into an actual spaceship. Maybe it happened on a "mystical landscape." Maybe it was a kind of consciousness event we are yet to comprehend.

On the ship I was shown babies that looked like "big bugs," in tanks of fluid. I was told that when I was older, I would teach the babies something. This, I, the child, took in stride. They weren't human babies, I could plainly see. The only thing that bothered me was, how could they be asleep, submerged in water with their eyes open?

I want to see how this story, memory, or otherwise, intertwines with the Atlantis link, and later to the Jesus link, as subtle directors in my life. Was there a hidden agenda from early childhood, or before? Was I "infused" at birth? Was the Atlantis undercurrent based on past-life memory fragments, or was that a story imprinted for service to the real story that would eventually surface in contact and encounters?

Hypnotically regressed by Ruth Hover, Ph.D. in Scottsdale, Arizona, on August 15, 1995, I watched my five-year-old self enter a round spaceship that was much larger on the inside than it appeared to be from outside, from the perspective of the child.

At the back of the ship was a glass wall that gave view of a "whole 'nother world"—rocks, sand, desert terrain, and pale-red atmosphere—an environment different from the forest where the ship was parked. That happens to describe the country where I live now, and did when I engaged in the regression, as if the child were glimpsing her own future. The terrain around here is often compared to Mars, something to consider, along with dreams of being in the presence of aliens in a place with two moons, also characteristic of Mars.

Dr. Hover had suggested the ship was a portal that stood between two dimensions. Possibly. Still I wonder if these events could be "staged dramas" orchestrated in a new realm of consciousness. The nature of some of my experiences, and certain communications, point in this direction.

Other subtle signs of possible abduction in childhood: I was a frequent sleepwalker; one time at the age of six, I was found at the front door of the house in the middle of the night. I remember seeing "sparky eyes" in the night, and feeling my hands swell to enormous proportions, while a great pressure bore down on them. (But I never experienced paralysis.) This sensation I would experience many times in my life, in that zone between awake and sleep. As an adult, always I would think, *what is this?* The question remained a mystery until 1994, when I was hyper-alert to extremely strange bodily sensations that were prelude to feeling I was disassembling, and transported to another dimension— perhaps it was out-of-body travel, but I feel it was more like "beaming up Scottie" on a *Star Trek* show (details in chapter 8).

I had a flying dream; I was leaping, diving, bouncing in a medium that felt to be a water-air mix. The buoyancy reminded me of these pressure points of compaction-expansion, just before I conk out, or disassemble. The air seems densely packed, and I am of a lighter weight that gives me spring. Navigation is by thought, with instant results, perhaps like a bird feels, but without the mechanics of moving the wings; one is simply propelled by thought, sometimes at incredible speeds. More than a couple of times, I have awakened, remembering having seen Earth from high in the sky: the most thrilling thing I've ever experienced.

The Atlantis link and my break with the Mormon Church are closely entwined in time. Possibly memories of Atlantis were obscured by my religious programming, or maybe the name Atlantis is a "consciousness tag," perhaps not reference to an actual place or civilization on Earth, but an ideal, or spiritual purpose; maybe it is a distortion of memories of life on another planet (Mars?), or in another dimension, or is Atlantis an echo from the future?

Whatever the truth, certain communications, beginning in 1993, support the notion that Atlantis existed as an actual civilization predating Sumer.

Following are excerpts from three early communications. All spoke to my soul like winds of memory. The first is an excerpt from a poemlike communication received December 5, 1993:

> Will is a gift,
> A powerful gift.
> Use it alone without guidance,
> You may succeed in blowing up the world.
> You almost did once.[3]

---

[3] Refers to a catastrophic event in Atlantis. I don't know the particulars, but my feelings align with researchers who speculate that worldwide legends of a conflagration accompanying Great Flood stories are suggestive of a nuclear explosion. Intuitively I feel it was a catastrophe that plunged the Earth into a lower vibration, from whence sprang stories of the human race having "fallen," which keys to cellular memory imprints of a lost paradisiacal world that we have collectively grieved for ever since, and have dreamed of restoring. Somewhere in here is also an intertwining of the story of a possible genetic alteration by extraterrestrials, linking to the "History of Humankind in Summary" in chapter 11 in *Summoned*, which I will explore further in chapter 10 here.

Which is why so many taboos
Were placed on that which you call the mystery.
Now unraveling, now coming back . . .
But again, hearts not ready.
But many (are) serving and seeking.
And this is a powerful deterrent.
And *will* move mountains that need to be moved. . . .

The second conversation, excerpted, occurred November 20, 1993, a couple of weeks after the Los Angelos visitation/dream, which was accompanied by a dream of a man of royal essence presenting a king with a lace indigo veil—an image that found its way into my novel, *Jonah*. The essence of the dream was about freeing people from captivity. I felt it spoke to a hidden agenda behind the UFO presence.

In the days of contact and work with letters and numbers, before the phenomenal events caused me to concentrate on the abduction dynamic, I felt I was given knowledge that hinted of a "high design" behind our lives, and that my role would be to leak this information through my novels. But the abduction phase of my experience would plunge me into a sea of confusion, causing me to doubt my role, the information, everything but the fact that I was deeply entrenched in a mystery that affected my body, as well as my mind, and shattered my life for a time.

In short, the story that evolved from my first recognition of the name Atlantis is a tale about a major disruption in our evolution, a fall to a lower state, making us vulnerable to exploitive beings who then established the world in orders of rulers and subservients, while those of a higher vibration retreated into other dimensions to act as guides, working in the shadows beyond our visual range and our conscious minds, until we evolved to a state where they could begin contacting us, to guide us toward transforming ourselves and the Earth; at which time, walls would collapse, veils would be lifted, and all would be windows. All would see.

Is this happening now? Are people all over the planet waking up and remembering our "calls" to help prepare the world for change? (The idea is best articulated in the "Hidden Message" in chapter 7.)

The second communication: I was journaling when they inserted themselves into my thoughts in the middle of a sentence. (Often the word "now" is announcement of the beginning of telepathic input.) The loose style of these communications shows them to be personal, not meant for the public, but I felt it was time to share them.

November 1993:

[N]ow we are speaking of your beloved Mayans and Atlantians, those who were taken up, and the ones left who would carry the story of the destruction into the world, in code, but preserved, now to be carefully lifted, now the veil, for soon all will be revealed, this being a preparation for those who are here to play a role, a gathering, yes, the ones called living to *all* eyes as ordinary people, kings and queens cloaked in rags, these are they who will inherit the Earth that was taken from them, and those who mind the webs, spinning, spinning . . . will be exposed. Imagine the horror . . . it is one thing to be spooked by a dream[4] . . . imagine when the veil is lifted . . . yes, those called must be notified to take their positions and stand ready at the portals, to soothe and nurture the ones who have been asleep.

Those severely captured are not evil, but they *are* severely captured and will interfere, sniffing the scent of anything that moves to reveal that which is forbidden.

Take heart, the kingdom is truly *among* you.

The third communication followed three days later. It is suggestive of an event that drastically affected human collective consciousness.

---

[4] Spooked by a dream: refers to the dream-visitation of Los Angelos.

November 23, 1993:

(Speaking of) . . . bringing upon your heads destruction and mass confusion and a wailing so forceful in and of itself, it did exert as a powerful destructive force to finish off all that remained erect, causing tidal waves that in fact did engulf that which you refer to as Atlantis; and yes, in all cultures there are flood stories . . . how "God" found all but "Noah" evil, destroying all with water . . . *God being a force used and abused in ignorance,*[5] so that over eons, it became in your minds . . . (?) . . . the information transmitted in sound vehicles[6] called word utterances became a force seeming to be separate and quite supercilious and finicky in its punishments and rewards, all being described in various stories, all warning again and again to . . . whatever you do, do *not* "take the Lord's name in vain" . . . do not utter it, this name representing the *house* of utterances associated . . . mind your p's and q's (and yes, your j's) . . . do not walk here/look here/ *think* here . . . see the veil? Behind it is a nasty secret that could destroy you.

You may think . . . Is it safe? Have we ever harmed you or a hair on your head? It is good for brothers and sisters to meet every 26,000 years or so, lest we forget we are related, all.

Whatever the truth about Atlantis, the name roused a "gathering story" in me, an impulse to find others whom I sensed were like me, not of this world . . .

---

[5] God being a force used and abused in ignorance: suggests that certain religious ideas about God may have developed as a metaphoric shield to protect against abuse of psychic powers, until our spiritual evolution caught up with our restored mental powers. There are links to this idea in a past life regression in the next chapter, and in chapter 10.

[6] Sound vehicles: From my work with letters and numbers, I sense they are speaking of something more fantastic than language, as we know it today. Glimmers here of the "Word made flesh"—the creative power of sound used in particular ways—in particular vehicles.

CHAPTER THREE:

Not of This World: The Jesus Link

The break with the Mormon Church was the beginning of a jagged path away from the story programmed in my young mind. Soon another story would emerge, at the recognition of the name Atlantis. . . .

The events that caused me to leave the church were petty on the surface, but the effect was a sudden loss of faith in the religion. Later I would learn that seekers of true religion tend to abandon institutions, but I did not know this at age eighteen. I suffered feelings of guilt and shame, without knowing precisely where I had gone wrong. The ominous warnings about leaving the fold were enough to explain such feelings, but I was young and inexperienced. I knew nothing about "hive minds" (chapter 8, *Summoned*), and I don't know much about them now, except that I see the "belief clusters," and people behaving like bees, buzzing, buzzing, but seldom questioning.

Leaving the church was similar to what I experienced at the breach when I became aware of the abduction-like activities. Certain beliefs were shattered, causing radical changes in my life. In the first shattering, religion was the issue, so I pursued its opposite, the world. In my young mind, the two were separate, church and world. The church was supposedly a shining city high on a hill overlooking the world. I was taught that we were God's elect. How could I have known this was a common worldly stance? The world was full of such posturing, people clustering together and believing themselves to be superior to others was so common, it seemed to be human nature.

Eventually I would forgive the Mormons for being "only human," and I would reclaim all that was good in my upbringing, and much was very good. The Mormons shaped my ethics and provided an environment of love and grounding for my independent spirit. While I had to go my own way, I am still linked to these roots, particularly in my interest in the genetic migrations of human beings. Like individuals, churches seem to be entities with purposes that do not show in outward appearances. I trust that my beginning in the Mormon church was no mistake, as I trust it was necessary to leave the church in order to fulfill my individual life purpose. Nonetheless, the severing was life shattering.

There were no warnings in youth that I would reject my religion. But in retrospect, there was an uneasiness in me around questions that I could not pose for the threat it would have been to my faith. One was: How could one small church be the *only true* church on Earth? If true, what would be the destiny of all who could not embrace it? Never mind the Catholics and Baptists and Methodists, what about the huge populations in China and India, and the Middle East countries—people who would not likely want to become Mormons? These were not questions I could pose to God, either, for God and the church were fused in my mind. So, leaving the church was tantamount to a break from the only god I knew, personified on Earth by men who wore suits and ties and stood at pulpits, claiming to speak for God.

At the age of eighteen, I was left with a story of doom. My impression was that "I" and my soul were the same. My soul was that which would rise at the death of the body, a kind of ghost person who lived inside me. If "I" could not reconcile with the church, my soul had not a chance, because there was no difference: except for a body that was like all other eighteen-year-old bodies, one hot to trot into bed with someone of the opposite sex.

As a symbol of whatever good I thought might be in me, I managed to remain a virgin until I was married the first time at the age of twenty-one. That my husband showed little interest in me sexually after we were married was one of those "sacred ironies," as Erianthmer in *Jonah* would say.

Employed at the Nevada Test Site, both John and I had "Q" (Top Secret) clearances. I flew to work five days a week in a DC-3, out to the desert where bombs were exploded underground. Another irony: That a young woman so naive about the nature of her own body, and life, would be working on such a serious project. But there was no "finishing school" I could have attended to bridge the gap between my upbringing as a daughter of Zion, and the world of bombs. It was a living, and by then, even married women were expected to work outside the home. (They called it "women's liberation.")

To give you a picture of a Mormon girl trying to hang on to a shred of purity, approaching marriage. . . . My mother-in-law asked discreetly if I had a diaphragm. I had no idea what she was talking about, so I made an appointment with a female physician for a pre-marital check-up. (I was much too modest to disrobe in front of a male doctor.) During the interview, the doctor asked if I had ever been pregnant. I told her I'd never engaged in intercourse. The woman dropped her pen and stared. I guess, even in 1964, virgins at age twenty-one were rare. (Women were liberated.)

The examination was humorous, looking back. At last, the doctor exclaimed, "All I can tell you, Dear, is to buy a large bottle of Vaseline, and drink a lot of wine."

The honeymoon was unremarkable, to say the least.

I had bought several sexy nightgowns. This scene stands out in memory. Soon after the honeymoon, at home, I put on a frilly nightgown and joined my husband on the couch where he was watching TV, a show about cowboys. At the end of the show, he stood up, stretched, yawned, said goodnight, and went to bed. I sat on the couch, wondering what I was supposed to do. . . .

We were divorced a few months later. So much for virginity! Now I was both doomed, and a "soiled" woman, in the terms of my upbringing.

I began to drink and did not stop until I was twenty-eight. In the meantime, I married twice more (trying it once more with husband number one), divorcing twice again, now with a beautiful daughter from my second husband to show for all my trouble.

There were no conscious events or even subtle signs of alien intrusion in my life during this period; but, curiously, a scene I would never have imagined emerged in hypnotic regression at this simple question: "When were you next contacted?"

In response to the simple question, my subconscious showed me at a weekend camp-over with revelers at Lake Pyramid near Reno, Nevada, where I lived then. We drank a lot. I was asleep, probably in a drunken stupor, in the back of a pickup on a mattress. The regression showed a clear star-studded sky, and a UFO, one of those round bright lights high in the sky.

I was being checked out, and was told they would not return until I was sober. Shortly afterward, at the age of twenty-eight, I did sober up. My recovery from besottedness was a bumpy ride the first year or so, culminating in a compromise that would break my heart again, but would set me firmly on a spiritual path.

Now I am going to reveal the most intimate of my human experiences, because I believe it may be a link in the "story behind the story."

After another divorce in Reno (an impulse marriage that lasted six weeks), I moved, with my daughter, to Denver to live near relatives.

Michelle was five years old. It was time to enroll her in kindergarten. I walked with her across a busy street in Denver, two blocks east and a block north. Hands clasped, we gazed up at multiple concrete stairs leading to the double doors of an immense, beige, brick school building. In memory's eyes, there were no other people about, no cars on the street, no one in the building . . . there were just Michelle and me.

Gazing up at the school, inexplicably I began to cry. Tears streamed down my face. *I can't do this*, I remember thinking. I don't remember what I told Michelle, but I continued to cry as we walked back to the duplex.

I called my relatives and asked if they would take Michelle for a few days. I was an emotional wreck and didn't know why. I packed up a few clothes and some of her toys and books, and her uncle came and got her.

I didn't see Michelle again for eleven years.

My boyfriend came over that night and I told him how desperate I felt, that I feared I would drink again, and it would ruin my daughter's life. (I could not turn to her father for help; he was in worse shape than I.) Art suggested I check into an alcoholism unit at a local hospital, and he brought me a New Testament, the Living Bible version.

That night I read the gift Bible, and felt a spark of hope. I read about a Jesus I had never heard about in church. This Jesus spoke right to me; I was one of the wretched he loved. Though it was nothing like instant conversion, what I had read awakened something in my soul.

The prior fascination with Atlantis was background noise muffled now by the stark sounds of shame and grief for the years lost on a barstool. But reading about Jesus, I experienced something similar to the recognition I had felt, hearing the name Atlantis. I did not have these words then, but now I can say it was as if the words of Jesus were "inscribed" inside me already. This may be literally true. We have just begun to explore DNA. I believe we are going to discover that there is an "energetic" language element in DNA that is a carrier of information beyond detectable physical characteristics. But our consciousness must expand before we can detect and read it.

However, that the words ascribed to Jesus sounded in me like a bell is not any kind of evidence that Jesus existed as the Bible stories describe. There is a mystery around Jesus I remain alert to understand.

Going into the recovery unit the fateful day after I had been unable to enroll Michelle in kindergarten, though I couldn't say it out loud in my mind yet, I knew what I had to do. I knew I had to give up my daughter, whether or not I stayed sober. Something in me knew that sober or not, my life was going to be hard. My relatives could provide my daughter a stable life with all of the dynamics a child needs. Plus, she would have brothers and a sister, too. I doubted I would have any more children, or ever marry again.

This was more than a sacrifice of a child. Michelle belonged to a dream that could never be, a dream from the Mormon story, the one I had to leave behind . . . all of it. But at the time of the decision, I had no such conscious insight. I was gripped in emotional and spiritual crisis.

In retrospect, I had to consider that in the moment when I stood with my daughter, gazing up at the school, my own hidden experiences at age five may have been speaking to me through my soul. In the undercurrents of emotion, did I feel that if I kept her, she would be inducted into the UFO drama? If so, does this suggest that subconsciously, I felt the business was negative? The question is moot because I was not consciously aware of my involvement. The "books are closed," Mehuki in *Jonah* would say, in regards to these two radical decisions: First to leave the church; second to surrender my daughter to the care of others.

But I have thought a lot about both decisions. Both seemed to "set me up" for a life that would not be ordinary. For an "alien purpose"? It may seem like I am creating a melodramatic justification for abandoning Michelle. At the time, it seemed the best thing I could do for her, but considering all that has transpired since, I am suspicious that something else influenced these two radical decisions. Although I take full responsibility for all of my decisions, I believe that to one degree or the other, or at one time or another, we are all affected by hidden influences.

Looking back, there is a sense of "sweptness," a log tossed on ocean waves until the bark is gone and the wood becomes smooth and supple. The log's journey is determined by the laws of nature and destiny. It is comical to envision a log trying to hoist itself into the air to fly, or to push itself onto a beach, or to plunge, of its own will, to the ocean floor. But I lived much like that—fighting the flow, thinking that's what a human being was supposed to do. But there were these times when I could feel life taking me, like a log in the waves—times like leaving the church, giving my daughter away, and the UFO catalyst—things impossible to explain, anti-culture acts with no peace for the actor, except over time, as the bark is stripped away, and the person you are begins to show. But in the living, it does not feel like anything as graceful or natural as a log riding the waves. A hundred decisions a day, sometimes one that seems anti-everything, water, air, earth, fire, alien acts impossible to understand. And yet, in the deciding, there seems no other way. You are a limb chopped off a tree, a log tossed in the ocean—too late to be paper, a rocking chair, wood in a fireplace. The way of the world is not the way of the soul.

After checking into the hospital, with a vague hope in Jesus, I prayed, asking God, is this right? Is this the best life for Michelle? Unexpectedly, I was flooded with feelings of peace, a sharp contrast to the grief that had racked me, body and soul. I interpreted the powerful feeling of peace as affirmation, and effectively then, I gave my daughter to God. Following three weeks of intensive therapy, I was released from the hospital. By then my relatives had agreed to adopt Michelle, and though I faced years of grief ahead, I felt my decision was some kind of spiritual imperative; nothing I would ever be able to explain to anyone, least of all my daughter.

(Michelle and I were reunited when she was sixteen. She loves and forgives me, a blessing undeserved. There are no signs of alien abduction in her life. She tolerates my involvement with UFOs . . . one more weird thing about her mother.)

Soon after release from the hospital, while living in a halfway house run by charismatic Christians, again I prayed, this time getting down on my knees. The grief I felt was almost unbearable. Was Jesus the answer? If I joined these people in their belief, would I survive the pain? Would I live?

That night, I was awakened from a nightmare. Something black was coming for me. Suddenly a shaft of white light fell on me, vaporizing the black form. Bathed in the light, spontaneously I laughed. It was a joy-filled light, which I took to mean that yes, I should join these hand-clapping, dancing people who sang praises to the Lord in indecipherable tongues. I was "born again." I was sure then I would never drink again (I didn't), and I would spend the rest of my days helping others get sober. I couldn't give Jesus to anyone else, but I could share my experience; asking for divine help worked. That, and not picking up a drink.

I was then "called" to be a housemother at another halfway house in the worst ghetto in Denver. The Hand of Hope was a huge, roach-infested house, filled to capacity with drunks rolling off trains, and vagrants in and out of the rain from skid row. Our food was leftover Salvation Army dinners, disassembled and remade into casseroles, and day-old bread from Safeway.

For a Mormon girl, raised and protected in suburbia, this was high drama that convinced me that I had been touched by Jesus, Lord of wretches like me. And somewhere in this, I would be forgiven for doing the worst thing a mother could do—giving up her child. I desperately needed a mission.

It was a violent neighborhood. One day a man was shot and killed on our front lawn, and many a night there were break-in attempts; the housefather grabbing the baseball bat, me dialing up the police, again. But I was in the light of Jesus, and maybe even a few people got and stayed sober.

It was not a special mission, but a common one shared by all recovering alcoholics. But after twenty-four years, I had to retreat from the fellowship, soon after the contact and encounters began. My view of myself, the world, the cosmos, and God were so challenged, I had trouble reciting the ABCs of recovery with clarity. A different mission emerged, then: Survival and adaptation to a new kind of consciousness, the purpose unclear.

The born-again feelings remained for awhile, but I was unable to abide any form of organized religion, even the enthusiasms of Charismatic Christianity; for here, too, were rows of chairs facing a pulpit, and a man there, translating meanings, which in my mind was not what Jesus had intended. My understanding was that he gave his life that the Holy Spirit would come and fill each person. Spirit would be our intimate guidance, and direct link to him. It was a radical view, I knew, that challenged all Earthly religious authorities. But it was my view.

I had two stories in me now: The Atlantis undercurrent, and now a vision of community and fellowship that had no Earthly leaders, but functioned as an ideal of love and cooperation, based on spiritual purpose; here an intertwining of Atlantis and a fellowship of individuals like the original followers of Jesus, before Paul organized them, and long before Christianity was absorbed into the Roman Empire and made to be part of the world, which, in my mind, was another divergence from the Word, because Jesus told his followers they were like him . . . not of this world.

For me, Jesus was a way-shower, a beckoner to the path of quest, which led me to study world religions, to discover the threads connecting all human beings; resulting in a universal view I call the "belonging story," subplot in a gathering story that includes brothers and sisters truly not of this world.

Chimes rang when I was thirty-three, in my bedroom, jarring me awake. It happened several times, a sound of gathering, an unknown purpose to perform ringing across the deeps of my soul . . . *remember*. Who knows what these things mean? I had to live in the world.

Throughout my thirties, I moved many times, changing jobs frequently, giving Department of Defense agents something to ponder when later I went to work for a defense contractor and required another top-secret clearance. (They told me I had the longest personal history they had ever seen. I believed them. I went places . . . did things . . . married men.)

One of the things I did was play violin in a Dixieland jazz group. These were the days of true fellowship of the spirit in a sub-society composed of wandering minstrel kinds, seeking God in everything and everyone. Painting became my first love, and my poetry flourished in the traveling years . . . not items that counted on an application for a top-secret clearance. My true life was hidden in the white spaces between the black statistics.

My fifth marriage was to a man incarcerated at Canyon City, Colorado. I married him to help commute his sentence. It worked. But I never saw him after he was released; the marriage was never consummated. Later, in a past life regression (if it is to be believed), I learned that helping Kerry was a karmic debt; I had walked out on him when he was jailed for a crime in which I was involved. This appealed to my logic, for my behavior to help this man, whom I barely knew, was bizarre; the lengths I went: Writing to the governor and other officials; driving from Laramie, Wyoming, down to Canyon City many weekends to see Kerry; marrying him by proxy up on a rock near Virginia Dale, Colorado, with his best friend standing as groom, after having convinced a bewildered minister to perform the ceremony.

35

Two other past life regressions revealed karmic ties, one to the Mormon church, and the other showing me dying of a drug overdose at the age of twenty-five, which might tie to my alcoholic drinking in this life. Several times, psychics have looked at my palms, tea leaves, cards, and asked about a tragic event when I was twenty-five.

By the time I was thirty-five, these karmic hangovers seemed resolved.

Nothing happened during the "traveling years" that hinted of an actual link with ETs, but sometime in my thirties, I became aware of the UFO presence. Old friends have reminded me that I was talking about extraterrestrials in the early 70s. I recall seeing a film, or reading a book about Erich Von Daniken's findings of archaeological evidences of past visitations by aliens. Today I am inclined to agree with Dr. A.C. Ross, a Lakota spiritual leader, author of a book titled *Mitakuye Oyasin "We are All Related"* (1997): "There are reports of UFOs landing today and they don't need landing strips." In Lakota history (and other native American histories), the landing strips were for their ancestors who had the technology and ability to fly. Misuse of this technology created a war, which was cause for a great flood, which destroyed the "third world." Shades of the Atlantis story.

However distorted, Von Daniken's findings sparked in me recognition that I associated with reports of UFO sightings. I remember this having the same effect as hearing the chimes ring in my bedroom. There were multiple subtle signals of these kinds during my thirties, but if ever I paused to analyze the meanings, I don't remember it. My life was full and challenging.

But I do remember feeling that I was living in a primitive and barbaric world. Was it my imagination, or was I beginning to remember living in a more advanced society? Atlantis? For instance, I envisioned crystals, as an energy source, suspended in the air above our homes; we programmed them with our minds. And sound vibrations were used to build structures, such as domes. But the strongest impression was of non-violence, and a mindedness for complete equality and respect for all beings.

As these "feeling memories" began to surface, I felt increasingly annoyed with such things as electrical cords and loud clunky machines of every kind. One day it struck me as weird to be moving down the street inside a boxy vehicle that smoked toxic gases into the air.

I was constantly observing others to learn the ways of cooperation and social intercourse without drawing too much attention to myself as the outsider I felt myself to be. Of course, I was kidded about coming from another planet, hatched in a pod in my parents' backyard. But in those days, it was sport to accuse friends of being ET—a joke, a merriment; it was *chic* to be from Mars or Jupiter. This was long before the stigma of contact and encounters seeped into the collective consciousness.

Reports of alien abduction, get thee behind us.

The theory of contact and encounters captures the imagination, as is so well rendered in Steven Spielberg's *E.T.* and *Close Encounters of the Third Kind*, but the reality is quite alien, and the human animal can sense it.

If there has been an alien agenda of social engineering over the ages, it is easy to understand why it would have to be hidden to succeed. The consensus is that we are in charge of our affairs. Even in a dictatorship, people join to overthrow the tyranny. But what say do we have in something that might be occurring beyond our conscious awareness? Maybe some of the UFO displays are meant to jar us awake.

Even in the freethinking 70s, I had the savvy not to be too vocal about my quiet awareness of the UFO presence. Always there was a sensing of the boundaries, always a strong sense of survival, knowing how far I could go, and still be socially acceptable, in whatever group I participated, be it a friendship between two or among many. In what social arrangement is it ever safe to reveal one's innermost thoughts? Few and rare are the affairs of the heart. But the truer one can be to one's own heart, the more often one will find brothers and sisters of the code, the hidden dynamic, true fellowship of the spirit.

But I was not so finely-tuned in my thirties, recent survivor of the alcohol catalyst, a fledgling in the big world, trying my wings, avoiding the many cages, learning to fly between the bars . . . I thought. It was a time of freedom and adventure, a broadening of education, and discovery that I could fit in society; all it took was going along, cooperating, on with the mask when necessary.

The inner agenda was subtle. In my early and mid-thirties, I was sure I was developing slick wings to escape all cages. But there was a constant call to surrender to the world. The mentors I most admired advised that I should give up the illusion that freedom could be *lived*, as was idealized in my mind. I had to admit that my sense of living in a primitive and barbaric world was based on nothing as concrete as actual memory of having lived in a more advanced society. "Feelings" were not guides to successful living then; I needed to get a "real life." Get real, get a real job, make some real money, get a bank account, a real house, a real car, get married for real . . . for, Sister, you are almost forty.

What designs of soul would ask that I plunge deeper into the world? I felt I was not of this world, but no one escapes the fire. Not even Jesus escaped. Who was I? A bit of crude lead poised at the door of another furnace, to be further tempered and refined, if I survived the heat.

Chin up. There are worse fates than eight-to-five employment and a wage skewed to keep you there, along with a traditional marriage to give you a proper name. An exercise was performed, a tinkering with "mentations" out of the 1972 book *The Center of the Cyclone: An Autobiography of Inner Space*, by John C. Lilly, M.D., and I was on my way to a life in suburbia, the American Dream, subtext of the lost religion. . . .

CHAPTER FOUR:

Living Double

Both the new job and the real marriage were sharp turns away from my former free-spirited life. It was nice for a change to feel applauded by the world. Renegade finally grows up and behaves correctly! I was proud of myself for making these leaps. And they were leaps.

The gathering story in me all but died, submerged now that I was "getting real" in the world. But throughout my thirties, everywhere I traveled, I looked for them, "my people," the ones I was supposed to find and join. And I found many; I saw it in their eyes, children of a destiny written in the heart. But none of us was inclined to actually join. Each was highly individualistic, not given to settling down—perhaps "wanderers" described in *The Ra Material* and the *Books of One* (Ra 1984). Although these books spoke to my heart across the deeps of time, nowhere in them was a message about a gathering of souls, matching the story in me.

A synchronicity: Unaware I was writing about a gathering story, out of the blue, a friend, Larry Schmitt, described the mystery in his life. In a letter, he wrote, "There is a gathering, Dana, and it involves me. I watch and wait for the next move, for the direction and guidance. It is coming, and it has power. I can feel it. . . ."

We are in the world, and the world has its story. Your name is on a certificate, you are issued a number, a camera snaps a photo of your face, you are foot- and finger-printed. Chapters in the Book of the World are Bloodlines, Race, Class, Gender, Appearance, Strength, Health, Talent, Intelligence—traits defined by the law of survival. To live, your body must thrive. In the Book of the World, we are human prototypes, elite or working class, and all between, in contest, striving to gain, or fighting to stay alive if face-down in a gutter, clutching a bottle.

The finer distinctions of the prototype are spelled out by the sun, the moon, the planets—astrology, gleaned from heavenly bodies once believed to be gods. The palms show the map, and your birth date reveals your personality. Even Carl Jung knew the story of the world; you are one of thirty-six types.

But the soul is an alien in the world, without name or number, a shadow behind the silver. A conspiracy is afoot, souls gathering in the wings of tomorrow, meeting in the invisible college, snatched up by UFOs, returned to form a fifth column, the trunk of a new tree rising up in the center of the world, the cosmic serpent uncoiling, a story in the secret Book of Life.

The story in me.

But there were no words for it yet, and if there had been, I doubt there would have been a marriage.

Suddenly after years of living as an outsider, I was embraced within the American Dream. I had a choice job in an aerospace company, and my husband was an engineer, a "rocket scientist," I called him fondly. He made me feel proud.

The glow lasted a couple of years, not an uncommon story. Changes in my job caused me to leave, and I became a realtor, selling seven houses in the first year. Then the bottom fell out of the real estate market and I was confronted with myself again, the self I thought I had superseded, now tilting on the whirling wheel of fortune. Though I was restless and confused at this point, life was good. We owned a home, Tom was a pilot and ham radio operator on the side, and I was an artist with a pack of wonderful friends.

The subject of UFOs did come up occasionally, but I would always roll my eyes, along with the others. I was in the world now, experiencing how that feels, the *stakes* . . . the need to conform, to *preserve* . . . the position, the reputation, the material goods, the small empire, the future. . . .

But always there was something working in the shadows of this dance I was doing, these roles I played. We are tricked into the experiences we need to fulfill the soul. We cannot dance the world without stumbling. The shadow loomed unseen, the thing that moved me, the soul working its mystery, feelings and impulses inserting, always calling for courage, for the world is a huge bubble in our minds . . . until life sticks a pin. . . .

Barely into the marriage, I was already on my way out.

But just as I thought it would collapse, it came to me in a flash; I could write a book! No sub-messages tweaking from a spaceship. No thought of UFOs then, just this clear impulse to write a book. My husband agreed to the "experiment." I told him I would know within a year whether or not I could write a book.

I wrote one in six months, an awful, wonderful, unpublishable thing. Of course, it was near-future, sci-fi fantasy, and, of course, the main character was a woman with a past in Atlantis. So in the name of research, I made an appointment with Dr. Helen Walker, to explore this business of reincarnation.

It scared me. A few years back, I had decided to list various possible past lives in my journal. I was alone, sitting on my bed. In those days, it was a mattress on the floor. The listing of past lives was a brave thing to do because reincarnation was a taboo in my mind; it was *occult*! Never mind the Atlantis story in me, I had these double things like a ladder, with contradictions running up both sides. (No doubt, my caution about things occult was influenced by fellowship with Christians, but it went deeper. In all of my studies of various world religions and metaphysics, I had a natural aversion to anything that smelled of the occult. The word means "hidden," not demonic, or evil, as some believe; nonetheless, it was a code in me for knowledge I instinctively avoided.)

But I had felt rather grown-up, sitting there on the bed, legs stretched out, as I listed possible past lives, with Atlantis at the top of the list. Something tweaked my big toe. It was just as if a person had pinched it. I jumped, and slammed shut my journal. Six years passed before I delved, again, into the subject of reincarnation.

So, when I went to see Dr. Walker in 1984, it was not with the intention of exploring my own past lives. I was just seeking information about reincarnation because it would be part of the book I was writing. (Secretly I *ached* to enter the mystery.) Dr. Walker assumed I had come to make an appointment for a personal regression, and like a man and a woman will pretend to just meet for a cup of coffee, the affair with my past began. "You mean me? Well, I suppose a regression would give me a feel for the character I'm writing about. . . ."

I returned to Dr. Walker a week later to be regressed. The trance state was so deep, I shivered, and my body vibrated; a blanket was provided (the altered state of mind affected my body temperature). It was the purest regression I've ever experienced; in future regressions, I never allowed myself to go so deep. I saw too much.

The most disturbing was a segment about Jesus. I was a follower, a young peasant woman with hair shorn close to the head, the cut of a slave. We called him the Master. His appearance differed from the archetypical pictures. I saw a robust man with blue eyes and long, reddish-blond hair. I saw him on the cross. We thought he had died, and I wept profusely. Dr. Walker moved me quickly to the next day. Sobbing, I said we knew the Master was alive. He had been placed in a tomb, but someone had come in the night and taken him away. We had no Bible then; all we knew was that Jesus was alive . . . and gone.

My belief about the resurrection of Jesus was rocked. But over time, I decided that the technical or political truth of resurrection was not important to me. (I believed in the eternalness of the soul.) In the same way that I don't insist that the Others are ETs, I don't insist that Jesus Christ existed in exactness to the stories in the New Testament. Certain myths, I learned, were tagged onto the story of Jesus, such as his birth to the virgin Mary. Still, I believed that there was truth in what I had viewed of the Master, while regressed. Later I experienced "recognition," reading Gnostic literature, especially the story of the Master in The Book of Thomas from *The Nag Hammadi Library* (Robinson 1990).

The effect of this sally into the reaches of "memory" was a heightened sense of Jesus in my history. Whoever he was, or is, Christ or Master, both or neither, he resides at my core as anchor for my faith, and super-link to God, the Great Mystery.

Both UFOs and experiences in hypnotic regressions can be belief smashers. What remains after the pulverization is mine, until that, too, is challenged in the next vortex. A quester walks a bridge of faith between experience and truth.

Atlantis was not on my mind when I told Dr. Walker I wanted to look for a possible prior relationship with my mother.

In the first scene, I was flying by means of a black box on my back, over a lush island I called Poseid (afterward, I learned this was another name for Atlantis). In the second scene, I was in a Roman-like bath with tall pillars and hieroglyphics on the glistening walls. I recognized my mother, a high priestess with snake bracelets on her upper arms. I was her servant, a lad with an Egyptian haircut, and eyes much larger than ours are today, as are depicted in some ancient statues and drawings on walls and tops of coffins, large, dark, slanted eyes.

There was a battle with men who had long brown hair all over their bodies. They used primitive but highly effective catapults to launch "fire balls" at our city. The building I was in was engulfed in flames, and I watched the lad die, the silver cord snapping as his spirit ascended. The lesson of that life was about abuse of psychic powers. (This "memory" keys to the communication in 1993, chapter 2, when the Others alluded to such abuses in Atlantis.)

Another link in this past life vision connects to the legend about Esau and Jacob in the Book of Genesis in the Bible. Readers of *Summoned* may recall my relating a dream in 1994 that keyed to the story of two kinds of human beings: One hairy like Esau, the other, smooth-skinned like Jacob, who draped goat skins around his neck to deceive his blind father into believing that he, Jacob, was the firstborn son. The seed of Jacob, the second born (a second kind of human being), would be "Lord over your brothers"—Esau's offspring, the hairy first-borns. (See Genesis 27:29.)

Messengers had told Dr. Karla Turner (now-deceased author of *Taken* [1994] and *Into the Fringe* [1992]) that the story of Jacob and Esau in the Bible was about the genetic alteration of humankind by extraterrestrials in our distant past. Three years after the dream that linked me with Dr. Turner, I would download a long "encoded" message that expanded on this story (chapter 11, *Summoned*).

This is an example of "recognition": In 1984, in the regression, I viewed hairy, caveman-like humans (offspring of Esau?) at battle with smooth-skinned people (Jacob's progeny?) on Poseid, an island believed to be mythical. One year after the regression, I read a book by Zecharia Sitchin that spoke of two kinds of human beings. Recognition: This matched my "memory" of Poseid. And ten years later, a dream keyed to a passage in Turner's book, which keyed to the Jacob-Esau story already in me. This is recognition.

Leaving Dr. Walker, going home to write my book . . . in my mind I was not a reincarnate of Atlantis, but merely an aspiring author who had just done some important research. I was not ready to accept what I had seen as real memories.

While I was weaving what I had envisioned in the regression into the plot of my novel, also from my pen flowed a story that was a distortion of the alien abduction phenomenon, which had not yet surfaced in my consciousness as real and present. There was nothing in the past-life regression that had been suggestive of anyone creating a breed of humans to serve as slaves to a master race, but this little horror story emerged in the memory of my protagonist's past life in Atlantis. But it was a story in sync with actual historical research done by Sumerian scholar Zecharia Sitchin, whose research I had not yet read.

After the novel was finished, when I did read *The 12th Planet* by Sitchin (1990), I experienced recognition. I read it like a history book about something I already knew (not all of the details, but the gist of the story). In my mind, links were clattering on a chain from Atlantis, to Sumer, to Egypt, to Jerusalem, to South America . . . the dark secret in our past rising up out of the sands, soul bones strewn on the deserts of memory. Eventually I read all of Sitchin's books in *The Earth Chronicles.* (Parallel to Sitchin's information, "The History of Humankind in Summary," chapter 11 in *Summoned,* focuses on the complications of the genetic alteration of humankind, as bears upon the evolution of souls.)

I had no idea in 1985 of the twists and turns that would occur in my own soul's journey in the near future. I thought I would write a few visionary novels, stay married, and live the golden dream of peaceable retirement. My heart was set upon it. Nonetheless, in the shadows of my dreams and cognizance, I was living double.

Upstairs, I was living the life of a traditional wife, while down in the basement, where I wrote, I was beginning to know that my difference was more than a past life in Poseid. I was beginning to know I was somehow involved in the UFO drama. The past life regressions and Sitchin's book had triggered something in me, beyond intellectual intrigue. It was all too familiar . . . something I knew deep inside . . . something taboo.

The stigma attached to contactees and abductees had not yet festered in the public mind, but instinctively I sensed the line that separated jokes about little green men from the reality of actual alien penetration into the affairs of humankind. There was a guardedness in me that preceded awareness of the dark story about alien abduction. There were dreams of running and hiding from UFOs. But I would awaken from them and laugh, and shake my head. Why was I having such dreams? I felt excited about ETs coming to Earth. I wanted to write a story about good ETs coming to Earth. But every time I began the story, I would be stopped by troubled thoughts; was there something to fear in the UFO? Around the time of discovering the evidences of implants in 1986, I remember feeling scared that something suspicious was going on in the background of my life. Later, when I began to seriously investigate my history, I went straight to certain dreams and nocturnal events that, at the times of these occurrences, had riveted my attention. But who would be *attracted* to the possibility of abduction? I was aware of the metaphysical law of attraction, and to some extent I believed that we create our own realities with our thoughts, so I gave no thought to these dreams and instances beyond the acknowledgment of them. I recorded them in my journals, then forgot them. Wife and writer were demanding roles, and I had a busy life beyond these functions, as well.

My second novel was about young children who are abducted, brainwashed, and developed into psychic spies by rogue CIA agents. The title is *Train Up a Child*, based on the Biblical scripture that says an adult will always return to her training. I meant to prove the scripture wrong. But which training did I mean to prove an adult could overcome? In my conscious mind, it was the programming in the church . . . but was there a deeper programming that predated?

When I discovered the evidences of implants, my daylight mind could not accept what it could not comprehend. An apple could fall from a tree and this was "scientifically real." But devices could not be inserted into my body without my knowledge, simply because I did not know how it could have occurred. I did not consider the implants with excitement about an unexplored reality. I was as bullheaded as any orthodox scientist in this respect. Never mind the actual triangular marks, showing blood, and the protrusion that indicated there was a small hard ball inside my hand. If I could not pose a theory about how they had come to be, forget it! And I did. Almost. My husband was impressed enough to snap photos of the marks on my hands . . . which came back blurred; a surprise, because he was an excellent close-up photographer. Not wanting anyone to think I suspected I'd been abducted, I downplayed the incident. Instinctively I knew the line not to cross, but inwardly I was truly spooked.

Next came *Ezekiel's Chariot*, written in 1987. Spaceships were not a part of the original draft. It was purely a story about a woman's guardian angel come to life in a little boy. But before the book was done, the extraterrestrial link had penetrated my consciousness to a degree that blurred lines between angels and ETs.

About the time I found a publisher for *Chariot* (Hampton Roads), Whitley Strieber's *Communion* (1988) had sparked international attention, and the media spotlight was on alien abduction. I did not experience recognition at the alien face on the cover of *Communion*, nor did I relate to Strieber's abduction experience. But his story left an impact. I knew it was a link in my own story, the one that was in me like a tide in an underground river, a story that would reveal missing links, if only I could write it. But, following the evidences of implants, *Chariot*, and Strieber's bold book, I wanted to retreat from the whole subject, and write something for a mainstream audience. Responses from various publishers during the course of shopping my novels, and vibrations in the media in general, were negative about new age literature, so I had my logic for wanting to shift to mainstream. But looking back, I can see the choice made in the shadows to distance myself from the emerging awareness that I was involved in something that I wasn't ready to know about.

Today, with my sense of timing of events, I suspect that I was not prepared emotionally, mentally, and physically to cope with full awareness of my involvement. Living double meant suppression of activities in hidden realms, as I lived out my private purposes as a human being in the material world.

Premature awakening to my role might have created problems beyond what I was equipped to handle.

Soon after the triangular surgeries on my hands in 1986, I began to study quantum physics, ancient history, genetics, and mythology. It was impossible to study these subjects and suppress the old story in me, triggered by Atlantis in '64, chimed in '75, and disturbed by dreams and phenomena in the 80s. But I was living side-by-side myself on the rungs of the ladder; on one side, wife and author; on the other, the stranger becoming.

When it was certain that *Chariot* would be published, I felt this would secure my marriage. In hindsight, it is plain to see that my husband and I were on different paths, and the gulf was becoming wider between them. But Tom was impressed by the publishing promise. He invested in new equipment for me, and designed bookmarks to announce the book to the world. Nonetheless, I was feeling more and more pulled to my life in the shadows.

The changes were subtle. I began to notice the image of a spinning globe in my mind whenever I thought about the world. And increasingly I was thinking about the whole world. I was drawn to watch educational shows on TV about the natives of the Earth in jungles and other remote places, and documentaries about animals, especially monkeys, apes, and chimps. I was struck with the intelligence of these creatures thought to not think or have self-awareness. In some ways, the natives I viewed seemed more advanced than "modern man." I watched a show about whales and tears streamed my face. I just knew they were highly intelligent creatures. Why didn't everyone know? I was waking up to the reality of interconnection of all Earth species, and with this, there was pain at realizing how separate we had made ourselves, how delusional the belief in our so-called superiority. People in this society, especially, seemed asleep to the very life system that supported us—this while beating our chests and bellowing about migration to other planets.

Feelings of alarm about wars were beginning to rise in me, too. When the Gulf War erupted, I wept. It was as if I woke up one day and discovered that my values were in conflict with the whole society. There was something wrong with us. All these wars, all this energy put into creating more powerful weapons of destruction. The world seemed crazy. But I didn't think of my husband as an ogre for working in the defense industry. . . . I had, too; and the men I had worked for were fine people. Our consensus was that we must maintain a strong defense against enemies, real or imagined, who would destroy us, if ever we lost the edge. I was no political philosopher or expert on matters of war; all I knew was: Wars had loomed large in our history, *and once again, we were in danger of blowing up the world.* . . .

This was the essence of feeling alien then . . . not feeling I was ET, but feeling I was living *among aliens*, people who seemed asleep to reality, people with stone hearts.

Unquestionably, my consciousness was undergoing a change. Was the UFO presence the activating force? In regards to the implantation of devices, the hypnotic regression with Dr. Walker, in 1995, suggested it was true. (The beings who performed the implanting were similar to Rowah in appearance; the "Sphinx people," I called them; they were all business.) Below is an excerpt from the regression (from page 59, *Summoned*).

Walker: Is this on a spaceship?
Redfield: Yes, but it's another scene. Very bright. Very bright. A lot of metal.
Walker: Where do you sense that it is?
Redfield: On some kind of craft. A laboratory.
Walker: On Earth, or is it in space?
Redfield: Space.
Walker: Are you the only one being sampled?
Redfield: No.
Walker: There are others?

Redfield: We're not being sampled. They put an activator in there. (*In my hand.*)

Walker: An activator?

Redfield: To speed things up.

Walker: What is the purpose of the activator?

Redfield: So you can be more directly taught. More directly guided.

Walker: Do they say why they want to teach you?

Redfield: We're planning something.

Walker: What are you planning?

Redfield: I don't have access to that information.

Activation had begun, but I was still striving to succeed at the dream of being a wife, while continuing the writing and studying. The story on the mystical landscape was quiet in comparison to the loud dream world I had constructed in a very real house on tangible ground. I did not want to lose home and husband, and this helped to suppress all indicators of alien intrusion. But at some level, I knew I was involved with the UFO presence. So as a kind of nervous handshake with the awareness, on my birthday in January, 1992, I returned to Dr. Walker for a regression that might show involvement with extraterrestrials . . . *before* this lifetime.

I viewed a scenario in the 1800s in Austria, supposedly my first encounter with aliens (like the tall, spindly ETs viewed when I probed the missing time events in childhood). The encounters began when I was young; the aliens wore robes with monk's cowls, hiding their faces until I was older and trusted them. They walk with their slender hips and legs seemingly going before them, in a graceful swanlike glide. Their heads are large, and mostly hairless, and their bodies are whitish, spindly, tall, and extremely thin. They seemed almost ethereal. If this "memory" is true, apparently this was when I was "recruited" as a participant in a drama that has been occurring all along in the shadows of human consciousness, not a part of the official story of human history.

It was the only audiotape of a past life regression that I never typed up.

I did not ask Dr. Walker to facilitate examination of possible encounters with aliens in *this lifetime*. That nothing "came up" seemed affirmation that I was not an abductee. Maybe I was just a sensitive person with *distant* ET connections? Maybe I was just picking up on the vibration. Maybe the whole notion of reincarnation was wrong. Maybe what I saw were scenes evoked from "cellular ancestral imprints." I'd never heard anyone pose such a theory, but consciousness and memory are mysteries, right? Did I think one of my ancestors encountered ETs? This was just as problematic. Maybe there was a "tag" in my bloodline. Maybe I was part of an evolutionary experiment. But I didn't see how I could be an abductee. The marks on my hands and all the rest were not *extraordinary* evidence. . . .

The demand for extraordinary evidence was the world's mandate. Like magic, it worked to discourage awareness of the UFO presence.

Extraordinary evidence or none, I was well into the becoming story before I even understood the gathering story. It was time for another leap. This time I had to be pushed.

Four months after the regression to probe for past life experience with extraterrestrials, my husband and I separated.

In five days, I was packed and gone.

CHAPTER FIVE:

Light Centers: Riding the Waves

For the soul, it was enough that we joined and loved each other, if only for ten years. But I am a human woman. Divorce sucks!

Four years later, I recorded this wisdom: "Respond to love as love beckons, but do not conclude where it will lead. Respond to the flames of passion as they may leap up, but do not imagine you know where such passion will lead. If you barely know of where you are being led, how can you know the path of another? If you could succeed at pulling another onto your path, then others could pull you onto their paths."

It was time to know my path. But "knowing thyself" takes time. How does one chart a map of unknown territory? It can only be discovered in the living.

I was full of knowing about the metaphysical concept, "you create your own reality." The divorce was a major conk on that head! It was not my intention to create that reality. In fact, I meant to create the opposite, a marriage that would endure until "death do us part." Maybe something died . . . which means that something new was born, or came to pass. Though I was not done struggling with the concept of reality creation, this communication, coming in November 1995, helped:

"You" create your own reality is a distortion. You do, to
limited extent, but you do not stand alone, ever, in any respect.
Together you create your reality . . . together you are forming a
large council, composed of many councils of two or more.
Together you are deciding what you want, what is to be.

But where in such wisdoms did the ET drama fit? Were
they, too, souls who chose paths and struggled to know their
destinies? Was there an interlinking of human and extraterrestrial destinies? Maybe, from a higher view, no differentiation
exists between them and us. Maybe we are all children of Life.

But as comfortable as I was with the *idea* of involvement
with extraterrestrials, the human had to be prepared to
encounter the alien Other on the mystical landscape.

Soon after leaving Denver, the grief lessened, and I was living in a comfortable home close to my parents in red rock country. Soon I was back in the writing groove, finishing *Lucy Blue*,
and starting another novel, *Once Upon a Starship*, an attempt to
write the gathering story. The gathering was of seven people
abducted onto a spaceship in outer space. Once they were back
on Earth, with memories suppressed, it would be a finding story.
The protagonist would remember some of what happened, and
a particular man. . . . But when I began the work with letters and
numbers in the fall of 1993, *Starship* went on the shelf, never to
be completed.

As stated before, contact began in tandem with the alpha-
betical work. In one of the first telepathic conversations, I
finally understood the gathering story. It was not necessarily
happening in a visible way on this physical plane. It had to do
with minds and hearts linking up on the mystical landscape. I
envisioned a matrix of thought forms generated by millions of
people all over the globe. Light workers, I called them, were
gathering and anchoring light, helping to stabilize energies, as
upheavals, wars, and "natural" catastrophes increased. But I was
told later, on January 7, 1994:

There will not be devastations at the scale that some prophecies imply. Some will *feel* such devastations, and upheavals will continue until the portals[7] close. Until that time, there is plenty of time for all to consider and choose.[8] You feel the urgency because your right foot stands beyond the portal. Your left foot is still in rhythm, tapping to the song of time.[9] Time swells and contracts, falls sideways, shoots into a beam, and swells again. You ride the waves, tapping, tapping, mapping the way. . . .

There was more. A geometric symbol was imparted to illustrate the look of the future in abstract; the reverse of a diamond—a triangle pointing downward—poised above an upright triangle, with points interpenetrating in a dynamic process. When the downward pointing triangle completes the descent, the two triangles will be interlocked in the Mogen David hexagon. This symbolizes completion of the current "wave movement," which I translate to mean a transformational event; but not the old millennial story, a "judgment-rescue" story, with the "good" glorified, and the "evil" cast to Hell.

That these events and mysteries were occurring around the flip of the big calendar seemed almost a joke orchestrated by Coyote the Trickster. Sponsored by Pope Gregory XIII, the Gregorian calendar, now in use in most parts of the world, was

---

[7] Portal: This word has several meanings for me. In general, it represents a gateway to another dimension, and a crosspoint event, or threshold. Literally, it symbolizes an actual opening, or door, inside me, where I "enfold" in the light body configuration to traverse finer dimensions. Having my right foot in the door describes my state of being when I am working in "split consciousness," grounded here, but aware in a visionary way of the other dimension.

[8] Time for all to consider and choose: This came up again and again, in reference to a choice each will make before the "portals close." (More in the "hidden message" in chapter 7.)

[9] Tapping to the song of time: pertains to the unfolding of events in this time/space dimension.

adopted by England and the colonies in 1752. Before that was the Julian calendar, inaugurated by Julius Caesar in 46 B.C. Association of end-time prophecies with a millennium is a fairly recent obsession. Time swells, and contracts . . . and we ride the waves.

Riding the waves describes a way of life, the way I was living mine, a path between creating one's own reality and "Thy will be done"; a dance between the old religious way and the new age mandate to grab the wheel and steer the ship. My way seemed to be to plunge, regularly, overboard into the waves, while hanging on to certain anchors, such as my faith in Jesus. Jonah, inspiration for my novel, personifies this way. His plunge overboard was a way to the shore. Regardless of our adventures, whether steering ships or falling into the sea, if we survive, always there is a shore, the ground of being for Earthbound · souls.

The communication about light centers was one of several that occurred in August and September, 1993. I was not yet seriously believing I was in contact with alien intelligences. I wanted to believe the transmitters were angelic, or "super-Muse," like Clio in 1989, guidance for a novel I would write. Why something as extraordinary as telepathic communication would be going on simply to guide in the writing of a novel never struck me as particularly odd. Looking back now, it does!

But in the quiet part of my mind, I had not forgotten the dream about the ETs commissioning me to write a book. I had tried to begin that book several times; but my daylight mind always sabotaged it, because . . . get real! It was simply forbidden to think about the dream as an actual encounter.

But I did think about the contact. I knew I was tapped into a "channel" that was different from what I'd heard and seen of channelers. There was no trance, and the writing was not "automatic." And I was certain this was not my Higher Self. Would my Higher Self transmit information on how aliens reproduce? (See chapter 7.) Some of the communications were frankly alien. But these, too, I took in stride, half-believing they were information for the novel I would write (half-knowing I was communicating with alien intelligences).

Was there ever a time in the early days when I felt I might be related to them—an ET soul here as a human link? Not then; that came later, after the breach.

I was riding the waves, going with the flow, recording what came. We have no language for this kind of experience, I understood, working with letters and numbers. We could make up words, such as "channeling," or borrow words from older cultures, such as "oracle" or "shaman," but European-Americans, for the most part, were uneducated about these kinds of experiences. Uneducated but opinionated! The message I picked up from mainstream America was that such experiences and activities were beneath our dignity. That, or it all fell under the heading of occult with emphasis on the negative. And regularly it was pointed out that such experiences were not "scientific," as if science were the ultimate voice of authority on reality. When people did use science to study these events, it was labeled "pseudo-science."

Naturally, I wanted to avoid being labeled as a pseudo-anything. The solution was to pretend that I was just playing around, experimenting, part of the living-double skill. But in my heart, I knew there was a serious side to this business.

Early on, I was receiving information that had nothing to do with preparation for a novel. Rather, it seemed for the purpose of preparing me so that I could grasp the importance of my small part. If it wasn't important, why work so hard, why go the lengths I did? But coming to understand the importance was a slow process. In the beginning, it was somewhat playful, as if I had tuned into an ET or angelic "chat room."

One of the early messages (mentioned in *Summoned*) warned that some government might stage a UFO landing. In the playful way they expressed themselves in the beginning, it began:

Once upon a time on planet Earth, humankind became very smart, very smart indeed, creating all manner of technologies to extend life and reduce disease, and communicating at lightning speeds and building machines that could fly to other planets. In their smartness, they built so many clever and truly helpful gadgets and gizmos that the entire face of the globe was cluttered with them, every tribe having many varieties and still more coming on the market to make life easier on one hand, while more difficult on the other; for in order to obtain the newest and best and most relieving, more work was required at higher salaries. Alas! Everyone was *very* busy working for and buying and sustaining and maintaining all these gadgets and gizmos. Not the least of which were television machines through which communications occurred worldwide in astonishing vividness that could only be believed— for the eyes and ears do not lie, there it was, on TV—the word, the action, what happened in Saudi Arabia, on the moon, inside the White House . . . there it was on the screen, *LIVE* . . .

And what will people think when the first spaceship lands and allows itself to be filmed by cameramen, and is shown to television viewers all over the globe?

(Me: They're real! We told you so!)

Could not a government *simulate,* mimic a UFO landing?

(Me: And its occupants?)

Did Hollywood create an ET? Aliens and third encounters?

(Me: But we knew it was Hollywood.)

But if you were not told it was Hollywood, could you discern the difference? Can you believe—discern—*anything* you see on film? How?

(Me: Inside, what my guts tell me.)

Why do you trust that?

(Me: Because I feel protected . . . guided . . . and I am skeptical of TV and governments.)
　　Why?

(Me: Because I know how we have been misled; I have experienced it, read about it, and know that others have, too.)
　　So *you* might not be fooled. But what of the masses who have developed no such discernment qualities?

(Me: I know. I realize. But how will my story help?)
　　Your work is simply one small preparation.

(Me: Point understood. Now, my problem, as you well know—please help me sort it out—I begin, I meander off, or my internal editor sticks in, over and over again. Why do I get muddled?)
　　Sometimes from interferences. Your part is small but powerful. All who participate are interfered with.

(Me: What about shields and protection?)
　　They cannot harm you or thwart your goal. You must write *through* . . .

(Me: *Crickets*! [Just then, the sound of crickets in the house leapt a decibel.] You mean, keep at it, don't give up?)
　　Yes, write through until you have it.

So, while I was communicating with them, I took it seriously enough, but up from the table or chair, going about my mundane affairs, or interacting with people, I was still living double.

The communication about light centers happened the same day as the above message:

　　The light centers you have identified as key are among you now, established and in process of being established, some with *those who have been planted and cultivated,*[10] some with volunteer Earthlings. *Your book—if you trust us and write what we direct* [11]—will trigger in these identification and will encourage and strengthen our joint efforts to lift consciousness in preparation for a revolutionary evolutionary transition that is necessary in order to diminish corruptive elements and establish among you leaders and guides who in generations to come will work to de-program, as it were, the false doctrines that frighten you so much. Do not fear false doctrines; in and of themselves they are not evil and have no power. Ultimately truth shines forth. Your feelings about false doctrines originated in your own experience, which was necessary in order for you to passionately agree to fulfill that which otherwise you might—would have—considered to be an intellectual problem, as is discussed in universities and other centers of higher learning where people who are without direct experience cogitate about the behavior of those with whom they cannot relate.

You know how it feels, in a deep way, to be taught something that does not fulfill the promises made. You know how it feels to believe something and embrace it, to have it crumble in your hands like dry leaves. A good metaphor, using the tree, the leaves connoting individuals, as relates to Jesus' story about branches being lopped off or withering and dying; true doctrine produces loving results, life, passion, fruit, whereas false doctrine produces confusion and fear and ultimately chaos.

---

[10] Those who have been planted and cultivated: Reference to ET souls planted into the human garden. I did not flinch or balk at this statement; the argumentative, reactionary daylight mind was partially suspended; I was more in the "knowing-remembering-recognizing" state of mind. It is only my daylight mind that has trouble believing it.
[11] Your book—if you trust us and write what we direct: Translated to mean a novel I would write . . . ignoring the part about them directing it. In time, "direction" would mean to me the imparting of certain messages, which I identified as such in *Summoned*. Direction does not mean force. Everything I share is my choice.

(Me: So . . . does the "doctrine" of abduction not produce fear? Please tell me about abduction again.)

We said a mimicking to create fear. [Reference to an earlier message.] If it were possible to defeat us in this way, we would continue helpless, no? So we came up with a plan they cannot so easily mimic, though *they* [12] are doing a good job.

(Me: They are mimicking light centers?)

Consider the channelers who leave such a bad taste in your mouth. Enough of you have come forward with "pap" that many have written this off, too. But light centers are different. These . . . are they—

(Me: CRICKETS DRIVING ME NUTS! What is the meaning of telephone . . . and crickets? [Ringing telephone, with no one on the line, and an intensifying of the sound of crickets during such communications.])

Interferences. Centers of light—each, alone, and in small groups of like-spirited—meditate, shielding themselves from interferences. They are dedicated channels of light. These literally become light centers, establishing light amidst the children of Earth, creating an environment into which *the new race/species* [13] can abide. The more light centers created, the more influence on

---

[12] They: They who are abducting, "mimicking light centers," and interfering: Reference to spiritual warfare (chapter 10, *Summoned*). Links also to information shared in the communications about Atlantis. Comes under the heading of "as above, so below." In this light, if warfare—battles of will—are activities down here on the material plane, they are activities "above" on the mental-spiritual plane. The call is to expand consciousness to become aware of the sources, and reasons for such battles of will.

[13] The new race/species: I put no asterisk by this phrase in my mind. It was taboo. While I did not believe the standard dark story of invasion, I felt that something was going on, having to do with creation of a new kind of human being.

harmonious radiations that are in discordance due to the great waves of fear and anger and hate. Yes, a wave and particle metaphor is applicable, light centers serving as powerful particles in relationship to waves. Yes, they are all one, but different in behavior—see the image of particles rolling over waves, lining them up, settling them down, regulating, harmonizing them into gentle undulations rather than the waves stirred up by the hurricane winds of fear and anger.

This is a good place to mention the hypnotic regression with Dr. Hover in August 1995, when I accessed "memory" of an examination scenario when I was sixteen years old, involving the beings we call greys (reference the face on the cover of Strieber's book *Communion*). This came as a complete surprise, because I had no consciousness tag for this kind of entity. And yet, so far as such "memories" go, it felt starkly realistic. I could feel their electrical energy buzzing over my body. The upshot of this scene was that Dr. Hover pulled out of me a confession that I was involved in a project to create a new kind of being. This is the part of the abduction enigma that caused me the most trouble.

Part of the purpose of this book is to lift my own consciousness as to the meaning of the birth drama. I'm not convinced I was literally abducted by "greys." Memory is a dynamic we don't know much about. When I was wrestling with whether or not to use hypnotic regression to probe for details of my experience, I was given this counsel (excerpted):
Recorded April 30, 1995:

Now we look at collective consciousness and the idea of ushers, those who serve as ushers into this new realm of perception; those who help facilitate the shift; for as it is that adults are there when a baby is born, you will be the nursemaids and nursehusbands of this fragile new child being born into consciousness.

"Memory recovery" . . . the value varying according to when it is accessed. If too soon, can be incomprehensible and frightening; needs to be at a point of maturity, so that the person can see beyond the drama, to sense the higher meaning. The value being to serve better as a helpmate to higher facilitators; when this is pushed, or prematurely experienced, this value is side railed, and the person can become fixated on false premises, having no way of interpreting the data, reaching wrong conclusions, and spreading this wrong information. This is why there is a strong taboo, why there are screens, etc. To protect you from seeing too soon what you cannot comprehend.

Yes, there is a point of readiness, and for some this is a crucial turning point, those who are here to serve in certain capacities; while for others it is better they do not probe just yet. Each serves to bring into light an aspect that broadens the picture, in preparation for the view that none see in total. And someday you will see how all these aspects relate, but for now it seems to you to be a confusing picture with many contradictory pieces; a waste of time to argue as to which is valid, which you cannot know, for you cannot make such determinations, lacking the big picture.

Remember, we are preparing all, taking into consideration a multitude of levels of awareness, while you can see only in part. So what is helpful to one group is foolishness to another. So yes, each writer or presenter has a specific audience, and the wise one does not criticize those who "don't get it," but understands that they get it a different way; as you can only get it in a particular way, in accordance with your level of development.

Along with the recordings about Atlantis in earlier chapters, I chose to share the message about the light centers to show that in the early days of contact, the communications dovetailed into stories already in me. The topics of conversation were familiar, and so were the transmitters, though I felt I should not ask their names. I was not as wary as I had been in 1989, when Clio came through, but I remembered that it was *me* who had asked for a name. I assumed these beings were like Clio, "spiritual" in nature, beyond names as we use to identify ourselves. When they finally did identify themselves as El, the servants of the Law of One, I understood it as only a "name tag" designating the kind of beings they were, their "nature." El is an extremely old name; we only have theories as to its original meaning. Joseph Campbell wrote that in the Hebrew mythologies of Yahweh (*The Hero's Journey* 1972), the traits of two gods are united as Yahweh, a storm god, and El, a solar god. Does this mean I'm in contact with a trait? Campbell was discussing ancient myths having to do with twin aspects of God as are expressed in various ways among cultures. The meaning of El, for me, is shorthand for Elohim, which means a pantheon of higher beings we have called, over the ages, gods or angels. Once they signed off as El "of the constellation you know as Alcyone in the Pleiades." Sounds ET . . . but what do I know?

If I'd had my way, I would have sat at the kitchen table working the letter/number designs, and recording the wisdoms, until the hearse came and packed me away to bury. But I was like Jonah, below deck, asleep, thinking I was the master of my ship. Jonah could not avoid experiencing the consequences of his choice, and neither could I, even if we were both in the dark as to when we had agreed to play such roles.

Going on four months, I had cheated sleep and eaten irregularly. The toll came as a sudden bout of flu at the end of December '93. Nothing I'd done in life thrilled me as much as the work with letters and numbers. I might have pursued it to the gates of insanity or death, had physical illness not stopped me.

It was more than an ordinary flu. For five nights in succession, when I went to bed, I was "made to feel," it seemed, the sorrows of all mankind since day one, and the devastations created by our ignorance. These emotions surging up in the weakness of illness were a torment, in contrast to the heights of ecstasy I had experienced in recent months. It felt as if my psyche was being wrenched apart. Although I am a private person, I could not keep from wailing; the pain was so deep and unrelenting. I was sure the neighbors could hear me, but I could not stop until I was emptied of the tears for that night.

That was six years ago, and I haven't had a cold or flu since. I don't know what to call the experience. But it was definitely a turning point, passage into a more serious zone of the mystery. I remembered the "visitation" of Los Angelos a couple of months prior. Something serious was at stake; maybe the survival of the human species. Inwardly I was trembling. I had seen the other side of our face, the prototypical species that cannot survive as we are. I didn't have these precise words then, but the story was unfolding in me. I was at a point—*we* were at a point—poised at a portal of change, some riding the waves, others bailing water out of a ship about to sink. And many were asleep.

And the light workers were gathering, remembering, beckoning to safer shores.

As of January, 1994, I had not yet been confronted with the call to perform as a messenger, except behind the veil of fiction, a no-risker. Only experience would show that my choice to go the path of least resistance was like Jonah hopping a boat to Tarshish. But before I realized I would have to do more than fiction, Jonah emerged in my mind as inspiration. I'm no prophet, but I recognized his predicament. My call was not so clear . . . no king to warn of coming devastations, no god rousing me with one simple message, no whale to clarify my choices. Nonetheless, there were correlates in the story to ponder . . . not only relative to my little personal drama, but also to the big story unfolding. Jonah and the whale, I believe, is a perennial story for any people, any time, anywhere.

For good or evil, the story provokes my gene for irreverence. (In chapter 7, I will resume the account of my experience.)

CHAPTER SIX:

The Messenger Link:

Jonah Blows It. . . .

All the sailors were afraid and each cried out to his own god. And they threw the cargo into the sea to lighten the ship. But Jonah had gone below deck where he lay down and fell into a deep sleep.

—*Jonah 1:5*

Let's pretend that the story of Jonah and the whale was based on an actual event. I bet, like abductees today, Jonah had no extraordinary evidence to prove that he spent three days and nights in the belly of a "big fish." The seaweed clinging to his body as he emerged on the beach would fail to impress scientists then, and of course, his testimony of experience would count for nothing.

Jonah might have delayed going to Nineveh to find others who had been swallowed by whales. He would meet gritty investigators who would interrogate him as to his mental stability and credibility. This would be good experience before he ventured into Nineveh.

Probably, initially, the investigators were impressed with Jonah's story—a multiple witness event! But then Jonah probably blew it by mentioning the contact with a divine personage. Oh, no, another deluded swallowee with a message to save the world! Just one city, Jonah explained, but the investigators were already rolling up their papyruses, shaking their heads, bemoaning the luckless find, one more babble artist with information from one more god.

On the road to Nineveh, Jonah must have experienced self-doubt, wondering if it was really God who had nearly sunk the ship and sicced the whale on him. Maybe it was a *demon* . . . maybe Lucifer himself! Maybe in the throes, Jonah was infused with *dis*information. Or maybe it was a hoax staged by the sailors. Jonah could picture them laughing their heads off, rolling on the deck, knowing he was such a sucker. He would probably actually go to the king and recite the message planted in his beam while he was drugged—that was it! The mariners put something in the wine.

Maybe he should heed the scripture in the Book of Luke, warning people to ignore signs and wonders; but Luke wasn't alive yet, the New Testament didn't yet exist. From what text could Jonah find reliable guidance? What if *all* scriptures were a scam, history contrived to produce believers as pawns in some demonically inspired agenda to control the masses to some end impossible for an ordinary human to comprehend? But he *did* hear that voice ordering him to deliver a message. The swallowing might not have impressed the investigators, but it sure got Jonah's attention! And all that business in the belly. How could he deny it? What if it *was* God? What would happen to Nineveh if he ditched the call a second time?

There is a whole chapter in *The Hero's Journey* describing the negative consequences for denying a call; but Joseph Campbell wasn't even a twinkle in God's eye yet . . . a book that wouldn't be written for a couple of millennia . . . what's a guy to do? Where's the script for messengers of the Divine? Would he be branded a prophet, expected to be a voice box for unseen gods, the Real Thing, or demons disguised? Who knew? And what if the king threw him out on his ear?

In the actual Bible story, the voice of God wakes Jonah up in the middle of the night to give him a message to proclaim to Nineveh in Assyria. Apparently reluctant to perform as a messenger, Jonah hops a boat for Tarshish in Spain. But God sends a storm to deter our boy, and then a whale to swallow Jonah whole. As the boat is rolling and heaving, about to sink, the sailors are bucketing water, and praying to their gods for deliverance. Where is Jonah? Down below, grabbing a snooze. Apparently free will was not quite a fully developed endowment in those days, never mind the story about the willful act of Eve that purportedly caused the fall of man. Whatever the quirks and glitches in the evolution, or endowment of will, Jonah was persuaded to change his mind in the belly of a whale.

As the story is writ down, we can wonder if Jonah was implanted with an activator, while inside the belly, considering his changed attitude after the whale barfed him out on the beach. But then, after the message was delivered, there was the typical human belligerence, expressed in complaints about being coerced to act as a messenger, to which God responded with an enigmatic statement about the necessity of using a middleman to communicate with "120,000 people who cannot tell their right hands from their left" (*Jonah* 4:11). Might this be because the right and left hemispheres in the brains of the Ninevites were not yet synchronized? Whatever the reason for messengers for the Divine, then or now, and despite his initial protest, Jonah fulfilled. The message? Nineveh would be overturned by rival forces in forty days.

Jonah didn't have to spell out the particulars of salvation; the king knew (*Jonah* 3:8-9): "Let [everyone] give up their evil ways and violence. Who knows? God may relent and with compassion turn from his fierce anger so that we will not perish." (In those days, the king was very religious, and God was fiercely angry.)

The part of the story that gets little press is what happened to the messenger after the message was delivered. The humility and quick compliance of the king and his people are not the only oddities in this story. After the event, Jonah was angry. ". . . God said to Jonah, 'Do you have a right to be angry about the vine?'"

"'I do,' he said. 'I am angry enough to die'" (*Jonah* 4:9).

God had grown up a vine to provide shade and protection against the hot sun and stinging wind. But then the vine withered, exposing Jonah's head to the harsh elements. Fine reward for a prophet. Why did he have to serve as a messenger? He knew God would be merciful, would spare the people destruction. Jonah felt used, could not see the sense of it. Why didn't God just speak to the king directly? he may have wondered.

But what if Jonah had faltered in delivery? For that story, we need a skeptical king. . . .

Jonah Blows It and Nineveh Blows Up

King of Nineveh: Cat got your tongue?

Jonah: No, Your Highness. I beg your patience. I'm new at this. [Jonah is on his knees in a respectful cower.]

King: [Deep sigh. A woman in a belly dancer's outfit sashays forward, offering the king a goblet of nectar. He takes a sip, glares at Jonah.] Why are your kind always so . . . disheveled? [The king sniffs.]

Jonah: Ordinarily I am quite neat, Your Highness. I beg your tolerance. Three days inside the belly of a whale, you would be disheveled, too!

King: [Jerks. Nectar sloshes out of goblet. Belly dancer hastens over with a cloth to blot the king's red velvet robe. King waves the woman away.] The belly of a whale! Your kind . . . your stories get more absurd with the passing of every equinox.

Jonah: [Sitting slightly taller now, but still on his knees.] No disrespect, Your Highness, but it happened, it really did. This whale—

King: Blue, grey, or humpback? [To the belly dancer:] Liza, bring my pipe. I've got a feeling this is going to be a long one. [Liza leaves, returns with an ornate bong. The king tamps herbs into it as Liza steps over to a palm frond to await his next command.]

Jonah: Blue, I think, a big mother! But I was hardly of a mind to notice the color.

King: You were fishing. . . . [King blows a wad of fragrant smoke, brings a leg up over the arm of the throne and gestures for Jonah to continue.]

Jonah: Not fishing. For reasons I would rather not go into, I was pushed overboard . . . I was on a ship.

King: Pushed overboard into the maw of a whale? What'd you do, try to make off with their stash?

Jonah: No, Your Highness. It's my God. Let me explain. This storm, a *very* dangerous storm came out of nowhere, and it looked like the ship was going to sink. The mariners cried to their gods to stop the storm, but no luck. By then, I knew the problem. It was my God venting his anger, because, well, I was reluctant to prophesy, which is the reason I—

King: We'll get to that. Go on with your story. Jonah, is it?

Jonah: [Nods.] Well, I could see the writing on the wall . . .

King: What wall?

Jonah: Figure of speech. Excuse me. My ancestors were Egyptian. I mean, I could see what was coming down. You don't have to be a king to. . . . Pardon me. Like I said, I'm new at this.

King: Get on with it! [Big wad of smoke erupts from bong.]

Jonah: I told the crew and shipmaster to throw me into the sea and the storm would stop. [Jonah spreads his arms in a gesture of helplessness.] It was either drown or be responsible for the deaths of all of the crew members. If I learned nothing else, I learned my God means business!

King: I'm shivering in my boots.

Jonah: [Huffs.] He's no one to take lightly. *That* I got in the belly of the whale. Three days, three nights!

King: [Sets the bong on the floor, waves Liza away before she can remove it. King bends forward, rests his elbows on his knees, gazes, dilated pupils.] Tell me, Jonah . . . what's it like inside a whale?

Jonah: To tell the truth, my memory is kind of hazy. Maybe they blocked my memories.

King: They? You had company inside the belly? I suppose a school of undigested fish. . . . [King rolls his eyes at Liza.]

Jonah: It was nothing like you might expect in the belly of a whale. It was actually like being inside a synagogue, except a lot darker. But definitely I wasn't alone! There were these . . . big, tall people. Looked like praying mantises.

King: [Voice cracks over a laugh he manages to swallow.] How tall?

Jonah: [Reaches his arm up, stretches.] *Way* tall. Like Siriuns.

King: [To Liza:] Borrows from one myth to feed another! [Liza flashes a knowing smile.] [To Jonah:] And what did you and these *way tall* praying mantises *do* for three days and three nights inside the belly of a blue whale? And speak swiftly. My vizier is on his way to conduct business.

Jonah: [Sinks lower, shoulders slump.] Details are hazy. Sorry. But I do remember praying.

King: That, I can imagine.

Jonah: And then I was encoded.

King: The hell . . .

Jonah: Don't ask me to explain. They did something to my . . . [Points to his head.]

King: No doubt! [To Liza:] Get rid of this . . . [Indicates bong.] And bring forth a fresh papyrus and a sharp quill.

Jonah: [Raises up, lifts a hand.] But the message . . .

King: [Jerks head.] Are you still here?

Jonah: I'm supposed to tell you . . .

King: [Snaps his fingers, and in strides a royal guard *almost* as tall as a praying mantis, belly-of-a-whale-kind; grabs Jonah under his armpits, hauls him up, packs him, sandaled feet kicking, across the intricately tiled floor.]

Jonah: [Just before the guard throws him down the stairs, Jonah shouts:] *Nineveh will be overturned in forty days!*

King: [Smirks at Liza, who is still smiling, knowingly.] Yeah, right. Like it rained for forty days after our supposed ancestor Noah launched an ark that housed two of every kind of flying, creeping, crawling, slithering, lumbering, defecating, fornicating creature on Earth—undoubtedly at the order of the same god who sent our derelict prophet into the yawning maw of a whale!

FORTY DAYS HENCE . . .

BOOM! Babylonians bomb Nineveh and swarm forth to seize the spoils.

Near a cluster of cacti on a desert close to the devastation, Jonah bursts from the tent he had erected to await the inevitable doom.

"Told you!" he yells, throwing a fist to the sky. Shakes his head, starts dismantling the tent.

"Jonah . . . "

Jonah trembles, hearing the voice of God. His knees wobble; he sinks to the sand. It's so hot, he can see waves of moist heat undulating over the sand. The sky is cloudless, and electric blue. Sweat rolls down the sides of his face. His gown is saturated, and only a third-cup of water remains in his pouch. His lips are parched; his tongue feels like the head of lizard.

"I tried, Lord. I did my best!" Jonah shivers, looks askance, wonders where his god is, exactly, afraid to get caught overtly looking for signs. Last time anyone saw the face of God, the seer was drafted to do a job you wouldn't wish on a leper. Even seeing a *finger* of God was dangerous. Men who saw fingers became prophets for *life*! The pay stinks, the material rewards are puny, and the ridicule *hurts*. (Jonah is a sensitive man.)

"I have a mission in mind for you, Jonah."

Oh, no . . .

"Consider it in the light of redemptive karma."

"But my heart was in the right place. . . ." Jonah pats his chest. "Doesn't that count for something?"

"Certainly," God replies. "You won't go to Hell."

Jonah's relief is so profound, he squeaks—not quite the squeal of zeal he feels. It's best not to be too emotional in the presence of God. His patience is sometimes short. Everyone knows the capricious, cantankerous, and not a little cruel nature of Jonah's god; one day he's pleased at the aroma of a burnt lamb sacrifice; the next, blasting a command to destroy some neighboring tribe that displeases him.

"What I have in mind for you, Jonah, is a kind of remedial school for messengers."

"School! I'm not complaining . . ." Jonah hastens to add, remembering the awful disgorgement out of the whale's belly onto the beach, and the humiliation he felt, trying to warn the king. But if God and Destiny have joined hands in the halls of time to write on the walls of his mind, what can he do?

"School," Jonah repeats, nodding his head, like a carpenter's hammer slamming down on a tent hook.

"Look up, Jonah."

Jonah stops bobbing his head and looks upward. "Holy fish!" he shouts, momentarily forgetting about God's annoyance at emotional outbursts. "What the blazes is . . ."

"Let's call it a chariot, Jonah. Come to carry you to that school I mentioned."

A blue cone light shoots down, as if from the belly of a silver, metallic . . . *whale*!

"I get it!" Jonah yelps. "Those *things* we called chariots are really whales!"

Doubt niggles at the edges of his mind. "Wait a minute. How'd a whale get in the sky?"

The blue light engulfs him. As Jonah is twirled upward, a snake curled up at the base of a cactus hears God mutter, "A little mystery is good for my children. It keeps them humble, and I *like* humble."

The snake slithers away from the cactus.

"Where do you think you're going?" God says.

"Knowing . . ." the snake hisses enigmatically. "I like *knowledge* . . . especially knowledge of good and evil. . . ."

For reasons we can only guess, God did nothing to stop the snake from going to the devastated city, to spread the same gospel preached under a certain tree in a certain garden in mythical antiquity. Perhaps there is Something Higher than gods, that likes a balance of knowledge and humility and the dance required to achieve that balance. Maybe (Frank DeMarco suggested) the Something Higher is a *humming being* . . . and with just the right balance of knowledge and humility, we can hear it humming deep within our bodies. (Co-owner and chairman of the board of Hampton Roads Publishing, editor of *Summoned*, and author of *Messenger* and *Muddy Tracks, Exploring an Unsuspected Reality*, Frank DeMarco is also an insightful friend!)

The story of Adam and Eve is another legend that has long fascinated me. Are we as naive and as manipulatable as were our prototypical parents? Are we as manageable as was Jonah, who tried to ditch the call of messenger? Some theologians perceive the story of Adam and Eve to be about the "downfall" of man, based on our parents' disobedience. The official story is that because of their disobedience, we, their offspring, were cursed with the work of survival, and the awesome job of the proliferation of the human species to six billion, and still counting.

But what would be the story if Eve and Adam had not eaten the fruit? There would be no human race. Adam and Eve would not have "known" each other. (The word "knowing" in the Bible is interpreted to mean sexual intercourse.) They would have remained in the garden, celibate and obedient. From the official religious view, it would seem that the endowment of will, along with sex, is a power we ought not to exercise. But to obey the command to resist the eating of the fruits of knowledge *is* exercising the will. Had Adam not chosen to give in to the temptation, had he been a "good boy," the result would have been innocence that never tastes of the trials and triumphs of embracing physical life as it is, in its fullness of contrasts and challenges.

I can make no sense of a god who creates a world of contrasts, creates children with powers of will, then forbids them to exercise that will in the positive. If we were to obey the dictates of such a schizoid god, effectively our lives would be like those of the animals who are governed by instinct and "training."

I question the paternity of a god who purportedly would drown the lot of us, save for Noah and crew, because there was "only evil in our hearts"; this after his "sons" came down and cavorted with the "daughters of man," according to Genesis 6. This odd scripture, which has long puzzled Biblical scholars, may be a distorted memory fragment from a breach in human evolution by extraterrestrials called the Nephilim or Anunnaki.

> The term [Anunnaki] literally means "Those Who From Heaven to Earth Came." They are spoken of in the Bible as the *Anakim*, and in chapter 6 of Genesis are also called *Nephilim*, which in Hebrew means the same thing: "Those Who Have Come Down From the Heavens to Earth." (Sitchin 1990)

What were Jonah's choices? Could he have refused to act as a messenger, even after the awesome experience inside the belly of the big fish? Or was he brainwashed, in effect, *made* to obey?

The question applies to the UFO presence. People report being snatched up into the bellies of "sky whales." Not all return with warnings similar to Jonah's message to Nineveh. In fact, if UFO experiencers return with messages, the messages differ so much, one from the other, as to seriously call into question all information emerging from alien sources.

In this way, the UFO is different from the stories of old. Rather than one clear and coherent message, as is set down in holy scriptures, there is a confusion of messages, altogether a babble . . . reminiscent of the Tower of Babel story, when the gods (plural, according to scripture), conspired to produce confusion to thwart the progress of human beings. The story says we were becoming too god-like, represented in the symbol of a tower, which the prevailing gods destroyed. Before this event, we spoke and understood one language, the Good Book says. As insurance to prevent us from building another "tower of power," the gods did something to confound language, which resulted in the scattering of peoples all over the globe.

The Bible and other sacred literature are the results of multiple confounding stories, worked over to reflect the beliefs and intents of the book makers. We could do the same today: Cull from the multiplicity of stories about UFO experiences a new gospel of sky gods. Or we could pause and wonder about the similarities to the story of Babel and the current phenomenon. Is there a "league of gods" at work to confound communication, just as we begin again to assert our independence and advance our creative powers?

The effect of my contact and UFO experiences has been to excite the questions that were in me before the breach in my physical domain. It has caused me to probe deeper into the mysteries of our history and nature. I am not satisfied with the "face" of the UFO, the appearance of a puzzle possibly meant to baffle and thwart us, as is illustrated in the story of the destruction of the Tower of Babel. I am inclined to believe that the activities of the UFO compose a complex message about human will and consciousness, about beliefs and choices, a message about our creative potentials; and a message about hidden counterforces that may intend to interrupt progress in the direction of our becoming the masters of our own reality and destiny. (But this is just another story, remember.)

Stories such as Adam and Eve, the Tree and the Serpent, the Tower, and Jonah, may contain clues about matters of will, evolution of consciousness, and the correlate mystery we call soul or spirit. The Serpent, who advises our parents to eat of the Tree of Knowledge, may represent the DNA coil. I'm not the only one with this theory. For anyone who is studying along these lines, I recommend a brilliant little book by Swiss anthropologist, Jeremy Narby (*The Cosmic Serpent: DNA and the Origins of Knowledge* 1998).

> So I decided to call Fritz-Albert Popp in his university laboratory in Germany. . . . I ended up asking him whether he had considered the possibility of a connection between DNA's photon emission and consciousness. He replied, "Yes, consciousness could be the electromagnetic field constituted by the sum of those emissions. But, as you know, our understanding of the neurological basis of consciousness is still very limited."

If the stories of Adam and Eve and the Serpent, and the Tower of Babel are myths about human will and consciousness, in both cases, perhaps certain "gods" wanted us to stay ignorant and powerless.

Know thyself . . . know thy gods!

But the story of Jonah is curiously different. In this tale, Jonah is challenged, as are UFO experiencers today, to relay a message he was persuaded to believe and take seriously, during his experience in the belly of a whale—the equivalent of an alien spaceship. God, in this story, tells him that he is needed as a messenger because the people of Nineveh don't know their "right from their left hands." Did the writers of this story know of the link between right and left hemispheres of the brain, and the hands? I suspect that the story of Jonah is about mediation between the daylight mind and the non-language realm we assign to the right brain.

Is it possible that before the destruction of the Tower (as symbol for a level of consciousness), we *did* speak and understand one language? That is, the left and right hemispheres of the human brain were once synchronized? Did something happen, as was communicated about Atlantis, that caused us to regress in consciousness? Do native American legends about the destruction and creation of worlds contain clues about an evolutionary plan? Do we "peak out" in knowledge and power just before a cycle ends/begins?

But my sources say that this time there will be an unprecedented change. Maybe this time, the "control tower" in our brains will not be destroyed, but will be enhanced.

In the story of Jonah, the Ninevites were vulnerable to attack because they were unaware of the potential for destruction. But Jonah is aware—made aware, first by a "voice" that roused him from "sleep," and second, by activation inside a big fish; a story as fantastic as our reports of UFO experiences. But before Jonah is swallowed, he tries to escape the call, retreating to sleep, below deck—equitable with the virtual sleep of the right brain, in terms of whole brain awareness.

If in some cases,[14] the UFO is a catalyst for awakening the sleeping beauty in the right brain, I can attest to the challenge it is to work to "stay awake" and deal with being overwhelmed

---

[14] In some cases, I believe what I was told: there are "mimics" and "simulations"—interferences by counter forces that mean to thwart the work of lifting consciousness.

by expanded consciousness. Such increases in consciousness don't mean that a person now knows *the* truth; simply there is more information, which means more to work with.

We are all messengers, all linked on the sacred grapevine. And knowledge of good and evil is still dangerous. It causes us to question, and questions can lead to journeys into the unknown, and some very alien experiences. . . .

PART II:
FRANKLY ALIEN

PRELUDE:

Take Heart

We live in a world of contrasts. On the path to light, if our eyes are open, sooner or later we meet the dark, internally and externally.

The enlightened view is that there is no evil because God is All, and God is Good, and all together we are One. I agree. But experientially, there is a missing link in this sunshiny vision. That is the will link. Where there is will, it is exercised in every direction and to every degree that we understand to span from positive and negative poles. Achieving balance and harmony between negative and positive poles is a daunting challenge. We barely conceive what we are up against in our dream of realizing peace and the freedom to create the paradise in our minds. Part of the challenge is to wake up to reality in its wholeness, which calls for courage to face the parts we don't like, the business thriving at the negative poles . . . in ourselves, and in the world.

When we are aware of such polarities, we tend to gear up for battle. But the principles of creation teach that battle only strengthens the opposition. What we fight, we give life to. The result is never-ending battles, which has been our history.

Speaking of parts we do not like, enlightenment that shuts its eyes to what needs to be acknowledged, healed, or set free, is like the Biblical character Herod, who shrugged and let Christ be crucified on the cross. "Thy will be done," Herod seemed to say by his failure to intercede on behalf of Christ. But *whose* will was done? That is the question.

Part 2 of this book wends into an unknown most would as soon not know. Denial is a skill of forgetfulness, but in my case, it did not serve me well. I was visited by the dark. The challenge was to meet it face on, and not flinch. But I still flinch sometimes, so there is more work to do. Part 2 requires the most courage, for I am aware of the taboo against acknowledging that anything slinks in the shadows of the Good Dream. But slinking is part of the human-alien drama, for there is no escape from the awesome endowment of will. The freedom that can achieve the dream of birthing Heaven on Earth calls for the courage to expand our powers of will. The story of Jonah shows that potent will knows its enemies. No enemy is greater than ignorance. From it stem all forms of fear, selfishness, and arrogance.

The art of bringing in light and anchoring it is partly to know where and how to apply it. Words on a page can be light, if the words are true. The purpose here is not to frighten; it is to include parts of my story that are as true as my visions of our becoming. The only light I can bring is the light in my own life. Quotes of enlightened souls are uplifts, but no one achieves personal light by hitching on to another's wings. Each creates his or her own light link. Each works out personal salvation, or enlightenment, sometimes in fear and trembling. Dark nights of the soul are as much a part of the human adventure as are travels with angels as companions. Jonah had his time in the belly, and I, times in the bellies of UFOs. Whatever the personal catalyst, each will be confronted with the face behind the silver.

Take heart is the word. The face is you and I, we and they. *Mitakuye oyasin*. . . .

CHAPTER SEVEN:

Hidden Message (the "Big Event")

A leap of will may be nothing so clear as a conscious decision. It might be a plunge into the waves, to be swept wherever it takes us. Maybe into the belly of a whale, maybe to be washed upon a foreign shore, to wander without a map. I didn't feel I was making a major decision after the five nights of sorrow. It was never more clear that I was already committed. But where was the script for me as messenger? Aren't messengers "knowers"? What does a quester on the path of mystery know? Nothing to teach or preach . . . but to be an instrument, like a string strummed by an unseen harpist. That was the right idea, but I was shy—a mask of fear and pride.

There was much more to experience before I was pliable, but the words were there on the pages, notes for a story I was afraid to tell. That would mean exposure. Those who call experiencers "little nobodies" do not understand. A little nobody is somebody. To truly be a nobody is to be all but invisible—transparent, like glass. The best a human can hope for is to be a mirror with only a thin coating of silver at the back, scratched for a little light to shine through.

But in my mind, I was not a messenger, I was a novelist. So I hid the first real message. The harpist must have known I wasn't ready to be strummed.

Although the hidden message struck a deep chord in me, I didn't share it in *Summoned* because it just sounds too fantastic. I was ultra-sensitive to criticism then. It is a fantastic message, but I feel there is something in it for others. Some of the material I record is coded; it speaks to the heart in bypass of the intellect. If the mysterious big event *does* happen, I'm pretty sure all of our great technological expertise and vast knowledge won't count for much as preparation. It is a message for the heart, and about the heart.

The message was literally slipped in, like the left hand not acknowledging what the right is doing. At the time of the recording, I thought I was receiving information for the novel that I was preparing to write. Strangely, after recording the message, I resumed the note-taking, as if nothing unusual had happened.

When the fiction story evolved into the first version of *Jonah*, I forgot about the tablet with the message tucked between the notes; like the missing times, like the evidence of implants, like not asking Dr. Walker to probe for an abduction event in this life.

Eight months passed before I found the hidden message and typed it up. By then I was pretty sure I was an "abductee." A confirmation of sorts came four days after I typed up the hidden message. On November 2, 1994, I was conscious during the beginning of an event that sounded like what others had described as abduction. (Details in chapter 8.)

In the spring of 1994, I was having "suspicious dreams," UFO related, and there was an increase of paranormal activity. To explain the phenomenal activity, it made sense to me that as a contactee, I might be having out-of-body experiences as part of my education. Maybe I was involved in an "invisible college" course. I'd had many dreams of being in classrooms with others, and some of the information recorded was suggestive of such "higher education." (But there were also many dreams about spaceships, surgeries, pregnancies, taking care of "smart babies," and encounters with various alien beings.)

In the appendix in *Summoned,* I included suspicious (UFO-related) dreams and nocturnal events over nine years. Those notes show that on March 1, 1994, I dreamt of stepping through a screen and encountering a very tall woman who looked like a man; a video about government propaganda was shown. On March 3, I dreamt about a cat woman; on May 11, while conscious, I heard a sound like the tail of a whale swishing in water, and I dreamt about a form that transformed into a whale, and a child transforming into an ET. May 19, 1994, while awake, I saw for the first time, an actual light display, like a matrix, displayed in my dark bedroom.

I had begun the novel in March, calling it "Having a Whale of a Time, Love, Jonah." About a dozen chapters into the writing, in May, I purchased the book *Abduction,* by Pulitzer Prize winner John Mack, M.D. Previously, reading about other abduction accounts, I had always been able to eliminate myself as a candidate. But there were so many details in Mack's book that were like my own experiences, I was in shock. Suddenly all of the hidden signs of my life—the missing times in childhood, the marks on my hands, the many suspicious dreams and phenomena—rushed at me like a stinging wind.

As if Mack's book were a trigger, activating phenomena, the first light display happened on May 19, 1994. It happened again on June 3. On June 11, I heard a humming sound in my room, and my bed vibrated. I snapped on the light, pressed my hand on the mattress, to make sure I wasn't hallucinating. On June 12, I dreamt about alien intruders, and on the sixteenth, a "bird visitor"—an apparition, I assumed—flew at me, while I was conscious. On June 26, I saw a "curtain" of light before going to sleep, and waking up, I heard a man's voice say, "One year . . ." (I had dreamt of talking with an Asian man, after a very vivid dream about being in a place like a large parking garage, with aliens; and seeing a mother ship in the sky, one alien giving me a hard time about bringing me back home.)

The suspicious dreams, lights, and sounds intensified, and on August 18, for the first time, I felt the "tinglings," like pins and needles and vibrations on my body. Reviewing the record, I am hard-pressed to explain how I could have continued to hold out then, and not declare myself an abductee. In addition to the signs in my personal history, I also found an inch-long straight-line scar on my left knee, and I wondered if it had anything to do with a past "dream" about "Orientals" performing surgery on my knees. There was also a jagged scar on my right knee. I had never noticed these scars before. Once you suspect you might be an abductee, you check your body thoroughly.

But still . . . *was* I an abductee? Were the phenomenal events, the lights, the sounds, the tinglings, the vibrations, the scars, the implants (?), the missing times, the contact . . . *proofs?* God, as I understood God, was merciful in responding to my prayer the night of November 2, when I pleaded to know what was going on.

After that experience, I could no longer deny that I was involved with actual Other beings. But that didn't solve the mystery. What exactly is abduction? This was late 1994; the experiences increased and became more intense, and I recorded a lot more information, some of it "encoded" (chapter 8).

And yet . . . nothing touched me deeper than the "hidden message." After the catalyst ended (though the phenomena have never completely stopped), and I reviewed the whole of my experiences, it seemed to me that I might have given short shrift to some of the purest communications. That is, the communications that occurred before the shake, rattle, and roll, when I was conscious of being taken. There were "interferences" suggestive of spiritual warfare. My guides harped on me about discernment, warning me that my mind was open territory, and I had better wise up and learn to distinguish between my own thoughts and those from other sources, and the quality of the "inserted" thought-forms. All this was confusing, and life-disruptive. Was I being initiated into a fourth dimension?

Before I share the message about the big mysterious event, remember that I do not consider anything that I record as gospel truth. None of it can be proven, and I am unable to confirm the identity of the transmitters. If the information speaks to the heart as true, that is the value.

To show the contrast, I have included my notes before and after the message. I was working on a fiction story about a being from another dimension who would alter his form to express as a human in this environment. The being I had in mind, "Eluxui," was a typical round-headed ET with big eyes. The notes are lengthy and complex (excerpted here). As I began recording the notes, they seemed to be my own thoughts, but then I became aware of another intelligence in my mental fields.

> *Notes:* Eating and disposal of unwanted food particles . . .
> perhaps they eat nothing but what is used by their
> bodies, eliminating the need for elimination. So
> that the process is . . . vaporous atmospheric.

The recycling process takes place through the pores, unneeded or excessive energies converting to particles that seep, as it were, through miniature pores in the skin. The seepage is small and slight when the entity "eats right," taking in no more than is needed to fuel the fires that keep the mechanism going. So what do they eat? Plants that refine into liquids. There is a ritual of reverence for the ingesting of other life forms, permission granted and thanks for the offering. There is no sensual gratification. It is an act that invokes reverence and gratitude, each ingestion serving as a reminder that all systems are interdependent. The small energy particles that seep out of the pores return to the air and are recycled, to blend with moisture that returns to the living plants that feed *us.*[15] It is a gentle system after many eons of refinement.

"You never eat animals?"

Only those on a microscopic level that inhabit the plants ingested. They come along for the ride, for the thrill of experiencing

---

[15] Us: I am now aware that another intelligence is communicating, so I address him/it directly.

the worlds within the entity. In the process, they too are changed, emerging in a refined form, each contributing to the flow of energy that continues to cycle.

"You don't need to wash, to remove toxins?"

No more. We ingest nothing that produces toxins. All is efficient. However, in your environment, there is need for precautions. Your plant life is unrefined. It must be altered before it is ingestible to our systems. This requires further steps before it can be safely ingested. . . .

(And, here, without comment, I shift into the message.)

As we approach the juncture, the veils between forms we normally see and forms we are not accustomed to seeing become thin and sometimes flap.

A frenzy of activity as we approach, old systems asserting force against fear, based on an innate knowledge that all systems are about to undergo a radical change. The spellbound ego knows only to fight harder to retain dominion.

But among us are many present specifically to help us transit, and many others are at a point of development that sees the "insanity."

Alignments must be made. The ones here to perform specific tasks must remember and begin if they have not, the "courage of convictions," to inform, instruct, and otherwise organize those who are ready . . . and await this leadership.

The first instruction is that we will not fight to keep intact systems.

The second instruction is we will instruct *hearts* . . .
- to help awaken ancient teachings;
- to activate centers of compassion;
- to fuel fires of love;
- to *act* on principles of spirit, allowing the material to sort or heave or shatter, attending to creatures who would die of fright otherwise;

- to prepare to inherit a world savaged by disharmonious creation;
- to survive the shock of "seeing" more than was thought possible then,
- to nurture during the preparatory stage of rebuilding the world with a conscious understanding of balance, order, and harmony, which will present new challenges.

We are not alone. We are all "connected," interdependent individualities who receive guidance from entities on "higher planes." While we are endowed with choice, that choice is not all-inclusive unto a given individual. If what an individual chooses does not resonate on a level of clan, tribe, or collective, it "plays out vertically," so to speak, alienating that individual from the community. Such choices in a series will ultimately weaken the individual, so that he or she will "gravitate" toward other realities with other agendas.

What of defective DNA that produces beings with weakened systems? Some are living examples of where a series of non-resonate choices leads. Others are in need of "restructuring," and each knows what it is and all will know who is who. Great caution must be taught to judge not. Some have chosen, others are "lost," and still others will make "eleventh hour" choices. All choose. But not all have chosen with the same degree of consciousness. All will be sorted out, not by you. You are the ushers and caretakers and builders and instructors and transmitters and receivers and information centers. You attend to your immediate tasks and leave the rest for others. Most is worked out "between worlds," where consciousness is uninhabited, free of physical limitations.

The work is to become keenly aware of the levels of consciousness, to see the purpose of ego, not to dominate but to serve. "Surrender the ego"; see it as a child aspect that must "behave" so that the adult can assert and do the work of evolution. Fear is to be identified as dual in nature. Learn to distinguish between fear that warns of danger, and fear that seeks to protect the ego. The second fear is evidence the ego resists surrender to guidance. It usually acts out in anger. Also: The aspect of diffused/focused awareness—dual natures of awareness. Powerful behavioral structures for all life on this plane. Become aware of polarities, end conflicts, and learn to utilize energies to balance so that all life operates in symphony.

A deep respect for all *forms* of life and "non-life" is essential.

To prepare as many as possible: When all glows with the Light of Life, some will sing, others will scream. There will be major announcements, veils lifted, all in preparation for the unveiling of the screens over consciousness, at this stage. You will be taught, and compassion will continue until that time to prepare as many as possible.

It is a part of the design that some will serve as "teachers of the left side," for those who have not yet *experienced* the depths of compassion necessary to do their jobs effectively. Some of you have experienced a taste of the grief to be felt at seeing the cruel results of disharmonious growth patterns.

These demonstrations will work to deepen or initiate the fires of compassion. You will see emotion do a great work. You will see "heart" in action. You will see the heroics of love like unto none before observed. All will seem hyper-energized and many will feel they will burst from their skins.

At a point of buildup, there will be a kind of explosion that will, in effect, "establish" the new order. At that point, all who belong will be present. And all who belong elsewhere will be absent. None will have seen this happen, but what you will see afterward will be enough to challenge your attention for a long time to come, as you work together to adapt.

Take heart. You will not make the leap alone. We will be among you, some in form, others behind the veil. Three to your one.

(Me: What of those who have died?)

They will "be present" . . . the ones who "belong" . . . *that* veil will fall.

(Me: But the sheer numbers!)

Some surprises await you. Some have played many roles. You will see.

(And then . . . as if nothing untoward had happened, I resumed the notes.)

> *Notes:* "Eluxui" explains that he is a fragment of a complex entity named VO-EKTU. Because he is only a fragment—though fully a being in his own right—he cannot express all that the complex can—it will be a strain to explain his reality . . . best he can do is outline.

Don't forget vibration aspect; to be here, the vibrations are slowed, so that he can enter our domain. But since he inhabits an earthly form and is vibrating at a slower rate, he cannot express what can only be expressed at higher speeds of vibration.

(Some rocks, minerals, such as sandstone, allow for transmigration . . . porous, contain water, essential. Others enter through other mediums, waterfalls, certain trees, and other natural living gateways.)

We meet on "ground" between realities, in a foggy no-man's-land, where we mingle as intelligences in a vaporous, swirling atmosphere that accommodates, a place where we meet in ethereal form. . . .

His metamorphosis: He must migrate through all stages. (Again, the Other intelligence inserts itself:)

> The gateways here are like unto the Fourth Passage.[16] A fellow can get quite banged up passing through passages three and two, however, and perhaps miss the target altogether. One must zigzag and travel at speeds that during the push cause temporary blackout. The astral belt surrounding your planet can be tricky. One must be alert to dodge some rather monstrous projections that you should pray never materialize. . . .

---

[16] Fourth Passage: I have no idea if this refers to anything real or not.

Several more pages of notes followed.

Around this time (February 7, 1994), I had drawn a big picture of an alien, as I envisioned "Eluxui," on a large graph pad. Around the edges, I jotted various characteristics and tidbits of information for the novel I thought that I was preparing to write. And again something was communicating to me. This felt to be a more remote intelligence . . . truly alien. In time I would wrestle the big sheet of paper back to the computer room and type up the information:

We are an outer system, one of many.

(My notes: They monitor us. We interact with them in regions between our world and theirs. We leave our bodies during dream stages and meet with them to discuss development. Many levels of development on our planet. Many are fairly new creations. Many experienced at many levels.)

This cycle is a crucial evolutionary juncture where a division will occur, a "new world" emerging. Some will transfer to higher "octaves."[17] Others will remain to usher in the new cycle for the many who still have cycles to complete.[18] Great upheavals, requiring more interaction between spheres of realities.

To make as smooth a transition as possible (many experienced ones will be leaving), you need to impart as much as possible so that "new world" leaders can better lead.

Danger? At this point (we are) vulnerable to other entities in other realities with different agendas, whence come mythological tales of demons and gods warring for men's souls and "harvest" tales. All is "sorted out" or "in"—not a danger of death, but [a matter] of where you want to be. At your level, many are not capable of making *conscious* choice. So they are like children whom you are responsible to influence.

---

[17] Octaves: Higher dimensions.
[18] The many who still have cycles to complete: reference to evolution of the soul. More on this subject later.

The drive to join together [is] our influence. To be where you want in groups. These groups will translate in the new world as forceful clans that will act with the power of ONE-S.[19] No *one* alone will pass over. Alone, you are prey to scavengers who can divert an entity to an entirely radical reality whose agenda would be unfavorable to most.

"Where two or more are gathered . . ." is an *instruction*.

In the new world, all will be conscious of all, so that you will need the nurturance of clan order to adapt. This will begin the *conscious* use of collective will. Which is why those who have developed conscious personal will, will more easily make the change and will serve as leaders for those who have succumbed to deep programming, but who are conditionally ready and desirous to enter this stage as fledglings. These may one day serve as leaders in the ushering in of the next Great Cycle.

The following are notes about "them," also jotted on the graph pad:

Notes: None of them dies alone. Groups (complexes?) decide to transmigrate to other realities or higher octaves. Reproduction is a clan affair, involving no fewer than three, in conjunction with tribal and collective decisions. Beings are created to fulfill purposes; as new challenges emerge, groups produce needed entities having characteristics that will fill the needs. Conscious knowledge of "gene codes"—engineering of DNA, each group

---

[19]ONE-S: The feeling is that ONE-S refers to "soul complexes" in the making (also called clans). Perhaps (as later messages suggest), when an individual soul reaches a certain point of maturation, a "gathering" occurs among souls of like minds and hearts to begin the work of forming a soul complex or community. This will be discussed in chapter 9.

member contributing cells (contributors chosen for strength of certain traits). Sperm-egg? Ours is a dual-system, theirs is a trio—"positive/negative and the spark."[20] They meld together? Skin grafts? Egg "fertilized"—cells duplicating themselves. What gets it started? They can mix together. But what causes the "entrance" of life? Mystery . . . a "mineral" participation.

When groups abandon form (to transfer to other realms), the abandoned forms are subjected to light treatments that "freeze" them in molds that will serve as containers for the gestation of new beings created. These forms retain a low-energy imprinting that supports and enhances gestation. (This sounds like the liquid-filled containers that hold hybrid babies, which many of us have seen.)

Hearing is at top/back of head. Blood like honey. Life force. Nose holes—vapors as refined vegetation in form of liquids is ingested. Central system like a honeycomb, graduating out in an ever more refined meshwork. Through microscopic pores energy emanates outward, blending

---

[20] The third element of reproduction: They know the combination codes to create a form into which the life force will activate, attracting a non-formed intelligence. Very intricate work, splicing together "combs" from three or more entities in a fashion that interlocks, creating *within* a geometric opening, through which the intelligence can insert. Like us, they can only "set the stage," watch, and wait for results. When it fails, other attempts are made. When successful, the form will begin to glow and pulsate, and is then nurtured in the container until the being has grown to a stage when it is safe to remove it and begin the process of introducing it to the environment. (This comb-combining business does not sound likely to work to produce a human-alien hybrid. Our biological systems seem too different.)

with vapors from the plants ingested, so that all life forms are interdependent, cycling systems for light. . . .

Frankly alien.

Was I recording transmissions from actual extraterrestrials? If I were being prepared to participate in a human transformational event, why would they transmit this kind of information? What did it lend to my task? Maybe awareness that we are interconnected with Others in parallel dimensions.

Maybe our lives as human beings belong to a larger "nature matrix" than most are aware. Maybe being human is a stage before becoming cosmic beings. Except, unlike our experiences here, where we can see the progression from child to adult, the "human becoming" cosmic stage is veiled, perhaps because it is something we experience in community, not individually. In other words, in this (speculative) phase of evolution, we first develop as individuals (develop light bodies, or souls) in community settings. In the early days of tribal development, we acted all together as one mind units (speaking "one language"). When evolution of the individual is activated, although we continue to live in groups, we begin to develop "minds of our own" (and develop diverse languages). The next step may be that we join together again to form councils of minds, or complexes, with each member having a mind of his/her own, to begin to learn "collective conscious creation."

This might sound very threatening—wrong to individuals who prize their independent minds and wills. But do we ever become so individualized that we can break from the chain of life? A possible and troubling scenario about what that might lead to is in chapter 12.

In another communication, 1993, this was said (in excerpt):

Here is the challenge: to develop awareness of the correlations. Spirit descending into matter is highly experienced and intelligent, but enters a realm where there are no identifiable markers. You enter literally as infants, vulnerable and dependent on the care and guidance of those more experienced. Here, see a correlation between human infants and parents, and spirits struggling to make contact with higher intelligences you call gods or angels. On all levels, physical and otherwise, you need guidance until such time that you become guidance, which is yet another level of experience and challenge.

(Me: So, that which guides us can have the quality of apprenticeship?)

Indeed. You as the seeker may be a teacher in reverse for a spirit learning the ways of guidance.

I like that. It affirms and extends the "belonging story." But why such mystery, why so secret, why such lengths to keep us in the dark? I hope to shed a little light on these questions in examining the rest of my experience to date. But before venturing into the gathering and becoming stories, more frankly alien pieces in the puzzle. . . .

By grace, it feels, I was able to remember enough of one encounter to know that we are being helped by beings of a higher order. Can I help it that they look like giant insects?

CHAPTER EIGHT:

ENCODED: Inner Vision
and Hidden Realms

I was encoded by a giant insect? This doesn't sound very Christian. Doesn't sound like the typical alien abduction scenario, either. But it does sound Hopi. . . .

"So the people began their migrations, climbing up a high mountain. They were accompanied by two insect people. . . ."

"The real *kachinas*, as we know, are spirits from other planets and stars. . . ."

(Waters 1977)

Excerpts above belong to a story about the Hopi people who survived the destruction of the "first world" as told in Frank Waters's *Book of the Hopi*. It was a time when people began to draw away from each other. Suspicion and accusations of wrongdoing increased, and many had become warlike. But there were a few people among the different races who still lived by the laws of creation.

"Sotuknang" (a spiritual being) appeared to these people, "coming with a sound like a mighty wind." He told them the world was going to be destroyed and another one created. These people were chosen to survive.

Sotuknang instructed them to go to a certain place. Their *kopavi* (the vibratory center at the top of their heads) would lead them. Their "inner vision" would give them sight of a certain cloud by day, and a certain star by night. They were to follow the cloud and the star.

All over the world the chosen ones began the journey. And people laughed at them, saying *they* did not see the cloud or the star. (But a few people believed them, and joined the migration.)

The ones who laughed had lost the inner vision, the story states. "The door was closed to them." At the end of the journey, Sotuknang appeared again and led the survivors to a big mound where the Ant People lived. . . .

To lose inner vision is to imply it was once functional—the door was once open, the crown chakra (energy center) at the top of the head was once activated. The implication is that the faculty in the brain for inner vision shuts down when people became warlike. Or, did the loss of inner vision happen first, resulting in warlike behavior? I wish I knew the whole story. Knowing it might shed light on why some have inner vision today, and others do not.

"Recognition" was the attracting force for the story about the ancient Hopi. In all ancient stories there is something that can enlighten us today. The past is not another planet populated by aliens. Just because people in the past used different words to describe their experiences doesn't mean they were less intelligent. What might people two thousand years from now think of us? Those dolts of the twenty-first century, they were barely awake. . . . Or, by then, will we even see time and history as we do now? It is doubtful. Both concepts are swiftly evolving.

It makes sense that our survival as biological children of Earth might be determined by respect and cooperation with the "laws of creation." Maybe in our DNA, besides codes that reveal various diseases and characteristics, there are codes for the activation of higher faculties, such as inner vision.

I am reminded of the story of Atlantis, of the catastrophe that purportedly destroyed the civilization. We tend to blame nature—for instance, an asteroid hurtling into the Earth—for the destruction of certain species. But ancient legends suggest that we have powers of mind to prevent such devastations, or at least to survive ourselves. Maybe these higher powers of mind only sustain when we take care of the world that is our life. Or, could it be, some people don't have the capacity to act as conscious stewards? Maybe evolved states of mind and heart reflect as responsible behavior. In early stages of evolution, maybe we are like children. Unsupervised children can be warlike. Some kill other children. Where are our parents? Maybe people with inner vision are those who are more evolved, like wise elders, compared to children gone wild. We try, but we don't succeed very well at supervising one another. Supervision comes from higher powers, when we ask for it. Otherwise, we are "closed doors."

The religion of my youth teaches a story about rewards and eternal life in Heaven—"up there" if we behave well "down here." But what if Heaven is within us? Jesus said it was. The Word says God is closer than our breath, and His/Her/Its laws are written on our hearts. In the Book of Acts in the Bible, the Holy Spirit appeared as flames that leapt off the tops of believers' heads, when they gathered in the "upper room." Sounds like activation of the crown chakra.

Maybe there is a Bible inside us . . . the Book of Life . . . DNA. If it is discovered that DNA is the text for the Book of Life—including evolution of consciousness—old religion will be out of business. So will old science. Maybe a merge will happen, a "spiritual science."

Again the story of Adam, Eve, the serpent, and the Tree of Knowledge comes to mind. A serpent resembles the intertwined DNA coil. The serpent is in the know—knows that knowledge leads to the development of god-like powers. He also knows that Adam and Eve have free will. But maybe will was such a new endowment, Adam and Eve weren't fully aware of their ability to consciously make choices. They were accustomed to God telling them what to do. A clue about the state of Adam's and Eve's new consciousness is in God's question, "Who told you, you were naked?" Who told you that you were an individual self, capable of making your own decisions?

When the serpent encouraged Eve to eat the fruit of knowledge, I doubt she thought: "Wow, knowledge of good and evil sounds cool—I think I'll believe Mr. Snake, the heck with God." Something was awakened in Eve, a new inner dynamic, a boost in consciousness, perhaps, of which will, as we understand it, was a part of the package, like a new software program.

But Western religions tell the story as an example of man's inherent rebellious nature. Maybe it is true that in the baby stages of a new consciousness, we must listen to "god wisdom," in order to survive and thrive. Exercise of will without such guidance might be like children playing with matches in a field of dry hay.

There was a catch in the Serpent's enticement to eat of the fruits that would make of us gods. Knowing suggests consciousness, and consciousness suggests awareness of the laws of creation and destruction—good and evil, right and wrong, what works, what does not. But if our parents' former experience was instinctual, how, emerging from the cradle of instincts, could they be fully cognizant of the workings of God's or Nature's laws? History shows that we learn though experience. History also shows that we don't learn much from history; rather, it seems that each child born is like an Adam or an Eve—completely new to this level of consciousness. Maybe Adam and Eve represent archetypes for a phase in the evolution of human consciousness.

Does it seem a little cruel to oust children of a new consciousness to fend for themselves in a world they do not understand? I think it is impossible to understand evolution without awareness that we are more than prototypical human beings. I predict that the debate on evolution will persist until we awaken to the awareness that we are more than personalities and minds that spring from bodies and brains, to live fleeting lives of trials, with little or no understanding of who and what we are in relation to not only this world, but to a vast cosmos we have barely begun to explore.

Maybe in the beginning of the human journey, we were as innocent and inexperienced as babies, and, as a newborn has to be taught, and cannot survive without parental nurture, we have been taught and nurtured by higher powers, throughout our evolution. As we mature, the teachings become internalized. But maybe internalization refers to a light body, or soul. Though the seed spirit is in everyone, maybe not all choose to evolve light bodies (more in chapter 12). The experience of our ancestors is written in our genes, and in addition, we can tune to the guidance of higher powers, if we choose to seek the "inner vision," and sustain the connection.

The story about extraterrestrials genetically altering certain human beings in the distant past, in order to elevate their consciousness enough to perform as slaves in gold mines, is another myth that may be based on something that actually happened. Gold has long been a symbol for the highest "spiritual" attainment. I've heard all my life that we are tempered in the fire to become gold. It's awfully hot in gold mines, I hear. Did association between fire, gold, and godliness originate from a new breed of ET-humans created by actual walking, talking gods, to work in actual gold mines?

This controversial history is expounded in the books of scholar Zecharia Sitchin, and is being further investigated by other researchers and scholars. But missing from these studies is mention of the soul or spirit aspect . . . I suppose because it is such a risk for "serious" scholars and scientists to bring into their works anything that smells of religion.

But it isn't about a battle between science and religion or ufology. I am not scientific or religious or political or ufological.

I study all and have thoughts about all, which are constantly changing. And the more I study and think, the less often I can find the lines of difference between these schools of thought.

But perhaps there are various religious, or political, or educational, or cultural, or scientific "hive minds." I don't begin to understand biological hive minds. The El, who said we were governed by them, did not expound. I equate hive minds to morphic fields, as are described by scientist Rupert Sheldrake in *The Rebirth of Nature: The Greening of Science and God* (1994). Jeremy Narby is pursuing study of the connections between biology and consciousness, and so are others, such as Gary Swartz and Linda Russek, Ph.D. authors of *The Living Energy Universe* (1999).

At the time I wrote the chapter on hive mind in *Summoned*, I was not aware of the film *Star Trek: First Contact*. I watched it on TV, April 23, 2000. The enemy in this 1996 science fiction thriller is the Borg—a "hive mind" with an evil queen mind and her drones, who can quickly adapt themselves to any weapon. "We evolve," explains Captain Picard. But the Borg conquer and assimilate—virtually overtake minds and bodies, like predators. I think the hive minds the El refer to are much more subtle, and are not an evil, but a natural element in the evolution of consciousness. But anything not understood in nature can seem to be evil, even the bearing of children . . . in extreme interpretations of Biblical scripture.

Think of a tribe in a jungle. Amazingly, among the members born in a given generational span, there is always the perfect mix of intelligence, talent, and potential for skills that are needed for the tribe to survive. Something, a "hive mind" perhaps, is functioning behind our awareness of the designs of nature.

In recent years, quantum physicists discovered that everything is composed of light/energy. Nothing is really solid, through and through . . . including human beings. Instead of a "basic building block" to explain tangible material, scientists discovered in photons and quarks and all those other deceptively and infinitesimally small micro-units, universes of infinite magnitude. In other words, inside everything are gateways to an inverse cosmos. This is perhaps hardest to accept about ourselves.

We are very close to discovering the links between mind and matter. We are very close to knowing that light and intelligence are the same stuff. Inner-vision-wise, I see it, but my area of expertise is not in articulation of mysteries so new to our consciousness. This is in the realm of scientific endeavor. And contrary to opinions that scientists are all "closed doors," it isn't true. Naturally the ones pursuing new knowledge aren't on the six o'clock news, any more than experiencers like me are encouraged to share our stories. What we are discovering is too new, and new is always greeted with tremendous resistance. New is like a bear's paw plunged into a beehive to get the honey. In this case, the honey is what people think. New ideas are like a direct attack on a hive mind.

Soul or spirit may have nothing to do with institutionalized religion. In "The History of Humankind in Summary," the El say that religion, as we know it today, was introduced to control a wild population of beings who jumped some steps in evolution in breach of the natural unfolding laws of creation. I am speaking of dictatorial religions, not the inherent knowing in us that higher powers exist and life is eternal. Archaeologists always look for signs of religion at burial sites, and in artifacts. But they don't find Bibles or crosses or stars of David; they find evidences that our distant ancestors believed in higher powers, and in life beyond death. Dictatorial religions concerned with human behavior—and politics—came later, when civilization appeared so suddenly it registers as an aberration in the story of a long, plodding evolution that suits the linear mind.

Whether working to expand knowledge of our biological nature or the consciousness of our spiritual nature, we are all striving to know ourselves, our external bodies, and our internal being. Perhaps we will soon be able to analyze and measure the energy fields of mind and consciousness. People are working on it now, while others are working to free consciousness out of hive minds. The inner impulses we feel and describe as "calls" may be evolutionary directives to begin to disconnect from hive minds, in preparation to cross a new threshold of consciousness. And sometimes the consciousness is boosted by external forces—activation by implants?

We don't know the purpose of implants. Sometimes I suspect they are not really "technologies," but are gimmicks to distract from what is really going on. Sometimes I think they are a kind of language etched on the body—"Look here, Sister, we are closer than you think."

Hypnotically regressed, I reported that the devices put in my hands (if there were devices) were "activators" so that I could be more "closely taught." And boy, does that mean *close*. Part of the awakening of new consciousness in me is awareness of the "inner cosmos." As with any new awareness, it was first experiential, then the struggle to find words to describe. Sometimes it takes whole books just to capture the barest essence. The best I can describe comes from remembering part of an abduction-like experience, which I am about to share in some detail.

My part is small but powerful, I was told. The smallness is evident . . . I am yet to see the power. But even small parts are fraught with perils. The "loyal opposition" is always working to stop the flow of light. Light seekers are "psychically greeted" by the dark, is Carla Rueckert's[21] gentle attitude toward the "loyal opposition," also her term. Her seasoned experience and sound, gentle wisdom helped me through some challenging times.

Am I speaking of demons and angels? These are just names of beings of different energies and agendas, who interact with us, usually unseen. Evolving, expanding, or raising consciousness

---

[21] Carla is an experienced conscious channeler, author of *A Channeling Handbook* (1987), L/L Research, Louisville, KY; and co-author of *The Ra Material* (1989), Schiffer Publishing, Atglen, PA.

means we become aware of such presences. "Spiritual warrior" is an apt term, except warriorship of the spirit is not violent. A spiritual warrior knows how to hold power and use the will for creative or healing purpose.

In chapter 4, I mentioned a time in April, 1995, when I decided to seriously consider hypnotic regression to discover more about what I was experiencing. This was triggered by a "nocturnal event" that I felt was negative. In a disturbing "dream," a small entity jumped on my bed and grasped my upper arms. He was small but incredibly strong. I felt something like an electrical jolt, which snapped me awake. That morning, while preparing breakfast, I felt a surge of energy from my waist down to my feet. The surging electrical feeling repeated every day, persisting for many months. It was not the dreams or visual and audial experiences that compelled me to seek professional help—it was the physical changes in my body, resulting from such experiences. "Psychic greetings" are calls to awaken to such realities, to take responsibility for them, and to learn to use the will. "Demons" or dark forces have no more willpower than we do. But they may want us to think so, to invoke fear, which results in our feeling powerless. My view of spiritual warfare is a clash of wills. The warfare is different in the realm of the spirit from what it is here, where we act everything out. But the polarities are the same. Why do some beings want darkness? Maybe because they feel it empowers them. But dark is delusion. There are only gradations of light.

In the training of our children, at some point we have to release them to the risks and dangers of the world. Likewise, in the maturation of souls, our "guardian angels" have to let us experience the dark along with the light so that we can become like them, god-like beings. What a concept—human life is school to become gods. I wonder if I'm even in kindergarten yet.

I didn't feel that I was "seeking light" the night of November 2, 1994, when I half remembered an abduction event. But I was seeking to know, and knowing is light. When I probed this event ten months later in hypnotic regression, I found that it was not a negative experience. The fear I felt was typical human reaction at encountering an unknown.

Neither did I feel that the possible implant event in 1986 was negative (but I was not ready to know more then). Should the whole phenomenal business scare me? Remember . . . although at the level of my daylight mind, I was challenged and mystified, deep down—or high up—I knew why all this was happening. The work is to enlighten the daylight mind, to wake up and remember who we are and why we are here.

But I was suspicious about another possible implant event that happened while I was working on this chapter. This one may have been a "psychic greeting." (It may have been a "mimic," an attempt to rouse feelings of powerlessness to interrupt the flow of my work.) I certainly didn't need any more physical evidence that the UFO phenomenon is not solely in our minds. But there it was, a triangular scab on my chest. . . .

This happened in March, 2000. The first thing to grab attention was a dream. But later I would go back and note that the business had started two nights earlier. The first night, I awoke sometime in the night and started at what I thought was a "big cricket" in my room. A hallucination, I decided, and went back to sleep. The next night I thought I heard a male voice say something. This was not unusual, and I ignored it.

I dreamt I was at a friend's house. Several of us were preparing food to eat together. Then there was an "insert"—something that didn't belong to the dream scenario. I saw a woman plunge a long needle into my friend's chest in the area above her heart, close to the collarbone. I was very upset, but no one else seemed concerned, not even my friend, who had been stabbed, or her husband. I asked my friend, the stabber, and her mother, each in turn: "Why?" Why was this done? No one answered. Everyone just stared at me. I was worried my friend might die, and wondered why no one was doing anything.

The next day, I reported the dark dream to my friend via e-mail. She couldn't relate to it, and had no insight to offer as to the meaning.

That night, I was jolted awake. My body whapped forward from the waist, as if I was trying to do a head bend to my knees. I have experienced head jolts before, assumably awakening from out-of-body journeys, but nothing ever this dramatic before. Wide awake, I couldn't go back to sleep until it was light outdoors.

Late in the afternoon I took a shower, and discovered a scab on my upper left chest. The scab was thick but smaller than my smallest fingernail, and precisely an equilateral triangle. I could see something tiny and white in the center. I examined my lapis lazuli crystal pendant, which is about an inch long and pyramidal shaped at both ends. I played with it to see if I could have slept on it hard. But I couldn't see how it could have caused such a tiny, precise three-sided scar. Wouldn't I have felt pain at such an injury? And it takes a little time for such an injury to scar over. Wouldn't I have felt or noticed something in previous days?

Then I remembered the dream. The scab was in the same position on my chest, as I had seen on my friend in the dream, where the needle had been plunged.

I went over to my mother's house to show her and my brother the scab, and to ask if either thought it could have been caused by sleeping on my crystal—and me not being aware that such an injury had occurred. But the scab was gone by the time I showed them. Only a pale pink spot remained. Mom said she saw a "pimple." At home I scraped off the pimple. It was a tiny hard white thing, like a mustard seed. Dried fluid from an injection? A dot in the center of a triangle is a meaningful symbol to me. Earlier I described the interlocking of two triangles in a Mogen David hexagon. Always I draw a dot in the middle to symbolize completion. Was something messing with my mind? Or was I injected or implanted? But *why?* And I remembered my "why" question in the dream. Was this event like an "annual checkup" that required an "infusion"?

For several nights after finding the scar, I was "messed with," or so I believed. One night, I woke feeling a palpable energy form pressing against my backside. I commanded it gone in the name of Jesus, and it left. There were sounds of rustling in the room and "electrical popping" sounds. The third night, an energy buzzed my face. This one scared me, but I told it to buzz off, and it worked. The fear was brief, the human-animal reaction to something unknown, so close. But overall, I was more annoyed than frightened.

The business culminated in a dark dream about intruders in my apartment: birds, cats, dogs; a lamp I could not get to work. And I saw a new TV set with a screen four times as wide as my little tube. The message could be, yes, you are being messed with, Sister. But look, your consciousness is expanding (symbolized in the wide TV screen).

All this business felt dark, but maybe it was a test to see my responses after another "adjustment" (see transcript, which follows later). Maybe I needed to see that I'm not as easily spooked as I was in the beginning. And I am more aware of the power of my will. I'm not living *as* double, not so much on the ladder between seemingly disparate poles. But I still live in the mystery, in the humble differential zone between knowing a little, and not knowing a lot.

The recent event is nothing I would check out in hypnotic regression. It felt like psychic greeting energy, nothing I wanted to give energy to. In these cases, it is best to acknowledge "their" right to express, then turn the attention to trying to anchor a little light.

But sometimes we are swept up, anchors and all, into the unknown. Some call this abduction. It always seemed to me to be more like a summoning. . . .

On the night of November 2, 1994, I went to bed about 1:00 A.M. Within minutes, I heard a "ting" in my ear, then the pins-and-needle tinglings began in my feet, then intensified into electrical-like vibrations that swept over my entire body. The bed vibrated as well, as happens when such vibrations are intense. The tingling and vibrations continued for about an hour. I was hyper-alert because I had seriously prayed to be shown what was going on, and expected something to happen.

There were subtle, suspicious sounds in the room. I felt a presence and heard weird "chitty" sounds. My body felt heavy, as if I were a water-filled balloon, two-thirds full. As the business progressed, the heavy, watery feeling gave way to such a feeling of lightness that it felt as though I were spreading apart. It is at this stage that usually I lose consciousness.

Not this night. Something alerted me that I was at a crucial point. I thought, *This is it! Pay attention!* After a confusion of images, I was suddenly flying down the hallway. Sharp left turn, whisking past the kitchen table, I thought, *should have grabbed my glasses*!

At the window in the back door, my mind and body seemed to explode like a fireworks display. This was the look in "inner vision," but not the feel of it.

Next instant, I was sitting hunched over in a darkish environment, experiencing extreme disorientation. But I could vividly feel an arm around my waist. I felt I was naked. I looked down, saw a small, thin arm around my waist. I probed the arm with my hand. (I have no recall of seeing the entity's face or body, just the arm.) The arm felt rubbery . . . no bone. I thought, *shit . . . this is real*!

In the next recalled instant, I felt the pierce of a needle into a muscle near my spine on the right side. I felt cold liquid enter my body. Next, I snapped awake in my bed.

About flying down the hall and "exploding" through the back door window: It makes no sense to me that this route would be used when there were windows in my bedroom. I suspect that the "transfer" occurred right where I lay, in bed. I remembered a jumble of thoughts just before the flying event. It seemed I was doing something to the clock in my dressing room, like running up the time (which makes no sense). Maybe the "hands" inside the clock in my head were spinning!

I suspect that what I remembered was my brain's best translation. We can't "know" something we have not observed, heard about, been taught, or experienced. Our left brains are like a computer with file cabinets. I had asked to remain conscious, and to a limited extent, that was granted. But there were no file cabinets for this experience! I had no words or pictures for it, so my brain did the best it could. It was *like* flying down the hallway, *like* exploding through a window. Back door window might represent the inner portal through which I enfold into another dimension.

My description under the hypnotic trance, though clumsy, is much more revealing, I believe, of what actually happened.

I perceived myself to be inside a domed structure. While I believe I was in the company of ET kinds, there is a question about the accuracy of my mental images. The dome might represent the house around the "portal" in my consciousness, from which I am experiencing the events in the other dimension; i.e., the dome might signify my *head*, a mental image constructed to provide an identifier my daylight mind can recognize. You will see what I mean. I was truly in an environment alien to my ordinary consciousness. But . . . maybe I really was on a huge spaceship with a domed top.

Coming awake after the event, I quickly wrote 2:07 A.M. at the top of the journal page. Remember, I said the tinglings and vibrations began around one o'clock and continued for more than an hour. I was very meticulous in recording times. Apparently this event happened very quickly, in a matter of moments, "Earth-time." As I recorded what I could remember, I also recalled having seen the moon bright outside my bedroom window before I whisked down the hall. This may have been an add-on image that was part of the transfer experience.

After recording the event, as I lay down to sleep, the tinglings and vibrations started up again, and then I felt, and heard, a loud "charge" or rush of energy inside my head, as if a motor had just revved, then died. Abruptly, the tingling business stopped, and I was able to sleep.

Next I will share the complete transcription of the hypnotic regression session that I underwent to discover the details of the event. Remember, it is difficult enough describing alien experience. This is compounded in the trance state, which, more right-brain focused than left, is thought to be the area for language. So, no matter the event explored, alien or prosaic, there is a stumbling around for words. Every time I say "Hmmm . . ." it means some time lapsed as I was trying to focus on what I was seeing.

TRANSCRIPT: August 15, 1995, Scottsdale, Arizona; facilitator: Ruth Hover, Ph.D. psychologist, referral of PEER, Dr. John Mack's support organization in Cambridge, Massachusetts.

Hover: Do you see yourself getting up and going into the dressing room?

Redfield: It's just like I remember it . . . I don't feel like I'm re-experiencing it.

Hover: Let yourself remember the details. Describe what you're doing. . . .

Redfield: I'm flying down the hall.

Hover: You're flying down the hall. . . .

Redfield: I'm getting away with something because I know that's what I'm doing, flying down the hall. I'm so excited because I don't . . . uh, usually get to know what's going on . . . but I'm awake . . . it's happening. . . .

Hover: Re-live what's happening.

Redfield: It's so fast, it happens so fast.

Hover: Re-live going through the kitchen.

Redfield: Went through the glass in the door.

Hover: Are you through the door now?

Redfield: Yeah, it didn't hurt . . . ohhh. . . .

Hover: Are you outside now?

Redfield: No, I'm on the ship.

Hover: Immediately.

Redfield: Yeah, you hit the door and you're in the ship. . . .

Hover: What's it like there?

Redfield: I see this very, very high domed ceiling . . . it's gray and hmmm. . . .

Hover: Can you see much?

Redfield: No, I'm trying . . . I'm having some kind of space problem. One minute it feels like I'm a giant person in a tiny leprechaun ship, and the next minute it seems big and vast above me. I can't . . . I'm just having some kind of space problem, like my body . . .

Hover: Sounds like you're disoriented. If you look around, can you get a fix on it, so you can stabilize a little?

Redfield: This . . . domed ceiling . . . seems as big as a bus depot, or something . . . or the top of, um . . . a Jewish . . . domed cathedral. . . . (*"Synagogue" is the word I'm groping for.*)

Hover: Huge.

Redfield: I can see four sides, I can see this big seam, and there's this top part in the center of it.

Hover: Look down and see what you're wearing.

Redfield: I want to say a sheet, but I don't think there're any sheets here.

Hover: You're on this table in this huge dome . . .

Redfield: I don't think I'm on a table.

Hover: Are you alone?

Redfield: No. I saw a glimpse of one. They have hair . . . but it's not like our hair. It's kind of scare-crowy hair. It's black!

Hover: Black?

Redfield: Um hmm. Black hair.

Hover: Are they looking at you?

Redfield: Yeah . . . this is a very insectile kind of creature. No wonder I don't like those crickets. Scary. Hmmm . . .

Hover: What are they doing with you?

Redfield: I don't know what they're doing with me. I don't know what . . . hmmm . . . there's some kind of communication going on.

Hover: With you or them?

Redfield: Between us. I see this one, very insectile, tall, spindly, bent-over kind of being . . . you know . . . their eyes are big, but more oval, (*vertically*) elongated. I don't think this is evil, I think this is okay. This is, I feel deep wisdom . . . and acceptance.

Hover: So even though you're disoriented, you're not frightened.

Redfield: I'm afraid . . . I'm very discombobulated, but I don't feel I'm afraid of this entity. It seems there's a bunch of communication going on, but I can't bring it back in English . . . like this is a checkpoint, this . . .

Hover: You understand it there.

Redfield: Yeah, it could be . . . it's almost like . . . it's like an infusion of information. It's like I absorb it, and it bypasses . . .

Hover: Goes straight to your brain.

Redfield: It bypasses the computer brain and goes to the records . . . you know . . . the mind to draw upon, you know. . . .

Hover: So, an infusion of wisdom. You don't even have to think about it.

Redfield: Yeah, it's just there, available, when you're ready for it, or something. The whole body . . . we think of our body and our brain and our this and our that, but it's a holistic component, so it's, um, the information is like everywhere, all around, and, um, maybe you can process it through your brain to some extent, but it's everywhere, it's there, it, well, it . . . um . . . we're just so much more than we think we are.

Hover: You're absorbing it, even though you're feeling disoriented.

Redfield: Yeah . . . I don't know how it works, maybe just being in their presence. It just . . . transfers. Somehow. On that level, you can experience it like that. Down here we have to write all these words and put them into books, and . . .

Hover: Think them in order . . .

Redfield: Yeah, and talk it and hear it and draw it, and (*chuckle*) there's this separation between the knowing and the knowledge and the body, and the body is the . . . block, er, something you have to contend with, and up in that other realm, it's just, you're not blocked that way.

Hover: You're absorbing wisdom, you're nurtured.

Redfield: Yeah, but it's a body-total thing. The body-mind, it's all one component.

Hover: This being, the tall, spindly being is the only—

Redfield: There are others around.

Hover: Close to you.

Redfield: Busy, around . . . those short guys.

Hover: Let yourself look at yourself with the short guys and see if you can observe the one that comes and puts his arm around you to hold you in position. Perhaps that didn't happen?

Redfield: Hmmm . . . I don't know.

Hover: You are still absorbing information?

Redfield: Yeah . . . I think I get to look at it like a window. I don't get to like be there and re-live it. I'm seeing kind of a static picture here . . . got some feeling about . . . wonder if they really do look like that.

Hover: Is anything going on?

Redfield: I'm interested in this ship . . . it's kind of a big . . . steel doors and stuff . . . almost the look of a mausoleum or a . . . thick heavy steel look to it . . . a vault . . . I don't know . . . just not like anything I've ever thought of, or seen.

Hover: It looks different from the one previously experienced.

Redfield: Oh, yeah, this is totally different. This is . . . I don't know if it's a ship or not. I don't know where this is. It's, uh, I'm almost trying to do an inside-outside thing on it. One minute it's like what I'm seeing is the interior or the wall, then all of a sudden, it's like the outside. But then I don't know where I am . . . really disorienting.

Hover: Check your body. Other than feeling disoriented, having your visual information coming differently . . . how does your body feel?

Redfield: I don't think . . . this isn't my body like it is down here. This is . . . I don't know how to explain it.

Hover: Are you non-corporeal?

Redfield: It's like something in-between . . . it's . . . I want to say the consistency of jelly. . . .

Hover: It's very unusual.

Redfield: It's . . . uh . . . just necessary to be in this form in order to communicate that closely. There's no way in this body, you could be there.

Hover: Can they do anything to this body? Can he put his arm around your waist?

Redfield: You can feel, yeah, you've got . . . there's substance. Whatever they do, it might have something to do with the amino acids, or something, the way your body processes the, um, it's the electrical system . . . if you're traveling back and forth a lot, your body has to be able to withstand that.

Hover: So the alterations probably assist you.

Redfield: Has to change, yeah, you have to . . . there has to be an adjustment.

Hover: Do you think the cold liquid and the needle in your muscle on your backside aid in this process?

Redfield: Yes, it's necessary. But I don't know if it's a needle or if that's what I did with it with my mind.

Hover: To put it in terms—

Redfield: Yeah, whatever they do is . . . we don't have any words. I don't even have a picture for it, because I just felt it.

Hover: Beyond the comprehension of our frames of reference.

Redfield: Yes.

Hover: This enables you to have this close communication with these beings.

Redfield: Yeah, you have to go be with them to get this information, because you can't . . . it takes too long the other way, and it needs to be as close to . . .

Hover: Like osmosis.

Redfield: As close to what it is as possible. When you're down here, there's too much distance between us, too many levels, so that's why you have to go be there with them in that form, to be able to get it in a form.

Hover: So much of the experience is governed by the need to transmute you into the form to get the information. Is the information coming in a way that you can understand what you're getting?

Redfield: No. It comes to you almost like an energy infusion. Then it . . . you process it down here . . . with the language that you use, and the images that you have.

Hover: Translate it into human terms.

Redfield: Yes. The source is available to you like a library, in a way. And then there are things that will trigger it. You can't consciously go in and just say, okay, I'm going to go find out about this or that. No, you're not conscious of how it works.

Hover: You don't know the triggers.

Redfield: But something will trigger and then you go sit and write, and you go, Wow! what's this about? Because you don't connect that you've been up, and, well, you don't really know what's going on, so you don't, you don't think, oh, this is coming from that time when I went up to get that infusion of energy.

Hover: But you can remember the physical feelings.

Redfield: Yeah . . . I don't know why they don't just tell you more.

Hover: Perhaps you wouldn't understand it if they did.

Redfield: Well, why couldn't I just wake up and remember seeing that being?

Hover: What you remember is feeling it. Feeling the arm, feeling the cold. Can you watch yourself and see what you do after you get this information?

Redfield: Humpf. I saw myself kind of go into a whirlwind.

Hover: Energy.

Redfield: Yeah, my whole self.

Hover: Does that enable you to return?

Redfield: Yeah, yeah . . . it's almost like you turn into a whirlpool, come down like a tornado funnel, back down through the vortexes.

Hover: So it seems you are converted into energy so you can move through—

Redfield: And then you're moving back down and the light body has to go through all these readjustments . . . by the time it hits your physical body, they match.

Hover: Okay. You're back in your body.

Redfield: Yeah . . . you don't . . . it's a blend.

Hover: Your body carried some memories in it.

Redfield: The body is . . . doesn't have a clue. It's like . . . I see now. The body freaks out.

Hover: Sounds like a necessity.

Redfield: There's the blend, then it's . . . what's the word . . . something other than adjustment . . . there's a gestation . . . or integration . . . integration, then the body becomes accustomed to the change.

Hover: When you get back to your body, do you suddenly wake up?

Redfield: Yes, you know, you're lying there, you don't know anything's missing until it comes back, or something. It's jarring. There's no smooth way to do it. I mean, for me to do it.

Hover: But you brought back what you observed as far as knowledge and wisdom and information.

Redfield: Yes. It's been activated.

Hover: So it's hard for you to have precise memories because you're not in a precise form.

Redfield: Right.

Hover: But what you can remember is when you come back into your body.

Redfield: You process it however you can, but you can only talk about it and around it; you can't see it precisely, because it's a whole different language, a whole different mode of being.

Hover: Some of it doesn't translate in human terms.

Redfield: Uh-uh. The best you can do is tell little stories about it.

Hover: Do you have the impression that you have a friendly relationship with the beings who are giving you information?

Redfield: Yes (*said softly, emotionally*). These kind of tall insectile looking ones, they're very gentle. Maybe they're like the historians and educators. There are whole civilizations out there, all kinds of stuff.

Hover: They seem to have a motive to want to share with you. Do you feel like you communicated anything back?

Redfield: They know everything (*chuckle*).

Hover: No need to.

Redfield: They know everything about you. I mean, it's just like— we're so simple to them. It's like we're easily accessible.

Hover: Do you feel you could ask for information and get it?

Redfield: Well, you could ask, but whether or not they give it to you depends on what they . . . what their purpose is. They don't waste time on trivialities. The thing is, most of the questions we ask are like . . . irrelevant. You don't know enough to ask the right questions. It would be like asking a dog what his astrological chart is . . . asking a dog . . . I can't . . . (*SIGH*) . . . asking a dog, where are your wings?

Hover: The experience has enough reality for you that you bring back pieces of it.

Redfield: You bring back what you need to do, whatever you are here to do, and the rest is . . . never mind.

Hover: Does this happen to you more than once in this manner?

Redfield: Yes, I think . . . there's certainly a familiarity.

But familiarity is not what I felt a couple of years later about a dream that featured adult-sized aliens, or human-alien hybrids (next chapter). But if I were to explore, by hypnotic regression, this dream as a possible real event, would I discover that it too was a positive experience that only seemed negative to my daylight mind?

Either way, negative or positive, something else was key to the source of this business. Metaphysicians teach that we create our own realities with thought, emotion, and will. While I believed I was responsible for my life, particularly in my reactions to people, conditions, and events, if I was the creator of everything in my life, including activities such as I just described, I was unconscious of my designer and orchestrator! What is free will if so much of our lives seems to "happen to us," rather than our directly and consciously creating them? And how was I responsible for my life if my will was limited?

Maybe some of us choose to allow for certain limitations of will. Maybe such choices precede our births. Maybe will is like intelligence, a characteristic that expresses in different ways and degrees in each; but like intelligence, will can be developed and expanded. Maybe that describes the challenge that some of us choose. Maybe we choose to experience certain events as a catalyst to advance evolution. Or am I just optimizing my experience? I doubt that the purpose of the UFO presence can be stated in a sentence, paragraph, chapter, or even in a book. It is too closely linked to our lives. But I have my work.

The next focus is on will.

Did I choose to participate in the UFO drama? If so, when did I choose? And if it was a pre-birth decision, how could I have known what it would entail, any better than I can predict the outcome of any choice I make, as an embodied being? Life was challenging enough before all this alien business. Did I need this?

Look into the eyes of any newborn human being. How many appear to be wise to this world, lying there so helplessly they cannot even feed themselves? We may see glimmers of "old souls" in their wunderkind eyes, but we see utter amazement, too.

If I'm a wise old soul . . . I feel tricked.

CHAPTER NINE:

Human (ET) Link: Will and *Sanctum Sanctorum*

Dark, light, night, day,
Whether in joy or in pain,
Revelation is the game.
We don't care how you do it,
Just do.
Error is divine—
An arrow shot,
Better than not.

Later I will share a frankly alien dream, and a communication that followed. The poem above captures the tone of the communication, which is about will—the least understood of human powers, I was told.

During the UFO catalyst, many of my former beliefs were shattered, and my foundation of faith was rocked. How could something as awesome as contact and encounters, or abductions, be happening to so many people and yet our reports of these activities be so vilified by the intelligent public? Even if I'd known about hive minds, blaming the reactions on them seemed a flimsy explanation for the public response to our accounts. I was aware that some of the most intelligent among us could not fathom the possibility that we were reporting the truth. After studying this human mind phenomenon for several years, I concluded that the problem had little to do with all of the reasons presented for the inability or refusal to believe us. While the debates I read about in books and magazines, and viewed on TV, began on rational grounds, inevitably they would break down and sound like the squabbling of children. There had to be something beyond the rationales argued to explain the gap I perceived in communication. The "recognition" factor is definitely missing in the minds of debunkers and skeptics. I suspect that the answer involves more than the gap between left and right hemispheres of the brain; but, at least, this was a place to begin in studying the mystery, which is as much a puzzle as is the UFO enigma itself.

So, there were these two parts of the puzzle—the UFOs and the ETs—and the response of the public to our stories. The second was by far the hardest to understand and accept. In the question about possible ET origins, it strikes me as odd that I would feel familiarity in the presence of an insect-like being, and yet be baffled by human beings in so many ways. While I believe my brain is constructed the same as any other human's, a little removed from the body-centered consciousness, the aliens and the activities do not arouse in me the alarm that my daylight mind thinks they should, and sometimes they leave me with feelings of connection with something more familiar than this planet and most of its peoples. Could this connection be with my soul? The question of ET origins is still there.

Looking back, what I experienced during the throes of the UFO catalyst was simply a heightening of what I had always experienced in this life. The alien activities underscored and emboldened what had always been true. It was always impossible to communicate with certain minds, beyond the ABCs and

1,2,3s. As one of an artistic and visionary temperament, always I was an oddball in a society that seemed to worship logic and reason above all. The description of the gulf is expressed as science over religion or mysticism, but these broad generalizations hardly begin to shed light on the mystery of our differences; for it is hard to decide where one starts and the other ends. Science tries not to be religious, and religion tries to be scientific, and mystics try to mediate between the two, but end up annoying both.

If, as metaphysicians say, we are the creators of our reality, it is the content of our minds that keeps the world intact and ever-changing. Observing the world at present, one wonders if minds have gone berserk. Truth is a clown laughing behind a UFO. Now you see it, now you don't. Smile. Caught in the flash of a cosmic camera, photo pending.

Beliefs, choices, and faith seem to be at the roots of our differences and disagreements. And yet we speak so little of choices. More often the debates are about what is real and true, with no comment about choices to believe as we do. This links back to consciousness.

If most (?) are governed by hive minds, then maybe most do not consciously choose to believe as they do. But the ones calling themselves the El imply that many could be aware if they wanted to be, implying that a state of spellbound consciousness is a choice, at least in some cases.

They had this to say on November 30, 1997:

> Belief is substance. Not whimsical desire, or wishful thinking, but belief is a substance with which you build what you will.
>
> Your thoughts are the designers, your actions are the carpenters. Faith is the inspector-watcher who trusts that the structure will closely resemble what hope, belief, and thoughts aspired to build.

(Me: If believing is knowing, how can a belief also be a lie? In a lie, faith is misleading, isn't it?)

All know, but some pretend to believe; they lie, and what they build does not last, for all lies collapse, and only truth survives.

(Me: If they know they lie, why do they pretend to believe?)

What they know, they cannot abide, so they deign to build replicas, flimsy beliefs that will not hold, fashioned of their refusal to confront what they know but refuse to accept. Pride is their master, and they live by what he bids.

whew!

Do not let what they build in replica fool you by its brilliance or fine workmanship. Impressed, you worry you cannot build anything so fine—you who doubt what you know. *Dare* to believe what you know, and trust that, of this substance, you can build as fine a structure. And know yours will last long after theirs collapse.

That is the secret, Little Sister. You *know*. Now trust that you do. And *believe* it. Your belief shall be as a boat to carry you across these troubled channels. You *will* arrive on the shore of your content, and discover the home you *knew* was there, all along. *That* is belief made manifest, evidence of what you know to be true.

The "channels" were still troubled in 1997, and the shore of content looked awfully distant. After *Summoned* was completed, and even after the rewrite of *Jonah*, when the phenomena and communications had all but ceased, I was having trouble with the idea of "home." Looking back, I'd always had trouble feeling at home anywhere, but now it was pronounced. It seemed I had *perhaps* never completely submerged myself in a home, even the one I co-owned when married to Tom. It was his home, and I was playing house. The closest I ever felt at home was in a little brick house on Moenkopi Street where, after the divorce, I began the work with letters and numbers. Financial and family problems caused me to abandon that home, and for a long time I mourned the loss. But that was confusing a physical place with a state of consciousness. It wasn't the house or the location that was home, it was the connection I experienced during the work with letters and numbers, and in the communications, particularly in the days before the phenomenal activities breached my bliss.

In the fall of 1993, I felt more at home on this planet than I had ever before. Now my secretiveness about the contact makes more sense. I wanted nothing to breach the wonderful feelings of familiarity and being at home *in myself*. But I was selfishly clutching, I see now, like a child who does not want to leave the comforts of home for the work at school; or, like many of us who would like to ditch our jobs and sail to a remote island to live free of the challenges of civilization.

But regardless of our origins, life on Earth is a community affair. We are here to work out something together, and though many of us try, we cannot escape the belonging story. Despite our amazing intelligence (which we think we have), and our freedom (again, we think), we are all interconnected, like leaves on a tree. Regardless of our apparent separateness, emphasized by limbs and branches, we all share a common trunk, and our roots are intertwined. And regardless of our current alienation from nature, like the tree that interacts with the sun, water, wind, land, other plants and animals, so we are all a part of the larger life chain.

Beyond exercising our wills to create our mundane lives is another level of choice that mystifies. Some call it fate or destiny, but in these concepts, personal choice seems to be missing. "There are no coincidences, and no mistakes," is the emergent awareness, and I believe it's true. So how do we reconcile conditions, events, or circumstances that seem not of our conscious choosing? I don't like feeling like a victim. In the quandary caused by the seeming contradiction between will and destiny, people can get entangled in a search for root beliefs, thinking that they have set into motion choices made behind the back of conscious desire.

Specifically I wanted to know: Why did the first version of *Jonah* fail to excite my agent, and the several publishing houses I contacted? There were problems in the book but nothing that could not be fixed, which was proven when finally there was a contract, and I rewrote it. But at the failure, I was mortified. Was I no messenger? I had been encouraged to believe the novel would fulfill my task. Was I misguided? Once the phenomenal events breached my life, my trust issues were huge. Was I seduced to write a "new age" book to cover up the true dirty business? Was I completely deluded, used, betrayed with no care that my life was on the brink of destruction? Without a contract on the novel that I had practically eaten fire to produce, I looked like just one more victim of alien abduction. I could feel them, people all around, tapping toes, sniffling, waiting for me to confess that either I had imagined the whole business, or I was suffering from a "syndrome" that needed immediate professional attention.

Basically I felt that no one cared. I felt that even my loved ones thought I was just acting nutty and creating a personal soap opera. I could not comprehend that they could not comprehend what I was experiencing. Why couldn't they hear me? Intellectually, I knew that you can't know a thing until you have experienced it directly, but I didn't really believe it. I learned the truth of it—by direct experience. And now I understand that I had to experience a lot more, and change, before I was ready to make a contribution.

Jonah was not a failure; it was just on hold, on a time-event schedule unknown until I experienced it, month after month, year after year. Suffering the ridicule and isolation was part of the package. What did I think—I could sail through it all and be the darling of messengers? Always I try to circumnavigate trouble. Who plunges off the cliff or into the fire, screaming *"Take me"*? And yet I could not find any comfortable spots in the dungheap of victimhood, either. Always the damn thing was staring me in the face—the choice thing. But I managed to do my share of wallowing in the awfulness of it all, anyway.

If I had embraced the following (excerpted) message communicated in September 1993, my way through the catalyst would not have been so tumultuous. But then, I had to live the truth of these words before I could accept them as true, before they influenced my future choices.

> On a higher level than you can conceive, all is in agreement as to the design and outworking of all that occurs on your plane. Within containment (embodiment) in your dimension, much that happens is as a result of decisions agreed upon in cooperation with this higher plane we speak of. Because of the nature of your containment in form, it is impossible for you to grasp the higher workings that manifest on your level. It is like a bellows, an inhalation process, both actions working together to accomplish what you actively desire—the creation of a fire, so to speak. Does the exhalation understand the inhalation? Perhaps that which pushes out feels frustrated by the push that occurs in opposition, and feeling frustrated, it breathes out again, only to encounter again the push back; and in the excitement of this perceived battle, a fire is created. Does the exhalation perceive itself as a cooperative agent in the making of a fire? Or knowing only its sole purpose, is it simply behaving as exhalation?
>
> It is enough to do your job, Little Sister. The rest is being looked after.

(Me: Easy for you to say! I'm supposed to communicate this stuff intelligibly.)

> And are you not in the process of doing that?

(Me: Like an exhalation that fights against the inhalation?)

> Keep exhaling. It's your job. And the fire will spark.

It more than sparked. At times I felt engulfed in a four-alarm fire. Maybe because I was such a neophyte to water—metaphor for feelings and emotions.

Our lives and our nature may demonstrate in metaphors more than we realize. Even as a baby I fought my mother when she laid me down on the kitchen counter to wash my hair under the faucet. As a child learning to swim, I was pushed off the diving board by a zealous instructor who apparently believed that all human beings are naturally amphibious. Aren't we all composed mostly of water, and didn't we all begin in the swimming pool inside Mother's belly? Maybe I didn't like that, either! Emotions scared me, and so did water, especially water in my face.

Frequently I have referred to the bliss it was to work with letters and numbers. But beneath the work with the alphabet, and behind the communications that stood out in memory, was a feeling-emotion link I have never tried to put into words. A "feeling" story about hay begins *Summoned*, but that was deep into the vortex. It described the feeling of carrying a burden of wisdom that no one seemed to want to hear. But also, in the beginning there were emotions around the "call," feelings not conveyed in writing about the curious dream of space folk commissioning me to write a book, nor in my amused wariness in the contact of Clio, nor in feeling spooked by the appearances of implants in my hands, nor in the feelings of familiarity in the contact in the fall of 1993.

Earlier I wrote of the changes in my consciousness beginning in the 80s, when I became aware of the plight of native peoples and endangered animals. Like many others, I was almost numb to wars and environmental exploits—until modern-day communication systems made the pictures of human suffering, and animal and plant life extinctions, all too real. My heart was being prepared for the work and experience ahead, if I chose to continue the course. But I was living double, so never did I allow my emotions full expression. I made my choices in dim light, always doubting myself, my right hand never understanding what my left was doing, or why. But always I was trying to understand what was happening, get a handle on it, steer it—and especially be able to explain it—to justify my strange life—to not seem too weird to others. My stumbling block was intellectualism, and it still is. The UFO confronts the heart and demands that we make hard choices.

The heart is a bird caged by a bound mind, and will is the key. As we choose, so we experience. But how can I choose the right course in the blindness of my proud mind? Probably it is natural that we would become enamored with our brain power at this evolutionary stage. Probably it was meant that our "right brains" would be suppressed for the purpose of developing our rational minds. Maybe it was expected that we would make of our left brains a throne, and seat our thoughts as king there. There from the throne in the left, we have exercised our wills to create dynamic empires and civilizations. Natural that we, the little enthroned creators, would feel proud of our accomplishments, and would feel righteously indignant at the proposition of "higher powers"—after success in dethroning all such "mythical characters." But like the Ninevites in the story of Jonah, in the dazzle of our accomplishments, we too are unaware that our left hands are working in the blind of what we think we are making with our right hands. But, unlike the Ninevites, not many of us are likely to be moved by recitations of Holy Scriptures. Although certain scriptures ring for me, the Bible was not the whole bell for this Mormon-escaped mystical Christian, Hopi, Tantric, Sufi, Taoist, Buddhist, New Age renegade. The quickening didn't happen in my head—it happened in my heart. My mind was a constant skeptic, and denier. I was a product of evolution, a prototype of left-brain success. Nothing like a UFO to knock a proud mind off her throne. But at every experience designed to move me off the throne, I was, knee-jerk, right up there again, defending my position in our made world.

The divorce helped . . . a painful way to further open the heart, but pain is one way. In the way of pain, emotions are unleashed like wild animals that have been penned and half starved. Early in my life I was taught that emotional displays were unbecoming. There is a strong stoic gene in my family. Playing the violin helped in youth to release and direct my emotions. I remember playing in concert on the stage, tears streaming down my face. The Muses helped with art, music, and writing; ways to direct the emotions in a society that judges tears to be a sign of weakness. But the arts are not big enough containers for the emotions once the heart is opened. I wept through many days and nights during the catalyst. The cool, detached heads who render judgments against UFO experiencers have no idea the emotional dimensions that are opened in us. My teachers were right about emotions being unbecoming. Suppress the emotions and it is very difficult to "become." The becoming requires the full presence of a person—mind, body, spirit, and soul.

In the fall of 1993, when the strings in my mind began to vibrate with communications from afar, one voice spoke of hearing the cries of the children of Earth. It was a group voice, responding to the outcry. What should they do, they asked me— and recited several possibilities. The overtone was like the Muse that expresses in poem or fable, and yet the voice rang true. I knew that too many of our children were suffering, victims of seeming imbalances in our evolution, especially native Earthlings: Hawaiians, Eskimos, Aborigines, and our Elder Brothers, the Kogi, hidden high in the Columbian mountains. Modernization was killing off the delicate remnants of a world lush with life since the passing of the last ice age. Were the natives right? Were we due for another major world change? This was the vibration that called me, not the dreams and phenomena. Those came later. My heart was already primed before the shake, rattle, and roll began. I was already in contact, already knew the UFO presence was real.

The accusations that UFO experiencers are only trying to steal limelight, or wrest fifteen minutes of fame, or sell books, or create dramas to elevate themselves in importance, are hollow cans clattering in a blind alley of misunderstanding.

When/if UFO experiencers get past the shocking appearance of the spectacle; when/if we transcend our fears, we are brought home to ourselves, the lost children we are in the midst of this mechanized world created in the success of elevating our minds to a throne in the left sector. In this state, brought to our knees, we clearly hear the cries of the children of Earth—reverberating off spaceships.

Some channel the voices of entities thought to be important ETs or Divine or famous personalities, embodied or discarnate. Reading about, or listening to, some of these voices can quickly bore us in the same way that voices of science put us to sleep, pontificating from left brains disconnected from the heart of what matters. But such channelings may be as close as we can come at present to breaking down the walls that divide intellect and feeling-knowing.

The language barrier between the two hemispheres in our brain is real. The seam between left and right must be entered to swim in the river that flows between the shores. In the external, land is not divided by waters. Land is continuous; it covers the whole Earth. The land on the ocean floors is the same land upon which we walk. And so it is in our brains. The separation between left and right is but an appearance of division. The left is like land, the right is like water. And the winds of mind playing over both seem another distinctly different element. Missing from this triad is a fourth element, fire. Prometheus was said to have brought fire down to Earth, which baptized us as creative beings. But still we barely conceive the meaning of the symbol of fire to our being, so fixated we have become on outward forms, thinking them to be all there is. Fire is both creation and destruction. Wisdom suggests it is time we noticed what we are doing and creating with our fire.

The UFO is no less than Prometheus, herald and bringer of new fire. Something is being ignited, something in the consciousness for all who are not too asleep. But it cannot be perceived or realized in the left brain alone. The fire the UFO brings is the breath of the cosmic dragon and the flaming swords the cherubim swing to protect the Tree of Life. It doesn't matter what we think about it; it is reality expressing in a new way, designed not only to provoke minds, but also to break every hard heart. We cannot continue to rule and dominate the Earth from a kingdom in the deserts of rationality alone. The Earth is showing us we cannot. She is whipping up her waters and winds. She is rocking and heaving, shaking us off our thrones.

The will is about to become free. But don't we already have free will? How free is a will when a mind is in half darkness? As stated, I was invited to believe that I chose to participate in UFO activities. But if I were fully conscious of these activities, would my conscious mind agree with the choice made, apparently before this prototype, that is I, was born? The mystery is in our whole being, and that *is* a mystery. I can tell stories about flowers to show you my perception (chapter 13); I can report my experience and tell you what I was told. But I am no different from any other experiencer—much is still veiled. I live much in faith, guided by feelings.

I was very uneasy after the dream I am about to report. The communication that followed was rare in that I felt the transmitter was female in quality. By female I don't mean softer or gentler! There was a punch to the message, and I felt the transmitter's impatience at my denial, pretending to innocence. The voice sounds stern and authoritarian, but keep in mind, this came in late 1996. I was exhausted from the almost daily phenomena and recordings. My life was barely hanging together. I was in the Psalmist's valley of the shadow of death; a table had been prepared before me in the presence of my enemies. But I *did* fear evil, and I felt no oils or rods to comfort. So when I had dreams that seemed more than dreams, and they were dark, suggesting that there was nothing "spiritual" about this business, it *was* an invasion scenario; I was being abducted to serve in some sort of hybrid, clone, or alternate body project. I did feel like a victim up against forces more powerful than I.

In this light, the stern communication worked to bolster my faith. It spoke to my soul.

It is said that ignorance is bliss, and I am a seeker of bliss! But bliss is hard achieved when up against frankly alien experience, even if experience of the dream kind. Some dreams are surficial—on the archetypical plane of consciousness. These kinds of dreams are thoroughly explored and analyzed by psychologists and other masters of mental symbols. But some dreams are of the memory quality, experiences distorted by mental images of things and events for which there are no file cabinets in the left brain. Not having full consciousness of other dimensions, one's "brain contained" mind reports the closest approximation to knowns in this dimension. In such translations, the feelings are more accurate reporters than the images the brain-mind provides. This is the same for memories in hypnotic regression, or even memories claimed to be "conscious recall." In either case, we are reporting of things alien to our daylight minds.

November 2, 1996: I was awakened by the jangle of a bell. Sometime in the night I remembered seeing a small red light.

The dream: I'm inside a spaceship. It's grounded on a barren, hilly place. (The light was dusky.) I see smaller vehicles parked around the ship. Inside I am "babysitting" fully mature beings. They're in tanks? Sleepers? Semi-awake, I think. Unnerving the way they stare. Extremely intelligent beings, I know. But also vulnerable because they don't understand us. And dangerous for the same reason. Human quality to skin, face, body, but lizard-snakelike eyes . . . that stare.

I'm out of this room. I lock them in, turn the key in lock. I'm nervous, afraid one will get out. I need to report to a leader. . . .

I'm worried about other human beings seeing this alien breed. I feel a need to inform. I'm scared, worried they might be moving among us, unseen. I feel relief when a "practitioner" comes to check on my wards.

Next, I am moving in a vehicle in an uncomfortable position, on my back with head down, at an angle. Don't like!

Bumping around in "hyperspace" where the ship hides. (I jotted the word "quarantine" at end of dream recording.)

After recording the dream, I wrote about my uneasy feelings. In the midst of communications, which were wisdoms I wouldn't mind imparting, were dreams like this one and phenomena that disturbed my sense of being a messenger of good tidings. Throughout the catalyst there was this duplicity, this unresolved conflict. Was I a dupe? Was the agenda to use people like me to promote a new age cosmic message, when in reality we were just being harvested for our genetic material to produce stare-eyed, half-human, half-reptilian creatures? More disturbing: I couldn't even claim I was a victim of that kind of abduction. I was acting in a *care-taking* capacity. And my "dream self" certainly was uncomfortable with the role.

Following the dream, end-notes: "Attempts to resolve the good-evil question just set me spinning. The goodness/badness is in the eye of the beholder, I guess."

And then They (she?) inserted themselves and I recorded the conversation. Keep in mind that when I shift attention to engage in telepathic communications, my "deeper self" comes to the forefront. In the shift, I am more "knowing" of what is going on.

> The experiencer has to decide for herself. Then present one way or the other. We don't care which. As long as it is presented. If you think it is bad, and present it as thus, those who think it is good will not be swayed, and vice-versa. What matters is that this information gets out. For the sake of all.

(Me: Why does it have to be this big melodrama?)

> Because this is how reality expresses on your plane. Here all is acted out, expressed, experienced in the physical. If it were a mental plane, it would be otherwise. But it is not. It is physical. So everything must manifest—truth is only perceived in manifestation. Otherwise it can be avoided, ignored, dismissed. And with no truth, on what basis do you exist?

This is not about what will you choose. This is about what you have chosen being manifested. You know what you chose by what is happening. So you can know you chose to be involved, because it is in fact manifesting. You fret because you do not remember choosing. And yet you accept that you chose your parents, etc. You would just like to be released from duty, for it is harder than you thought it would be. So goes existence on this plane. Yes, it is harder than imagined, but we feel you will agree—there is a greater potential for joy.

Now, in keeping with the nature of this book [*Summoned*], you will not include such messages [above], except in brief excerpts, as the spirit moves you. Some is contaminated, distorted, and you don't know which. Some are "sparkers"—and these you will include. You will be guided. Some will serve to ward off those who would move to censor if it were too obviously "true." The "lightness" [humor] will serve to ward them off.

And thus you will play your part.

(Me: Why was I so overwhelmed [with information], if only to use snippets?)

It is not for you to question the purpose. You are a link, but cannot see the shape of the chain. Don't like the metaphor? What bothers of a human chain? Do you wish to be free of the chain? On your own? We think not. No one crosses alone. Think of a chain-link fence around all that is holy. Sanctum Sanctorum. Envision an electrified fence. No one can enter/pass if not of the vibration to be immune to electrocution.

Yes, you long to share the "el"oquence, but is too late. Too many have poisoned the waters. Now we make haste to alert all who are ready to hear.

It will all happen as chosen, by all. It will be manifest.[22] This is the law. This is the essence of this plane of existence. Truth is *revealed*.

---

[22] It will be manifest: I assume this refers to the "big event" mentioned in other messages.

(Me: But if it's a done deal—why would the defeated want to play their parts?)

Because they are shut off. They don't know they are defeated. And won't know until it manifests. Does anyone seek God before defeated? And how can you help them learn the truth, if not to help them reach the defeat that gives them opportunity to choose something different?

Do not try to protect them. You forestall the revelation of truth. The sooner it manifests, the sooner the truth is revealed. If you are devoted to truth, you will not try to forestall.

Your book, while light, will challenge. If done right, it will reach the ones intended. The guidance will continue, as before.

(Me: Why is it taking so long?)

You were not ready. You needed the time to assimilate, to sort, to decide. You could have opted out. And suffered the consequences. You cannot set conditions. You are either in or out. If in, you must act on guidance and forgo personal wishes. Proceed . . . and trust. You are ready now.

Yes, there are many who have opted out. They do not want to participate in manifestation. They want to be on the sidelines, not involved. And so they do not reap full benefits.

Respect all choices!

This took me back. I remembered the feelings during the five nights of sorrow. I remembered the pain of knowing that the disasters and cruelties experienced over the ages were as result of our ignorance. I then believed a shift in consciousness *had* to happen . . . and that nature had provided us a way to break free and realize our creative potential as the stewards of Earth, as was intended in the original design.

The stern communication helped me get in touch again with why I was suffering the trials of this particular catalyst. I was doing it "for the sake of all." What does that mean? I can't explain it to my head, or yours, but my heart knows the meaning in the same way that I know what the whole communication means. It is futile to analyze the words and lines of such communications. They are understood in the feeling-knowing-remembering-recognizing way, if that aspect of consciousness is open.

But the communication only worked to quiet my beleaguered daylight mind for awhile. About six weeks later, I was up against the fears and frustration again. I had begun *Summoned*, and it appeared I would never be able to write a "true" book that anyone would want to read. At a point of frustration, I asked Them bluntly:

December 16, 1996:

(Me: Which is it? Free will or destiny?)

Both. It is a paradox. There is destiny … and there is choice. So why not discover your destiny so you can consciously choose it?

Yes, /

(Me: But if it's already decided, what does choice mean? I don't know about this paradox thing, but I figure you can't have it both ways.)

What if you chose before you were born? And that choice determined your destiny. Now, along the way, "life happens" in a creative way. You and everyone else, all together are creating your environment. Your destiny has little to do with these activities and much to do with the choice you made, before you were born. The choice was to follow a given path, and this set up definite limitations, and challenges, that are unalterable by you.

The goals and desires of this world are not the goals and desires of your souls, and therefore, often you feel lost, frustrated, or a failure. This is because you have an agenda you made as a physical being, but that agenda has no bearing on the choice you made, except to complicate, delay or otherwise create confusion.

The deeper you seek Spirit, the more you can become aware of the *nature* of the path you chose, and therefore, make less trouble for yourself, and live more "smoothly," more in accordance with that which was set—by you.

8-05

All this will pass; all this is temporary. All this is the physical manifestation of the path you chose. But do not try to interpret it in worldly terms. Do not say, "My poverty means I chose a spiritual path, not a material one," for everything is spiritual, and everything is material; nor say, "Because I am President, my path is one of leadership," nor say, "My destiny is to be a musician because doors opened and it came easy."

Your destiny has nothing to do with things of this world.

Destiny is like a new Rolls Royce. Pump fuel into the tank, engage the key, press the pedal, and away you go. Your journey will be pleasant, no matter the road you take. But if you have no fuel, nor can you find the keys, you will be better off with a bicycle. The form of transport does not matter. What matters is that you keep moving, keep choosing. Whether by bicycle, Rolls Royce, wheelchair, or on foot, eventually you will reach your *destination*.

A person who seeks to be true to destiny insists on neither poverty nor wealth; seclusion nor prestige; rebellion nor position; but meets each day as a mystery unfolding. And as the mystery unfolds, choices are made—in keeping with your destiny, if this is your level of awareness; or not, if you have yet to become aware.

So it is, so it was, and so it shall be. We are your brothers and sisters of the Fifth Order, children of El, servants of all. Adonai, adonai.

I had my chance . . . why didn't I ask . . . *are you extraterrestrials?* What is the Fifth Order? Who *are* you? I had many chances to ask. After Clio, I asked only once, and a voice "thundered" (vibration) "We are Elohim!" And "Are you embarrassed to use our name?" They knew I was. And this is why I had not asked for a name. Elohim is an emotion-laden name like God or Jesus. An ancient name, it means different things to different people. In reaction to the upsurge of various new age movements, some claiming contact with important ETs, there has been a backlash from people who are alarmed at signs of conspiracies they imagine are behind all this UFO or new world order business. Spare me! I wailed in my psyche when the name Elohim was thundered like some Old Testament prophet. (The full story of Elohim is in *Summoned*.) Well, it was my choice to reveal the names of El and Elohim too. My intention was to write a true book, as honestly as I could. The fear at using an old trigger name was ego-based. I just didn't want to be branded as one of "those people." As if everything else I was sharing would cast me in rosy light, wearing a white pinafore.

You read it—the choice I made meant I would forgo personal wishes once this work began. I jumped off the proverbial cliff to live from moment to moment in the mystery unfolding.

"Unfolding" at the end of part 3 of "The History of Humankind in Summary" was the name El: "We are those of the fifth order of the star you know as Alcyone in the constellation you know as the Pleiades."

There it was, the ET link, twinkling like a ruby in the sapphire sky. A link only in my mind? Which mind? Old or new? In part 3 here, I will explore what little I know of matters of mind.

I want to close part 2 with a communication like the last, one that applies to all, aliens or Earthlings. It is my contention that regardless of the time, space, or environment, the principles of belonging-gathering-becoming are universal in scope.

This wants-to-be-a-poem happened a couple of weeks after the five nights of sorrow. I was still trembling from the harsh shift from the bliss of working with the alphabet and the crash in the flu when I was racked, mind, body, and soul, by the grievous side of human history. me too after reading "The Big Questi

I was waxing a little philosophical, retreating into a comfort zone of thinking I could somehow sidestep the UFO business. And yet my heart would not let me . . . they reminded me. Whenever I feel confused by choices, I remember this "narrative poem." (In places it sounds like a blend of me and Them.) I hope it will inspire others who may feel confused by the paradox of making the choices that create our personal realities while also recognizing the almost imperceptible thing that pulls, feeling like a call we ought to respond to, if only we knew what it was. . . .

January 17, 1994, notes: What simple deep yearning in earlier life did I turn away from because something "better," something more sensible took precedence, with or without a vow that I would respond to the yearning later? Did I lose track of it altogether? Or was it a fool's dream, what we all wish for, but . . . we grow up and accept responsibility, or we screw up so badly, we believe it will never be possible, or we feel we don't deserve it. Not on a material level; to be rich, or own a big house, these are symbols . . .

deeper, deeper
in your heart
what you were so sure
you would do on this plane, what
you were so sure you would not forget.
perhaps you haven't,
perhaps you are accomplishing it.
but are you enjoying?
reaping the rewards?
or is it hard, hard . . .
is it too late to get in touch,
make the contact?
are you ready now to
allow Guidance to
direct your affairs?
even if it means letting go of
everything you have so
winningly put in place in
creating your own reality?
what do you seek Guidance for?
to help you create what you want,
according to your plans and specifications?
how about a deal.
help me with this

but these you leave alone.
but my Dear, we would say if you asked,
this and these are interwoven.
you ask that we remove an ear
but leave the bone and skin
connecting it to your face?
you line up your lessons,
you describe your problem
and submit it like a rough plan for a house,
inviting a little help in,
to provide the furnishings,
and the means and labor to build it
on a spot of your choosing,
in a nice neighborhood
with running water, hot and cold
and a garden in every yard.
you ask for knowledge, for strength,
to carry out your plan,
or to please tell you if there is a better one.
all the while these things you know and have.
and when you "receive inspiration,"
you say Thank you, God
and get busy with your plans,
claiming a go-ahead, a green light,
this must be the way.
or the deal falls through and
you say there must be something better.
and you go to work again,
in your mind, on your friends,
the answers will come,
they always do—
from you
on that level.
do you really want Guidance?
or do you want to know how you can carry out your plans?

if "Guidance" knows a different plan—
are you ready?
to let it all go?
or are there people and things and circumstances that
must stay . . . surely.
yes, you create your own reality.
you have all the tools,
though many are quite rusty
and some you do not know how to use.
obviously you have enough to do the job.
you do have a life and it is your creation.
including the help you sought on specific problems,
for Guidance responds to the limit it can
without trespassing your will.
seems a relinquishment of personal will,
the idea of turning completely to Guidance?
but that is a choice, too.
no one is forced. Ever. To any degree.
so that a choice to "turn it all over"
is actually one choice
that relinquishes all other choices?
Is this doubletalk?
a man cannot serve two masters.
you serve one at a time.
experientially it seems
you are sometimes in spaces
in between, torn, confused—
you stand at the edge.   yes,
will you jump?
on the edge you are still serving one master,
though your back is turned and
you face the one who waits.
will you jump?   yes,
the moment you do, you begin to serve that master.
during the time you are "growing" or "developing"

you may feel comforted
that you are moving toward
this surrender, though you are
careful not to go too close too fast,
after all, you are very busy,
creating your own reality.
you need balance,
a little of this, a lot of that,
and of course the hand
must remain on the wheel.
you are responsible, you accept it,
not like some you know,
who have created for themselves quite a mess
and then they blame!
the government
a bad childhood
hard times
not you.
you are responsible.
doing a pretty good job of creating your reality,
creating a pretty good one.
except for these few areas that need a little
Guidance.
please, just mend this,
can't you see? don't you care?
maybe you need a new concept of Guidance.
power! That's it!
describes exactly what you need.
empowerment.
you deserve the best,
you worked hard for it.
it's your turn
for smooth sailing ahead.
of course there will be problems,
that's life.

everyone says so.
maybe you should just
accept, count your blessings,
live loose,
and ask for nothing more.
did asking work?
what a surprise
to find
that every step
led to the cliff.
what then?
jump or turn back?
these are the only choices?
I thought I was in charge of my life.
you are.
will you jump? *Yes, !*
to what?
to the unknown.
to live now
minute to minute
not knowing
how to create a reality
that fills the void,
satisfies the yearning,
no matter what goes or stays.
you will only when
all that you alone have created
no longer tugs,
when you
truly
want
love *Simply, Love.*
at
any
price.

PART III:
THE GATHERING STORY:
MISSING LINKS AND
WHOLE BEING

To everything there is a season. . . . a time to be born,
and a time to die. . . . a time to plant, and a time to pluck up
that which is planted. . . . a time to cast away stones, and a
time to gather stones together. . . .

—Ecclesiastes 3:1-5

CHAPTER TEN:

History Mystery: Bloodlines, Codes, God Pretenders

Part of the gathering story is in the mystery of our connectedness, which has endured throughout the ages of warfare and other atrocities that seem to mock the word love. I cannot address the gathering story directly, but in the discussion of missing links and whole being, maybe the meaning of the gathering will emerge.

Some of the information in this book is foreign, alien to "society-think." The purpose is not to teach, educate, or change the collective mind. Whamming a baseball bat against a beehive would be as wise as to try and retrain a hive mind. When the term "hive mind" was communicated in the "History of Humankind," in context to the question: "Do you not realize you are biological entities?" it jolted me. "Do you know you have a collective hive mind?" (No, I did not!) "Do you not know that you have your high councils and you have your workers who perform the will of these councils?"

And then They said: "But there is trouble on your planet because of the breeding that was done in ancient times, when two species joined to make a third." This means that an ET breed and a human breed combined to produce a "second order" of humankind. The trouble is that the breeding interrupted the evolutionary design for humankind. But there is no historical evidence or record to validate the information that came as a "download." And the El do not give details that can be researched to prove their assertions. Some of what they say may be purposeful distortions of the truth, to discourage efforts to prove or disprove, because the purpose is not to educate the thinking mind. The purpose is to stir memory in the souls for whom the information is meant. I am not a teacher, scholar, historian, or spiritual guru. I serve as a messenger without being certain about the messages, except when they affirm old tested wisdoms. I share controversial, impossible-to-prove information because it stirred "recognition" in me, and because I know I am linked, and I trust others will "recognize." Trust is the guiding word here; I trust that good will come of my efforts to pass on information that may be links for others in the mystery unfolding.

But life is more than collecting information to solve the UFO mystery. My life did not stop for me to do this work. Whatever the nature of our tasks and roles in the mystery, we each still have a personal soul agenda (I believe), which is woven into the evolutionary plan for all our relatives. In other words, it seems to me that the extent to which we can perform our tasks largely depends on attending to our personal evolution. Persons of like minds and hearts naturally gather. In attending to our personal evolution, we will find the people with whom we belong, to serve in the larger plan.

The purpose of this chapter is to add to the information about the "troubles" the genetic alteration caused in ancient times, as bears upon the activities now in progress, as pertains to the ongoing saga of human caterpillars transforming into creator butterflies.

We don't have to understand evolution to evolve. I was invited to see that complex knowledge is not necessary for human survival or evolution. Knowledge is an ever-changing story. Yesterday's facts are tomorrow's myths. The knowledge we need to survive and evolve is simple enough to be understood by all humans, regardless of level of intelligence, or status in society. It matters not the race, culture, country, or how much money we have. All are linked on the human chain in some configuration on or around the Tree of Life. Civilizations rise and civilizations fall, but the human garden survives.

In the beginning, when I felt the communications were purer, before I experienced the "oppositional energies," and my trust was challenged by the trials in my physical environment, I received part 1 of the "History of Humankind in Summary." As stated in *Summoned*, I was less than impressed because it was just a few pages long. Summary of history, indeed! I was skeptical, had no idea more would come three years later, after I was thoroughly wrenched through the vortex that the UFO catalyst was for me.

The "rest of the story" was announced a day before the information came in December, 1996. Can't recall all of the details, the particular light and sound fanfare accompanying the vision, but I do vividly remember seeing in the air an expanded hologram of a one-inch square wood block with a magnet on the back that is on my refrigerator door. On the piece of wood is a painting of Little Orphan Annie, her dog, and the words, "Tomorrow is only a day away."

I had been obsessing on titles for the book, as I do when I'm blocked (wood block). "Tomorrow" was a word I had been working with, using the number-letter routines I employ to work out my thoughts on paper. So I thought the hologram of the Little Orphan Annie refrigerator magnet was a kind of salute from Them, underscoring the word "tomorrow" as good to use in the title. Months later it dawned on me that the hologram was announcement of the rest of the history story, which was transmitted the next day: ("Tomorrow" being December 6, 1996).

I don't want to make too much of this, as if to say I think the history story is so important as to call for ET fanfare to announce the transmission. It is not an important story for "mankind." But it is important to me. It resolved some questions, but as is true of all of the communications, the mystery was kept intact. While I do not share it as an answer to the puzzle about our origins and evolution—because I don't think that's the point—I knew that something important had been imparted, and it would be the heart of the book I was struggling to write. The impact of the history was so strong I felt my personal experiences were secondary, hardly worth mentioning, would only be an introduction to the message given me to pass on. I was so sure this was right, I contemplated printing up the history summary and distributing just that. Skip my contact-encounter story, which was not interesting to many investigators, since I had no proof or witnesses, just a story.

I struggled along, did my best to summarize my experiences as framework for the history message that was the flame that kept me working. The story of how the first book came to be is in *Summoned*. To my amazement, the publisher was more interested in my personal story than in the history message, which I was quite sure was the key to the mystery of all this alien business in my life. I surrendered to the guidance of Frank DeMarco, and the history sits in the center of the book, with my personal story all around it.

If I'm not sure it's an accurate account of actual history, why did I feel it was so important? The importance, I felt, was partly because it did bring several threads together, of a design always playing at the back of my mind: the mystery of the Atlantis story, side-by-side with the UFO enigma, haunting me all these years, like a song you are trying to remember. If the history wasn't "the story," it was a big piece of the puzzle I was trying to solve. The question about my personal link to UFOs and the El was subtext to the mystery that gripped me. It was the story of humankind I sought. It was frustrating to have to focus on the details of my alien drama, when I had spent so much time studying, researching, puzzling, seeking the answers to the larger mystery of the UFO presence.

But "alien abductee" seemed the only door open to present my pieces of the puzzle for others who had an interest in the UFO presence beyond the spectacle of hapless human beings being snatched up into spaceships by characters that would soon be appearing in cartoons and commercials and be made in replica in dolls and pen tops. The little buggers became the darlings of mass marketing.

I didn't like getting down to the nitty gritty of the abduction scenarios, seeing it all in black and white, glaring on the page like a blasphemy to the Little Sister I felt I was to the ones who spoke straight to my heart. If I had to experience all that to get down to the real business, so be it, was my attitude. It was a strange viewpoint, I came to realize, maybe impossible to communicate, unless you've been there. The messenger impulse throbbed strongly to the rhythm of my heart, but darn if I did not get caught up in the drama of wanting to convince people that my experiences were real, not some mental dysfunction, sport for debunkers and others with nothing better to do. Part of me wanted to join some kind of crusade to uplift the consciousness of the alien abduction phenomenon, which was taking hits from every school of thought. Comparisons to every negative story ever told or imagined by human beings were trotted out to show that we were people with more than implants to worry about; something must be fundamentally wrong with us, to be such "victims" at a time when the siren song was you create your own reality.

And so my focus shifted from all that I had experienced and recorded to noticing that I had moved somewhere so far west of the mainstream, not even my best old friends could relate to me anymore. Few, it seemed, cared about the history of humankind. Maybe we evolved from apes; maybe we were the accidental offspring of spores blown in after some random cosmic bang drama that sounded so sensible to the modern mind; maybe we could finally erase from the blackboard the god myth, for good and all. We had been to the moon and photographed other planets, and no sign of god ports were seen anywhere. If intelligent life existed in the heavens, it would speak first to the scientists in radio language, decipherable in numbers, because now we knew that numbers were the code for life, and any other intelligent beings would know it, too . . . so goes the logic.

Right or wrong, the cosmos was calling, and we were answering in extremely impressive vehicles made to storm the gates of Heaven, and enter the cosmic race. If there weren't a race, we would create one. Race we knew from every angle and meaning, from our faces to outer reaches, from racy humor to racing stripes, from the arms race to racing joggers. Race got us up in the morning, and raced us around every day. Speed impresses us, especially when accompanied by loud noises—machines blasting with power to tear up the sky to match all of the signs of our swift progression down on the ground. What goes around goes up, too, we discovered, good for the race away from the down, or, in so far, we can't get out.

We want off and up and away, and fast. Hell is down, Heaven is up, this much has always been clear. Fire is in the belly of the Earth, molten lava spilling over to remind us. The grass on Europa might not be greener, but it is up there, a garden spot to find to escape the downs down here where all is fast going to Hell.

No matter the direction or angle I start from, always my pen loops back to the subject at hand, the state of humankind, the story in me before the alien business erupted into my living space. I can tell you about the scars, the marks on my body, the lights and the sounds, and the dreams that were more than dreams. I can chart the links that woke me up and brought me here, but it is not to persuade you to believe that paranormal activity is some kind of real, or that ETs are actually on the scene. Greater minds and stouter hearts have tried . . . for eons. Focus on the signs and wonders captures the fancy for a time, and then the show is over, and it's back to business as usual . . . a theme replayed throughout history with predictable results.

Civilizations rise and they fall, a story that never ceases to enchant. Everyone on the human chain knows it, every link. The belonging story is us. And so is the gathering story on the way to our becoming.

Along the way we gather, and are gathered. Don't try to see it; the minute you try, it changes, like a pool of water disturbed by a rock skipped across the surface. The image of your face ripples, showing who you are in the biological scheme of things.

If we are souls passing through these bodies to "gain a wisdom of understanding," as was stated in part 1 of the history story, why should the history of the human being concern us? If our destiny is in the sky, by space station or mother ship, or by rapture or resurrection, why pause to give thought to the bodies of future human beings? Isn't the way up and away, no matter how you look at it, by religion or science? And down is down, either way, if down in the dirt, or down in the bowels of Hell. Either way, extinction is the end of the race, the face, the legs. To survive, the human body must adapt to changes, seen and unseen.

I can only answer these questions this way: Real or imagined, I am a link between the two stories that play at the poles of the human mind. It is not a role I studied to play. There was no script, no dress rehearsal, no stage, no banner announcing a show to be performed. Stand-up comic would have suited me more. From my writing table here in my little cave in this remote Martian-like terrain, I can see no audience. Every word I write is in the faith that I can trust my deepest instincts. The history story means something to someone besides me. But it is more than blind faith, more than a reach to make sense of inexplicable events, more than a drive to rise above the apologies that attend every story of involvement with beings impossible to introduce or even describe. Excuse me, but I have a story to tell you.

I was made to tell this story. My body had to be changed before I could record it. That's how I knew it wasn't all in my mind. My body was changed. In the beginning, I lacked the faith to tell this story. I doubted the words that fell on the page, even though I sometimes felt a presence, even though I knew I was conversing with a different intelligence, even though I could not deny the familiarity, the knowing that I was linked to brothers and sisters of some other plane or planet—that question was never important to me.

We do what we are made to do. I don't mean made as in force. I did not relinquish my will. Books have been written telling abductees how to stop abductions. I didn't need a book to tell me how. I knew how. Just say no. Just don't go there. Inherently I understood the consequences of the no decision, in the same way I knew I was in contact with Others. The consequences for saying no to my life would be the same as for anyone who goes a way they were not made for.

We ask, why am I here? What is my special task? What is the meaning of life—*my* life? The answers to all of these questions are in us—literally in us, I believe. But *in* is scary to many; it's too downward, not the up we are taught to seek, the head where we make sense of everything, not in the sky toward which human eyes roll when the word Heaven is spoken.

How did I know to seek the answers within, down below the head? I was told by other human beings who knew this way; but telling is only a clue, not the discovering. Once the way was pointed out, I focused there, and the results were positive and real. Because, I believe, this is how I was made. To do this, to turn within, to quest, to eventually connect, to do this little job, to tell this little piece of a story.

I and my task are obviously not any more important than the millions of people and the myriad tasks that they perform to help to keep me alive. If not for the people who grow and prepare and drive the food to this town, I would not survive, for I cannot live off the land . . . I was not made for that. If not for those who make the clothes I wear, I would be cold and wouldn't get far, because my body and feet were not made for that kind of hard going. If not for every human being who has taught, clothed, fed, nurtured, and provided me with everything I needed, I would be dead. I was not made to survive alone.

I did not know what I was made for until I began to work with letters and numbers, but this did not spell out my task in whole, nor did it wholly define me. The vision I had was not much like the reality that unfolded, and I fought it all the way, because little in my life had prepared my mind, and my body was responding to my daylight mind. As for what it knew to do— my body just knew! While I lay on the bed, completely baffled by what was happening to my body, it just did its thing. And although I was willing and anxious to write, believing that fiction was the way, it became apparent in a way impossible to explain—my hand knew, better than I did, my job.

The way was inward, and I went there. In the inner cosmos, I was infused and encoded, and my body was marked. The marks were not proof for anyone else, but a language my soul understood, like the triangles the child knew to draw at age three, to leave a little map for the bewildered adult who had lost the memories of where she had been before she began this journey to remember the silver.

The history in *Summoned* is too long to repeat here, and something is lost in summary. It *is* a summary, a whole as it is, but it is not the whole story, nor should we take it too literally, though some of it may be literally true.

As stated, part 1 came three years before parts 2, 3, and 4. The "voice" of part 1 was rather formal and stilted. A severing of communications between our creators and us was mentioned, and I said I did not know what that meant. But I did, sort of. I just wasn't prepared to put it into words yet. The severing belongs to the same elusive story about Atlantis. Something happened deep in our history . . . a shift of dimensions, a shift of consciousness, downward I think, and a shift in the powers that tend the human garden, or evolution. And now, it was announced, communications between us and our creators was being restored.

There are "tracks" to this story in *The Law of One* (Elkins 1991) books, Ra speaking through channel, Carla L. Ruekert (mentioned earlier). In the Ra version, a quarantine was placed around Earth after the genetic alteration. But the story in *The Law of One* books differs in details from the story transmitted to me. In the history summary, the Nephilim (Genesis 6) were the ones who created the second order of humankind. Those of the second order were part-Nephilim, or part-Anunnaki, from the planet Nibiru (which means "planet of the crossing"), which allegedly passes between Mars and Jupiter every 3,600 years; this according to Zecharia Sitchin in the book, *Genesis Revisited*. But according to Ra, the genetic alteration was enacted to transfer souls from Mars to Earth, after the Martians had rendered their planet inhabitable. Either way, there is a general agreement that a severing, or quarantine, happened as result of a genetic breach in the evolution of Earthlings.

The gathering story in me may refer to certain creators who are re-establishing conscious communication with their progeny. But now we are "brothers and sisters." We have evolved past childhood. Now we are adolescents, still needing guidance. But were we completely cut off during the severing, or the quarantine? In a way, yes (according to my information). But as was stated in part 1 of the history summary, "channels of communication were dedicated (in some bloodlines) that you might seek and receive guidance."

The El were not speaking as creators, but as mediators who were telling me a story about something we need to know about our past. As I said before, I feel that no one messenger has the whole correct story.

At the end of part 2 of the history, the El speak of a plan to correct the genetic breach. Their attitude is positive, but there is a subtle disapproval when they say the Nephilim "conspired to be our guardians and shepherds," deciding in councils to direct the affairs of humankind. In the Ra story, "guardians" initiated the quarantine. In the story told to me, the Nephilim instituted hive minds, which resulted in a severing of communication with the creators of the first order of humankind, which was then "two orders" (two kinds), the second order being part ET. The plan was to assimilate both orders. Toward the end of the history information, the El began speaking of an "unprecedented change" on the horizon, for which we are now being prepared.

At some point, we will be of a consciousness—"soon the light will shine brightly enough for all to see"—to "clean house, to restore order where chaos has long held the reins," and we will "oust those who have usurped the rule of free will in exploitation of the plan you have abided in faith."

Below are excerpts and discussion from a couple of communications in the early days, which may shed more light on the story.

November 21, 1993:

(Me: So, the gathering of the twelve tribes is both literal and symbolic?)

Literally there are no direct descendants on one hand, considering reincarnation; on the other, the bloodlines are still in existence, blood being the rivers that carry the blueprints—those of the descendants of this/these particular branches having received strong *anti*programming, to preserve, in some part, to some degree, patches of, remnants of the truth; the uncorrupted design. So that at such time that the restoration draws near, those with these remnants, those with some codes still intact, will respond to their calls and make ready to reclaim their rightful domain, that which was given to them in love, that which has been plundered by those who took power and enslaved you to the endless rebirthing cycles.

(Discussion: This reminds me of other conversations in the fall of 1993, included in chapter 2, having to do with Atlantis.

In review: Certain Atlantians and Mayans were "taken up" when a great catastrophe occurred, and others were left to carry the story of the destruction into the world. The information was "preserved in code." This could refer to either myths or DNA, or both. In essence, the Atlantis story informs us that rulership of the Earth shifted, and this happened because of human abuse of the "God force." This is not exactly the same story as the one about genetic alterations, but they could be chapters in the same story, told from different angles.)

(Me: Why? I ask in shorthand for several questions.)
They feed off negative emotional energy.

(Discussion: The "why" was shorthand for wondering how the "rulers" could have wielded power over us for so long—*endless* recycling? I thought reincarnation was a natural part of soul evolution. What is the nature of their hold on us? They feed off negative emotional energy? I can imagine the fear, shame, and grief the catastrophe and the consequent "fall" must have engendered. Suddenly reduced to a primitive consciousness, man becomes animal-like again, except we still have the mind and emotions of the human, and the ET influence. The fallen elites might be driven to regain status and power, and the "peasants" might see the downfall as an opportunity for revenge and gaining a stronghold. Quickly memories of the catastrophe are shredded by the crisis as survivors revert to wars to determine supremacy in the new ravaged realm.

Remember, the earlier communications informed us that our spiritual leaders were "taken up" to another dimension to allow us to live out the consequences of our actions. And they would serve as guides to help us re-evolve our consciousness. Might also the "archons" of gnostic literature rule from a parallel dimension that interpenetrates this world? This might be the story behind the story of spiritual warfare [angels and demons]. The implication is that we are influenced by beings in other dimensions, some who actively interfere with our will, and others who guide but do not interfere, in respect to the Law of One. As long as we are asleep to the presence of these forces, and are driven by fear, lust, and greed, resulting in wars to establish hierarchies at the level of the human animal, we provide negative emotional energy for the "archons" to continue their rule over our minds. In ignorance we recycle, until we wise up, make different choices and break free. The implication is that we are waking up.)

Earlier in the conversation, they said:

> "Spellbound," you cannot make right choices based on programmed information (hive minds). As you are not taught the complexities of consequences, you do not see the vast simplicity of interconnectedness, and so you choose what you believe to be right, trampling on your path all those who are in the way—therefore wrong—as you have been programmed, to wit, the many, many fine people who surrender to the justification of war. After all, you must defend what is right, and fairly speaking, sometimes the other does behave as an enemy, attacking first; *he* quite certain that *you* are wrong, and then of course, there are always those who need no justification, they being motivated purely by greed or riches or power, by-products of any war, nastily gained prizes, the victors *manage* to enjoy, despite the *bloodshed*.

(Me: Will people respond to the same old good-evil battle story? Seems to me we are all jaded on that one. The good news these days is that evil is a perception. We create our own realities.)

> Yes, some can manifest quite nicely, especially these days when the battle is heated up. Yes, some very good activities, some inspired, truly, for we have our troops, too, those who have been groomed, all these wonderful players convened with messages all; and as the battle wages, while the game becomes on one hand more blatantly clear, on the other hand, it appears more subtle.

And even the elect were almost deceived, for what was presented seemed ever so logical and right ...

(Me: But what difference does it make? If a person is working for peace, and behaving "in love," with loving motives, how
could this be wrong?)

Not wrong. But still the issues are not being addressed. These
good works and miracles can be hypnotic sleights of hand to distract from the waging battle ... eat, drink, be merry, for tomorrow
you die ... and are reborn. And because you were such a good kid
this time, next time will be a breeze, a prize this next life, so keep
doing these good works, you have never had it so good.

(Me: So in essence, some of the best works are the most
cunning diversions?)

From the reality that you are not yet gods and godlets and
godletesses. The only way to *become* these powerful models
shown to you is *in consciousness* ... exercising conscious will that
benefits ... harmonizes with *all*. ...

You must see the links ... you cannot choose rightly not seeing them. Though your choices on some levels *may* in fact be ben-
eficial to some, the overall pattern is not benefited, and therefore,
there is no gain toward freedom. All continues to cycle, the heroes
and heroines of today, thieves and murderers in some next life ...
where they are born ... *with memories blocked* ... perhaps in circumstances where it takes divine intervention to keep from developing murderous (for instance) impulses ... and taking into
consideration that in some cases the corruption is such that
people are born with codes so scrambled, they are, so to speak,
"destined" to create terrible havoc.

Yes, it is good to see each individual as a child of God; in
truth, all are. But also true is this corruption, this corrupted pattern,
design, blueprint, that if not for the guardians, would have built up
such a momentum of power that not even the most powerful
angels could have gotten through the web spun over your minds.

But you see now, there were instructions left, encoded—"holy books" encoded—and the guardians, those who were strong enough so many eons ago to understand and keep the secrets ... passing them down,

     down,

         down

             through the ages, threatening terrible punishments on those who failed their tasks, and in essence, the outcome for humankind would have been terrible if they had not kept to their tasks, if in fear and trembling, on *hairs* of faith, thin reeds, indeed.

(Me: I don't know what I've written here.)

And your green light is *not* on.

(This was one of those heads-up comments that reminded me this was not just me talking to myself. Often in the beginning they would make references to certain physical things to show me they were "other." I liked to write with a certain green light on, and I had not noticed it was off. The quick statement at a moment of disorientation snapped me alert again.)

(Me: So the 12 tribes . . .)

. . . are truly those with less corrupted blueprints, but these are not them in specific countries together as groups as to call Finlanders or Eskimos or those in the Mormon faith or the Jew, in or out of Israel.

Those who carry the seeds, the bloodlines ... no one knows their names. They themselves do not know who they are. But many, and progressively more, are sensing something ... "hearing" something, no less than the sound which is sounding, like that which your dogs howl at before you hear the sirens.

You are literally being called "home," being that which means to gather ye all, for your *real* fathers are returning, the "bridegroom," if you will.

A few days later, these subjects were again discussed. I had read a book by another experiencer that confused me, and when I addressed my confusion to Them, I got a very hot response! They have "buttons," too. I triggered something rarely communicated—a kind of spiritual fury at what was apparently perceived to have been lies by certain aliens, or "gods." My contacts sometimes sound very human. They get personal about God, too, but I feel it was protective of me.

I began the conversation by writing about the book I had read, which stated that some people would be taken off the planet, but not all, because the rescuing aliens "did not have room for everyone." And also certain statements in the book about "God's family" bothered me, which caused me to ask Them, "But isn't everyone part of God's family?"

It is a matter of origins, is it not? Why search out genealogical records—to baptize by proxy those who have died? (This refers to my childhood religion.) As if your god were truly this supercilious, finicky being we referred to earlier who would set up such requirements. A symbolic ticket into heaven, condemning those who were not fortunate enough to receive missionaries and surrender to that which ruffles the logical mind.

Who is that God?

One must be born of the body and of the spirit in order to enter "heaven," baptism being *symbolic* for physical birth, and seeking and accepting higher guidance is the essence of being born of the flame of spirit, each coming to these in his/her own times and ways.

Yes. Any system devised to exclude human beings based on failure to perform a symbolic ritual is *evil*, vile, a lie. If worship of *form* is not worship of an *idol*, what is?

One does wonder, does not one, how people so bright could be so blind. Perhaps blinded by the light that beckons them to *glory*. Self-glory. Crowns and scepters and white stones, a name chiseled in a book forever, gods, goddesses, sons and daughters of the *right* hand, those who obeyed the *rules*. With nary a thought, blind faith, abnegating that which their creators endowed them with, a little thing called a *will*. Accompanied by brains designed to grasp concepts much more complex than are imagined, as you know. You have dared to break the rules, descending the bars to break free. You did.

(Me: Not by myself!)

Never alone. True. The essence of guidance, nearer than your breath, ever present, ready to teach, instruct of the ways of love.

Yes, do look again at "friends" who would abduct, render pain for their own purposes, and *program to forget*, promising freedom and rescue, implying specialness. Yes, do look. Whom does it remind you of?

(Me: The human race!)

In general . . . and how did you get this way? Yes, look. If early in your history you were tampered with, your *gene banks scrambled*, and you were programmed, said programs imprinted upon your very blueprints to be passed on from generation to generation—is it any wonder today your world would be filled with those who justify rendering pain in the *name of right*? Who would justify leaving *most* behind because *we have not the room*?

(My pen was smoking.)

How small is this god? Is his throne a thimble? His scepter a toothpick? The prerequisite, "they" say, is that you believe in God. Now. Which God would they be referring to? The opposition is clever. One wonders if it were possible to outwit such as these. Why . . . even the *elect* were *almost* deceived. And what saved them? Perhaps . . . just consider a moment . . . yes, you are ahead, your tentacles out there grasping the sword . . . that during this time of upheaval when the balance of power "shifted," we were able to institute programs of our own in some, which does not imply that we did not love all the same; only that it was only possible to reach a few.

Yes, we are speaking of programs within programs, encoded, which distorted, tends to suggest there is a superior race among you, tending to make loathsome the idea of interbreeding, and, in fact, interbreeding of certain formulas *does* cause mutations, as is seen worldwide. We are speaking of the ones willing and able to respond to the call to become workers in the field as we prepare to call all who belong . . . all belong . . . all belong . . . let no man or beast put asunder.

Some choosing to challenge the order set up cycles of disorder, which, yes, as you can conceptualize now—which, in turn creates the chaos-to-order pattern, tireless in its devoted effort to regain a stronghold, thus the "wheel," the "Mandlebrot set," ever spinning, going nowhere, which, save for love would mandlebrot into eternity.

Yes, love comes with a sword in its mouth. To set right that which was set to upset that which was downset. The ever-spinningness never going anywhere, satisfying the wants of those who would if they could forever remain at the level of sensory satisfaction. It is the nature of the beast. It can't help itself.

Do you see? You do, yes.

(And they end on a playful note . . .)

Up and down the mind's ladder. In and out of the rooms of memory. Gathering daisies, strewing them, construing a stew, mustn't stew too much. Rest with the pearls, a pile becomes a cushion, where once it was as the pea beneath the mattress that made impossible sleep for the princess.

For everything physical there is a spiritual equivalent. A pearlmusement.

(Me: That means there's a spiritual me.)

Bingo. The thumb's turn to rule.

(Again, a "heads-up." My thumb was sore from writing.)

Now to link these three stories, of Atlantis, of a genetic alteration, and a scrambled bloodline story that seems to belong to another drama, unless we can see how all connect.

It may seem like evasion to say that details don't matter, because details are precisely what most of us desire to know. But I believe them when they say that we can't comprehend the intricacies of the evolutionary designs.

Maybe we *can* comprehend the intricacies, but always they are speaking in respect of individual will. My understanding is that it is an infringement on will to present information as the "word of God" because everyone has a different concept of God. For many, God is not an entity like a glorified ET. So anyone presenting such a god, demanding that all should bow to him or her, and all should live by the dictates of that god, well, you see the problem. We have lived it. Is it possible to live in harmony, respecting everyone's different views of God? It is declared as an ideal in our very Constitution, but in reality, people use beliefs in gods as excuses to battle one another, each claiming their god told them to punish or kill people who don't believe as they do.

This is my current understanding, which is limited: We are here to experience individually and together. It is in the togetherness that we have so much trouble. Individually we are evolving. Individually we each have will, and the very individual nature of our wills is bound to result in clashes. Simply, not everyone wants the same things, or perceives reality in the same way. Individual will would be pointless if we did. It is in the working out of our individual differences in communities that we evolve.

I think of how it is with parents and children here. If parents show favoritism, or interfere in childish squabbles too often, the children are hurt and don't learn, particularly if the parents show favoritism. And what are stories about different gods with different "chosen children," if not expressions of favoritism? What excites feelings of rejection and resentment more than showing favoritism? In the histories of such stories, we are led to believe that the chosen ones are truly better people. We are led to believe they are examples, and if we will but mimic them, we too will be as loved. But is this the way it really is on Earth? From every story of a chosen people arise stories of the failings and imperfections of the chosen ones. History shows that when a people decide they are uniquely special, such as Hitler's Germany, they often revert to the most terrible examples of humanity. In my perusal of history, I read that all chosen people stories end in jealousy, resentment, war, and destruction, providing plenty of "lunch" for those who dine on negative emotional energy, if that story is correct.

The El always speak of us as one whole family, which has diversified in some "interesting ways," as one contact put it. To do otherwise, to "name names," to point to certain people and say, "Ah ha!" would be like parents showing favoritism, or rejecting some of us as "not as evolved," and therefore less lovable.

In respect of a free will world, a "god" that loves all equally would not endow some with advantages and others with disadvantages, and then pamper the advantaged and punish the disadvantaged. Anyway, this is not my idea of love, upon which I base my most fundamental faith in everything I consider to be good and reasonable. *But* it is clear that *nature* produces every kind of being, and some are disadvantaged, handicapped, crippled, weak, etc. I believe that in the "together" part of our journey, in the community part, we work out our individual evolution by how we treat one another.

In short, I am saying that human beings are responsible for everything we have done, good or bad. I'm saying we can't blame gods or disadvantaged genes for our wars and the disharmonious patterns we have created. *But,* I also acknowledge that as nature produces patterns that are judged to be disadvantageous, so have more advanced, or advantaged, beings also interfered to create patterns of disharmony that were not there by nature, nor created by a Supreme Being. In other words, perhaps certain ETs did act as gods (and still do), interfering in the evolution of Earthlings.

I believe the El when they say that this world and its people were created to evolve in a natural, harmonious way. And that the pattern was disrupted. The Atlantis story? Nephilim? Martians? Orions? Some unidentified virus? What really happened? The details are not important. We can see the trouble caused by all these different groups warring over such details. No matter the details, we are still will-endowed beings. We choose what to believe, unconsciously or consciously, and by that we live.

I am inclined to believe that there was a breach in our history, and that measures were taken in certain bloodlines to insure that the basic messages about our wholeness as one race, and the simple principles of wise living were preserved on the "sacred grapevine" to be told in stories down through the ages so we could keep the faith in an inherent knowing in our hearts that we are all children of a Supreme Creator, and all are equally loved.

I cannot make sense of this simple faith I have. I cannot explain us, or our world, in a way that answers the myriad questions that arise in the daylight mind. I can't do it for myself, much less for anyone else. Because I cannot make sense of it, and yet it is so powerful in me, I can believe that faith is inherent in my very genes. I can believe that the driving force that has caused me to rise to the occasion of these books is literally in me, in my very blood.

"The message" in its many, many forms is going out all over the world. It is not all done in books; in fact, books may be a very small part. Do most people read? Do most read and understand English? And of all who do read English, how many give a hoot about UFOs, much less the origin, nature, and history of humankind?

The remaining chapters in part 3 in no way compose a religion or a science about mind, body, soul, or consciousness. Everything I wrote in this book is my personal bias. The El can only communicate through me, using my little dictionary of words, and my library of education and experience. It is the same for any conscious receiver of information.

It may seem a long meander in the chapters ahead before I return to the question of my personal ET link, but as I stated, my role as a human link is to impart certain information.

An old saying from the fellowship that loved me until I could love myself fits here: Take what you can use, and leave the rest. . . .

CHAPTER ELEVEN:

Infinite Mind, Heart, and Symphony

> Every one of the Faithful could hear a pronounced whisper that filled the wind. The destroyers seemed to hear nothing. We listened more closely and heard the voice of our Earth Mother as she spoke to us through the Language of Love. "Children of Earth, hear me," she said. . . . "It is up to each of you to gather the seeds, fruits, bits of bark, and roots from the Tree of Life while you can. . . ."
>
> —Jamie Sams and Twylah Nitsch,
> *Other Council Fires Were Here Before Ours:*
> *A Classic Native American Creation Story* (1991)

Mind on Religion

Religion was a dream in me, maybe carried over from a past life that I viewed as a Mormon in Missouri. Religion failed me in that life. Maybe I had unfinished business, or maybe it was a dream I could not let go of, an idealism I sought to live in the flesh. I think I have learned the lesson, seen the delusion, dropped the dream. But oh, the price I paid to break from that hive mind. I nearly died, and it was a long recovery that I doubt I could have accomplished without the help of a fellowship of seekers who loved me until I could love myself. If we are to live the golden rule, first we must love ourselves.

But today, religion seems least about love and most about competing dogmas. Religions went to our heads. Religions became big business, contending for the official story. Religion became political, competing with the state. Both religion and science now go to government on bended knees, because government is the big bank. Money determines success in the world, and both religion and science need lots of money to do their things. Life is big business now.

Long ago, before we split into hive minds, life was seamless. Religion, government, evolution, culture, and business were parts of one weave in a seamless fabric. But now that we see with divided eyes, histories that speak of life different from today's official story are deemed to be religion, or myths to be dismissed. Now the Native American legends can only be religion, because we cannot (and don't want to) affirm them as stories about actual events. They fail today's test of empirical proof. History over the past couple of thousand years is rife with stories about various human beings gathering in expectation that Jesus or some other godly being is going to return . . . soon. Such gatherings seem to be powered by a desire to escape the plight of human life. Sometimes such gatherings end in mass suicide.

Some gathering stories personify disconnection. In these stories, we are not "all related." There is no belonging, no continuation, no becoming story for such people; there is only a going away story from an imagined destruction that only a few—they—can escape by rigorous faith in separation from perceived enemies.

By the fact that we exist as separate physical entities, it seems self-evident that we mean (or Evolution or God intends for us) to accomplish or realize something as individuals. Perhaps we are gathering to become . . . ourselves.

Hive Minds and Religion

In the Seneca story of the cycles of life, the current cycle is called the "Fourth World of Separation." Soon, the legend informs, we will pass into the "Fifth World of Illumination."

On page 97 of *Other Council Fires Were Here Before Ours*, authors Sams and Nitsch say, "Each relation is being given the opportunity to seek out any conflict within the Self and heal it in order to stabilize the wobble that keeps us from personal balance and world harmony."

We've come a long way from gathering "seeds, fruits, bits of bark, and roots from the Tree of Life." Now we are gathering ourselves, getting our stuff together, preparing for the big mysterious event, after a long journey of separation by tribal hive minds.

But "illumination" does not describe the vision of the future in certain religions. Some hope for Armageddon; a near miss is the twentieth century, the bloodiest in recorded history.

> Between 1914 and 1945, seventy million people in Europe and the Soviet Union had died violent deaths.

And . . .

> For decades, men and women had dreamed of a final apocalypse wrought by God; now, it appeared, human beings no longer needed a supernatural deity to end the world. They had used their prodigious skill and learning to find the means of doing this very efficiently for themselves. (Armstrong 2000)

And since 1945, many more have been slaughtered in "ethnic cleansings." Whatever the stated motives for such mass slaughters, they all look to me to be playouts of beliefs about "chosen people," survival-of-the-fittest horror stories acted out by the most fearful among us—fear of not having enough, fear of annihilation, fear of loss of identity and status; hive minds fighting for their lives. If hive minds were a transitory phase between One Mind and individualized minds, all who have no individual identity outside a hive mind would feel threatened by the increasing signs of individuation. Probably they would not construe the changes that horrify them as signs of individuation. If a person has no sense of self beyond a hive mind identity, that person may not be able to conceive of individuation. From the hive mind perspective, everyone must belong to some other-defined group or category, some other wrong religion, "secularists," "liberals," "humanists," "new age," or some demonized political group. The definitions are endless, but they all have one thing in common: They all represent the enemy in the minds of people who know no other life than one governed by some hive mind.

Life may be telling us that we have outgrown the old hive minds, as we would training wheels on a bicycle. But individuation doesn't mean separation from all other human beings. The belonging story is still the story of life. No matter how individual we become, we are still social beings who gather in communities of one kind or another, if only families.

So far as we know, never have so many human beings walked on planet Earth at the same time. Never have there been as many individuals walking free of hive minds (speaking of unprecedented changes). But if tribal minds cannot recognize the new individualism as even in the realm of possibility, they can only construe the change in the terms of their understanding. Often the change is described as abandonment of God.

The gods are multiple, one for each hive mind, but all believers seem to agree that modern man worships the scientific or "humanist" mind, which, heedless of God's laws, can only be inspired by some demonic being. In the dualistic mind, if there is a good god, there must be an evil opposite. In this mind-set, fragmented into multiple conflicting hive minds, sans a rescuing god of some kind poised on the near horizon, their terror might be horrific, might be a driving force to cause them to take matters into their own hands, if to assume roles of the avenging angels, who, at the stroke of midnight at year 2000, were *supposed* to have descended to separate chaff from wheat, weeds from flowers, Corn Flakes from Honey Bunches, loafers from sandals, lead from gold, dirty from clean, white from black, brown, red, yellow, hetero- from homo-, beer guzzlers from wine sippers. The angels of separation were supposed to have rescued the good seed and plowed the evil seed under the ashes after the final cleansing conflagration.

All this because a couple of rebels in some ancient garden couldn't keep their hands off each other.

In the old hive mind-sets, if ETs exist, they can only be part of the pantheon of gods and demons believed to rule the heavenly abodes. If the hive mind cannot allow for the individuation of human beings, how could it entertain ETs from worlds not described in the holy books from which the beliefs originated?

Mind on Science

Thousands of years from now, will future man be as mystified by the artifacts of our civilization as we are by pyramids and Mayan astronomical calculators in stone? If our bodies, deteriorated to skeleton pieces, are not the stones to reconstruct a path to show an orderly, logical progression in evolution, how do we solve the creation-evolution puzzle? Where are the mind pieces? They show in hieroglyphics etched on stone, in exotic squiggles on parchments, in scratchings on papyri, in words and pictures and symbols . . . maps left for minds who can decipher the meanings.

But science insists on objects—called empirical evidence—to prove the claims to meanings deciphered by using the mind. The objects analyzed can be collective stumbling blocks. Infinite mind can create anything, and does. Brains are instruments for focusing infinite mind in particular ways, but without a consciousness to fathom the concept of infinite mind, how can we shift attention away from the instrument?

In *Gifts of Unknown Things: A True Story of Nature, Healing, and Initiation from Indonesia's "Dancing Island"* (1991), author Lyall Watson says, on page 216: "Looking for physical explanations of mind is like attacking a piano with a sledgehammer to get at the concerto imprisoned inside."

Maybe part of the purpose of this cycle was to increase knowledge of the instrument. And if the Seneca are right, next . . . illumination.

Now we begin to grasp the connections between brain and mind; now we begin to gather our knowledge to see the puzzle in new light, and in a new configuration, one that exceeds the thought pieces we labored to push into place, like squares jammed into circular holes, to make the picture match our beliefs.

Expansion of consciousness is not an abstract notion, lacking empirical borders and identifiable components. But the thinking must change. The thoughts must burst the boxes; the words must fly the coops and take wing; the feelings must be loosed from cages to roam the new terrain, unrestrained. Proud minds must at least touch the hem of Infinite Mind, at least to acknowledge that something exists beyond what can be readily apprehended by machine brains, ticking, clicking, calculating.

The challenge is neither philosophical nor mystical, words to brush off like crumbs of spiritual bread. Man does not live by bread alone; neither does man live solely by thoughts minced in laboratories and boiled over Bunsen burners.

Consider this from Karen Armstrong, *The Battle for God* (2000), page 365: "Confronted with the genocidal horrors of our century, reason has nothing to say. . . ."

Traditional science seems content in its compartmentalization. It is not yet a sign of alarm that the right hand does not know what the left is creating. Right and left hands are so pleased with their respective inventions, to suggest there might be a higher science is insulting to these much-revered leaders of the technological age. But it is not a childish balk. The consciousness has not shifted to see the interconnections and wholeness of the patterns of nature. Telling scientists won't move them. Consciousness is not religious or scientific; religion and science are expressions of particular kinds of consciousness.

The UFO presence is usually addressed from a religious, psychological, or scientific perspective, because these form the platform for current thinking. This makes it very difficult for an experiencer to communicate the truly alien ideas she has encountered. I write with a tension caused by the awareness that the meaning of some of what I share is lost. But that is my work, to try to mediate between two realms of consciousness. It is time to gather our thoughts, time to listen to the subtle harmony of the music we have been making with our mind harps. Time to tighten and tune strings, time to discover the conductor, and begin to hear and record the notes and write the score the human spirit knows. It is time for a symphony.

Neither religion nor science is the enemy of new consciousness. If the left hand offends, do we bind or chop it off? But hands lying listless in the lap don't work to resolve our dif ferences, nor do hands clenched double-fisted to smash everything we have accomplished together. One hand works the fingers up and down the neck of a violin, and the other draws the bow. Hands work best in coordination, and this is true for minds. The fear, criticism, competition, and violence will cease as more people awaken and realize that we are all one, as the body is one with all of its highly specialized parts. Does the collarbone feel superior to the knee? Do the eyes hate the sexual organs? Does the mind look down on the heart? Does the heart blame the head for the sorrows it feels?

Heart Link

The heart of the Earth may be high in the Columbian mountains. The Kogi believe so. Miraculously surviving the slaughter by the Spanish, the Kogi may be the last surviving high civilization of pre-Columbian America. They may also be a remnant of the "first order of humankind." Although they do not specify their creator as extraterrestrial, their story of origins includes elements that affirm the information from the El in "The History of Humankind in Summary."

"Much later, Serankua created another kind of human being, a Younger Brother to the original people. This was a creature with a butterfly mind, which paid no attention to Mother's teachings. . . . He [Younger Brother] was given a different way of knowing things, a can-do, technological knowledge, and [was] exiled [sic] to lands designated for him across the sea. The Elder Brothers, caring for everything spiritual and material, would take care of the heart of the world. . . . " (Ereira 1993)

The Kogi allowed London historian and filmmaker Alan Ereira and his crew into their hidden civilization to film them and their message to Younger Brother, which is compellingly rendered in the book *The Elder Brothers*. Ethnic cleansings aren't the only wars Younger Brother is waging. The Kogi are intimate observers of our war on nature. Consider this from page 113 of the same book:

> We are the Elder Brothers.
> We have not forgotten the old ways. . . .
> The Younger Brother, all he thinks about is plunder.
> The Mother looks after him, too, but he does not think. . . .
> When they kill all the Elder Brothers then they too will be
>   finished.
> We will all be finished. . . .

From the Elder Brother's perspective, Younger Brother does not think. From their view of observation high on the yellowing mountaintops, I can see their point. But Younger Brother does think. The problem seems to be not in the head but in the heart. It is as if, in the passage from the One Mind to tribal hive minds, the heart was severed from the head. It is as if the human chain was broken, links scattering everywhere.

What did the Creator have in mind, giving man a thinking mind and will, but seemingly not a heart big enough to guide either? A mystical view: When will was born, Mother (heart) retreated to the shadows, allowing Father (head) to take command. The will-empowered child was a law-burdened child with a harsh father who seemed to be terrified of the life-giving power of the woman. But now, after long separation, Mother and Father are falling in love again, softening Father's heart, releasing the fear. In union, law and love are embracing to create a new child of both, a wonder child.

Mind-Body Links

During the UFO catalyst, the most profound thing happening was in my mind, and body. The communications and downloading of encoded information were signs of changes in my consciousness, and my body was changing, too. The frequent tinglings and vibrations over my body were certainly something new. I knew few, personally, who were experiencing this, but from reading such books as Dr. John Mack's *Passport to the Cosmos: Human Transformation and Alien Encounters* (1999), I knew it wasn't uncommon. He writes, on page 81: "For abductees a strong physical vibration that seems to affect and even change the cells and molecules of their bodies is a central aspect of the encounters."

On page 82, Dr. Mack writes about the theories of astrophysicist Rudolf Schild: "Schild wonders if the UFOs and the 'aliens' have somehow discovered a way to master the quantum fluctuations of the vacuum energy field in order to transport themselves and enter the Earth's atmosphere. Perhaps, he speculates, they have found a way of 'introducing a fifth dimension,' a principle that would enable them 'to organize mass and energy in our own dimensions that we just haven't encountered yet.' It would not be surprising, he [Schild] suggests, that abductees would feel such intense vibrations as they encounter these unusual energies."

These statements seem to be about how the Others penetrate our physical environment, but I will go one step further to suggest that the energies demonstrating as vibrations are intelligent and informational. Perhaps such energies "speak" to our minds through our bodies. Where is the division between mind and body?

Those of us who sense a coming birth event are tapping our metaphorical toes, waiting for something more than a shoe to drop. In the months and years of waiting, we are doing "womb work," if barely aware of the meaning or significance. I don't understand the womb work given to me. These chapters in part 3 were a particular challenge. I knew that I couldn't add to understanding of the mechanics, or nature of the human body. This body has always seemed slightly foreign to me: dense, awkward, and restrictive. My body seems like a pet I have to feed, sleep, nurse, and nurture. For instance, we don't agree on sleep, body and I. Even as a toddler, much to my mother's chagrin, I thought sleep was a waste of time. But body has taught me that I function better if I sleep, so I surrendered to "my animal" who is the product of eons of cultivation in this environment. Some call the cultivation of the body form evolution. One thought is that the human body changes when human beings are challenged by some outward threat that stokes, in the brain, the fires of survival. This is supposed to "evolve" the brain. But maybe we've got it backwards.

The brain is not the mind. The brain is like a harp, and the mind is like intelligent music. Mind knows the score, orchestrates, and plucks the strings. Over time, more strings are activated and tuned. Mind knows survival, because Infinite Mind designed this world. It is the prototypical human being who functions with only a fragment of Mind who needs to experience, "hands on," all of the stages of creation, which happens in a time-unfolding program, or evolution, designed by Intelligent Spirit.

Higher Mind and Human Will

The popular view is that we use only 10 percent of our gray matter, and 90 percent of our communication is non-verbal. Add to these another pertinent statistic: Jeremy Narby says on page 139 of *The Cosmic Serpent*: "The molecular biology that considers that 97 percent of the DNA in our body is 'junk' reveals not only its degree of ignorance, but the extent to which it is prepared to belittle the unknown."

It is believed that nature governs the growth patterns of our bodies. If nature also governs leaps or shifts in consciousness, then knowledge that rests in the 97 percent of the DNA that scientists cannot read might also be governed, as to *when* it is read, and *by whom*. How many scientists have admitted to inspiration as the source of life-changing discoveries? Name it anything you wish, but the evidence of a higher mind is overwhelming. The silence of the 97 percent may be nature's way of insuring the survival of the living things of Earth by intelligent design. Human beings are not only intelligent and self-aware to some extent, human beings also have will. But not all humans are of a consciousness to be able to act responsibly with knowledge of certain principles of creation, in respect to the whole. It makes sense that nature would have checks and balances to safeguard higher knowledge until minds are ready to use it with awareness of the effects on the whole. With what is known now, strong impulses to destruction are demonstrated. Is man's will greater than nature, greater than the life that bore us? My mind cannot grasp the illogic of the parts exceeding the intelligence of the whole. But if people believe in a god who would singly set upon the whole of humankind destruction in a global flood, and the people identify with this god, then is it any wonder that many would aspire to mimic his power? As consciousness rises, the gods become, in direct proportion, gentler and more thoughtful.

Alien Mind

The latest buzz is that in such an enormous universe, with so many planets that could support life, it makes no sense that we would be the only, or the most evolved creatures. But many humans balk at the idea that any such creatures could be interacting with the population of Earth now, for a couple of reasons. One, surely a being evolved enough to travel here would know who our leaders were and would know to contact them. In this logic, the fact that only ordinary grassroots people are reporting contact and encounters means that UFOs can't be from outer space. "More evolved" to these minds means the ETs would look, think, and behave like us, and be just a tad more advanced, like Klaatu in the film *The Day the Earth Stood Still*. At least science fiction ETs have the sense to respect our hierarchies and protocols. But what if contact and meetings are determined by imprints in the DNA, and/or energy bodies invisible to most human eyes? Maybe you really can't judge a book—or a human—by its cover.

Two—(more circular logic): If there are intelligent beings in outer space, they haven't yet figured out how to travel here . . . because *we* haven't figured out how they could manage it; ergo, if we can't imagine it, or it isn't prophesied in scripture, or science can't explain it, it just can't be. But if ETs had reasons and means to come, would they be sensitive to our egos, and wait until we figured out how travel across light years (our measure) could be accomplished swiftly and expeditiously before revealing themselves to us in a way that would be undeniable?

The science minds have scoffed at our accounts of sightings and encounters because we have brought them no "extraordinary" evidence to prove we are telling the truth. It appears to me that the evidence is *too* extraordinary for the science mind to see. Restricted consciousness seems to be the perfect cover for the UFO presence. Some ETs play with our minds, the same way we tease animals or children. Maybe they want to wake us up. Shift the eyes of your mind. Look inward. Dare to ask your heart what is going on. These things we are experiencing are not happening to laboratory mice. They are happening to human beings. We are the message.

New Mind

In the early stages of this book, I composed a blithe thing I thought too tongue-in-cheek for the serious subject of mind. But play is the language of the Muses; our Mothers in Heaven speaking across the spheres, converting music to words.

In the first version of my visionary novel *Jonah*, J.Q. Mahoney is transported to the realm of our Mothers, where he receives education of a kind not easily captured in words—personification of my own plight. It is difficult, almost impossible for Jonah to accept that certain energies could be personified as embodied persons. But this is his experience, as baffling as meeting an intelligent alien of the insectile kind.

The chief Mother says to Jonah,

". . . Aiy, Earthman, we are your mothers. We appear to you as clouds, we bask in your sunsets. Sometimes we come as an eagle, a hummingbird, a mountain lion poised on a cliff. We whisper to you in the breezes that play in your trees and fields, we rest along the contours of your rainbows. You can hear us in a baby's laugh, and we are always there when lovers embrace. Aiy, we are everywhere, watching over our children. We are the songs in the wind, we hum in your rocks, we chant in a crackling fire, and if you listen, you can hear our voices in every drop of rain."

Too mystical for the hard-boiled science mind? I am tapping my toes, waiting for science to discover that every living thing is intelligent, including that which is considered by many to be inanimate, such as rock.

The terrain in part 3 is as vast as the Mothers' realm, and my path is narrow, winding, and dimly lighted, with hedge thoughts bordering and blocking view of the ground of our being. The going is rough and I am stumbling.

It is as impossible for me to define a mind as it is to study the wildness of a caged bird. But in the blithe thing I wrote about new mind, I think something of the native wildness of new consciousness is captured. At the least, readers of *Summoned* will appreciate that I am more relaxed than I was three years ago. I can joke about it all now, while continuing the quest to understand more of the mystery.

New Mind . . .

I seem to have a new mind. Maybe my old mind was traded out for a new one during one of my escapades with manipulative ETs. Whatever the dynamic or folly, the claim to a new mind I make without knowing exactly what a mind is. Is it like an invisible bonnet, streamers tying it to my brain?

My thinking changed. This I say, not sure what a thought is, much less the speeding thoughts we cavalierly call thinking. The secret to settling down my speeding mind was to slow the thinking. Put on the brakes, bring the mind train to a complete stop. Let the steam dissipate. Concentrate on the sky, the breezes, the sweet smell of wildness. Get quiet, feel the small still voice that speaks below the chattering thoughts.

Literally, I see more than I used to. This I confess, not fathoming the mechanics of an eyeball, much less what happens between orbs and object observed. What I see isn't particularly spectacular . . . a gold UFO in the sky, red roses or chrysanthemums floating in the air, flashes of light, geometric shapes. . . . Some people call this paranormal phenomena. But if it's normal for me, how is it "para"?

I hear more. This said in ignorance of the mechanics of the ear and the science by which the brain identifies sound. What I hear isn't especially unusual: trills, tones, buzzes, chimes, music from unknown spheres. Also, I hear what people say in a different way now, as if, along with a new mind and new ears, I got a new interpreter. This I claim without understanding how the brain processes language, or how we construe motives and meanings.

I read differently. I am sooner bored, left hungry for more, frustrated at what is missing, agitated at the repetition, pages and pages to say one thing, something I already know.

Another sign of new mind: Some of my dreams seem to be auditioning for real life by showing off clips of events that actually happen a day or two later in my real life. Hardly anyone believes in precognition, and here I am, having dream-cognition, one more thing making me a suspicious character. Dreams are thought to be confused thoughts wandering all over the place with no one in charge of them; or like a film resume of some mental pretender who wants to be me, who, as soon as I fall asleep, takes the wheel of my mind and drives it around like a stolen Mercedes Benz, leaping it over a guardrail to burst through a circus hoop and shoot up into space to perform wheelies on a planet in Upsilon Andromedae, just for the hell of it, because she can, while I am in slumber's cocoon.

For better or worse, new mind seems bigger; it seems to hold more. The world we have made feels too small now, too cramped and extremely cluttered. New mind squirms, pushes against the walls, seeking spaciousness. Getting used to new mind is like a five-year-old trying to live in a dollhouse.

New mind seems like a head too large swaying precariously on a body too small. That can't be right, but it describes a thought life that almost forgets there is a body. Balancing the energies of new mind with physical functioning is like trying to roller skate on a marsh.

The technologies we are so proud of seem to new mind to be crude and loud and lacking in elegance. New mind knows there are things more wondrous than whirring, whacking, clacking, belching machines, and predicts: When a certain number of people realize new mind, we will rebuild everything to reflect our consolidated genius. Then we will be Sapien homos.

But new mind is least apparent in what I say and write. There seem to be circuits not quite linked up. This I lament, not having the dimmest notion of the nature of whatever it is that communicates from my head to my wagging tongue, or the hand that scribes. Thoughts? I already said I don't know what a thought is.

> *A thought is*
> *Thought to be*
> *Like a byte,*
> *Popping like a lightbulb,*
> *One pop per thought.*

There seems to be a wind tunnel between my thoughts and what I say. What I thought I meant blows away like a feather in a Texas dirt storm. And when I try to speak my new mind, it's like trying to teach a dolphin to recite multiplication tables.

Same problem with writing. Attempts to communicate new mind hiccup down the page and jitter on to become essays that disturbingly resemble that censored crap I used to write. And it doesn't help, dressing it all up in fancy or important words.

Whence did words derive, anyway? Who crowned words with meaning? Who put them on, wore them, proclaiming *I am Divine?* Sometimes I am very wary of words. They are such chameleons, or stern schoolmasters shaking a stick in my face. I much prefer letters. I can fiddle with letters, experiment . . . and lo and behold, up pop new words like laughing clowns.

Thought, say the makers of *The American Heritage Dictionary* is . . . thinking. Turn to the word "think." We are informed: To have a thought. (Who edits dictionaries?) On mind: The human consciousness that originates in the brain. . . .

The statement that the mind originates in the brain is one of those theories we put a hat on and called a fact. But think of the problems if the makers of a dictionary did not fix, or originate, the mind in the brain. The very idea "it" might *not* be in the brain—this thing or process or totality we call the mind (or *human* consciousness—we know there are other kinds?), the idea, the very inkling that the mind might not be, or have originated, in the brain, threatens to spring open Pandora's Box, without even touching the dangerous thing.

Out would spill every cockamamie idea touted by every new ager since Copernicus, and even before when the Greeks used to debate such things, quoting new age scholars, poets, and oracles clear back to Egypt and Sumer. Thank God, it stops there. The hieroglyphics and whatnots left on stones by peoples predating the Sumerians and Egyptians are conveniently only decipherable so far as matters having to do with time and astronomy. The fact that these ancient dwellers knew the precise movements of stars and planets—planets *we* didn't discover until recently—doesn't mean they were smarter. Lacking our advanced technologies to slow them down and clutter their lives, they just had more time for sun, moon, planet, and star gazing. They thought the heavenly bodies were *gods*, for hell's sake. But if, like us, their minds were confined in their brains, this might explain why they thought the way we think they did.

If the mind *isn't* the brain, but is located *in* the brain (somewhere), maybe it's one of those invisible things like a quark; or, possibly, it is simply a literary device, like the Phoenix or Pandora's Box. If invisible—is the mind really real? Doesn't "real" mean something tangible, observable, and measurable, something that will sit still, like a cat dropped in a box inside the Laboratory where Scientists conduct experiments to determine what is real and what is not . . . and have you noticed? The list for what is *not* real is growing longer every day.

And time . . . oh my, time. I'm still on Tuesday (last week) and already it's Friday. Time has speeded up, leaving me like a turtle in the lurch. Now I need a clock divided seven ways for the days of the week. Forget seconds, minutes, and hours—particles drowned in the waves of days rolling over me, breakfast at four o'clock P.M., no dinner because now it's time for bed. New mind is a moon child working by nights; the banker doesn't care, the postmaster has no compassion, and the grocer, no pity. Up with the sun, down with the moon, old minds get along fine, while I write twiddly words into dawn's silvery light.

Are people with new minds smarter than old-minders? Smart is like pretty—smart is as smart does. Some psycho- and sociopaths are very smart (and pretty).

Is the mystery, simply, that my mind is now talking to my brain, like an alien teacher to a bewildered child? Is this the mystery behind the calls and missions and visions of UFOs? All along, *we* were the gods of mind, sounding like Old Testament prophets or Galactic Commanders, talking to brains lidded tightly like sealed jars? If so, is it any wonder there would be *-ifty* kinds of aliens from *-ifty* planets or dimensions, all telling us something different? Then what *are* the UFOs that jet pilots, astronauts, and people in radar towers have seen, tracked, or pursued across the sky? If human minds created them, as some have accused, the accusers in their ivory towers ought to ponder such power; for if cranks and grass rooters can produce flying objects that fool even NASA, the Military, and the White House, what next might we create?

If I figure out how I create rose and chrysanthemum holograms, I'll work next on figuring out how I created the spherical gold vessel I saw in the sky in August '96. That was wonderful. I would like to see it again.

When did I notice I had a new mind? A couple of years after I began experiencing the rock and roll business we call alien abduction.

CHAPTER TWELVE:

Material, Serial, and Light Body Link

Some of my experiences and some of the communications were scary. But so is life here, with or without UFOs. Observe any human infant. Without the nurturance of loving elders, every infant is terrified. As babies, we are lumps of howling hunger and cannot feed ourselves. We are cold and wet and cannot clothe ourselves. We cannot so much as cuddle a blanket around our tiny, frail, hairless bodies. We hurt and cannot tell anyone of the pain, except to scream. In our helplessness, we are suckers for food, warmth, and especially love. In our helplessness, we will do anything to please, to bring, to keep someone.

Until we are two.

Stop feeding her, my aunts jestingly advised my mother when I was a toddler. Don't give her any vitamins, another declared. I was infused, all right. Infused with incredible energy and curiosity. And I was born knowing I was loved.

And then I grew up . . . and became aware that I was living in a dangerous world. Everything here was eating up everything else! There were a hundred ways you could die every day, and if you lived, you had to watch out for emotional sabotage in the battle for prototypical supremacy. It was not enough that human beings were at the top of the chain. Many wanted to be at the top of the top, and that meant stepping on heads and crushing hearts on the scamper up the proverbial ladder. Anyone who survives into old age on Earth is made of hearty stuff!

The UFO is a mirror reflecting back on us, I often say, and for experiencers it can be a catalyst for change. Many of the stories about the abductors report that they are devoid of emotions, and terribly curious about ours. Maybe they bred emotions out of themselves, and hope to breed it back in by creating hybrids, some theorize. Well, then, do they know the emotion gene? Are scientists working on the human genome looking for an emotion gene?

My dictionary explains as much about emotion as it does thought. Emotion, it says, rises "subjectively" and often involves physiological changes. Sounds like we don't know if emotions originate in the body or the mind. Whichever, as soon as I entered the business world, quickly I learned to suppress emotions, to not let them show too much. Why is it so shocking to encounter aliens who show no emotion? It's not as if we are not familiar with such behavior. We teach it.

For some, the UFO is a catalyst to open the heart chakra, or expand the opening. There were many days and nights of tears during the catalyst. I wasn't crying about aliens; I was crying about what the mirror was showing me about myself and other human beings. How emotionally numb we seemed; how we disdain emotion, and applaud cynical wit. As much as was possible, I kept the crying private. Cry too much, people suspect you are crazy. I knew the rules, the protocols. I was in the business world before I could even begin to know the emotions felt in the sudden shift from a religious community to a world I had not been prepared to enter.

It used to frighten some people when, after achieving sobriety, I would say that although alcohol almost killed me, it also saved my life. Beneath the stoicism and behind the strength of endurance, I was a passionate person with an artistic temperament. Alcohol is a catalyst for repressed emotions. In a society that must suppress emotion in order to conduct business, there will be a high rate of alcoholism, because human beings are emotional beings, and will find outlets for the emotions, or die. I don't recommend alcohol as a catalyst for emotions. Unfortunately it tends to convert hurt into rage. If you survive it, you have to work down through the layers of rage to get to the pain, and it is a howling animal after so many years of abduction by alcohol. The UFO catalyst was much kinder and gentler.

Initiation into the world outside the grooming of the Mormon mind was brutal. And yet, plunged into the center of the battle for prototypical supremacy, even in the throes of alcohol, I never lost sight of our brotherly love, our simple humanity. I knew we were the worst and the best of creatures, the smartest and the most ignorant, the kindest and the cruelest . . . seeming glitches in the cosmic design, a puzzle to ourselves and a fright or delight to the other animals.

Losing religion was to lose God, for the two were entwined in my mind. In a way, I did not know I had a mind of my own. A mind that thinks on its own in a hive is like a lit match dropped in a bucket of kerosene. It is not tolerated. Far was I from imagining I might also have a body hidden from eyes that only knew themselves by what is reflected in a mirror.

During the catalyst, I was the anxious human going along, meticulously recording details of experiences, and typing up communications that contained information I wanted to preserve in the secret file I was building. I was certain I would never share certain information—the messages in this chapter.

It was bad enough having experiences that were cause for ridicule without compounding it with troublesome information. Was I being deceived to promote messages with lies woven into them? Old religious hive mind programs whispered to me: You know how Lucifer works; he slips his lies into provocative truths. Lucifer means light! He's beautiful! Only Jesus can resist him . . . that's why Jesus is the savior. Without Jesus, you haven't got a chance—you are *meat*. Lucifer is a very old, experienced soul, and you are just a frail human being, just a woman! (Women can't even get into Mormon heaven unless their husbands call their secret names on the other side, divulged to them in temple ceremonies.) I was a sitting duck for demons!

But something deep within me knew better, something older and wiser than the human prototype, daughter of DNA. Nonetheless, I was stuck with the imprints of a thousand hive minds, and frequent reminders that I was having incorrect experiences.

In the beginning, writing the first version of *Jonah* was my shield. Not only could I say that I was writing a novel (you know how eccentric writers can be), but I could reassure myself that in this way, I would fulfill my task, and then all of this alien business would settle down. If I *wasn't* a messenger—was all this communication business a ruse to keep me isolated and silent? Should I be reporting my experiences to serious investigators? Should I flop on a hypnotist's couch and get down to the awful truth? Become one more statistic on someone's case history report—no one special, just another body being harvested for reproductive materials? One problem with that scenario: I'd had a total hysterectomy in 1981 and these experiences did not begin to surface until 1986; I had no reproductive materials and no womb. There were no miscarriages, no abortions, no signs I was a breeder for aliens. Although I was engulfed in the mystery, knowing no more than anyone else at the level of the daylight mind, I balked at the notion that our bodies were the alien's primary interest. I did not have the words to articulate it then, but now I can say that this perception is expression of a body-centered consciousness. If bodies are our primary interest, then logically we would think it so for aliens. We project our beliefs. The world and the sky are mirrors. But if everything mirrors our beliefs, how do we ever see the truth? Perhaps, the higher the consciousness, the less the mirror effect. We see ourselves, others, and everything else more as they are, with less clouding of self-projection. The silver at the back of the mirror thins, more light shines through the dark glass.

But in the early years of the catalyst, I was as challenged as any experiencer to find a way to part the clouds and see the light behind these baffling events that were disrupting my life. Whatever I might see in hypnotic trance—would it convince my family and friends that I was embroiled in an abduction drama, seemingly against my will? Would people want to read the stuff I was recording? I tested that. With love, family and friends believed I was experiencing *something;* but ET contact or abductions? Get serious. Or they might decide I needed some serious counseling. . . .

When I finally let him know what had been transpiring, Frank DeMarco (editor of *Summoned*) asked, "Did you think you were crazy?" No, I answered honestly. But I was afraid I might wig out if I could not find my way back into the world. My reluctance to share my story resulted in more seclusion than is healthy for a person of my natural social affinities. Friends were blowing away from me like pistils on white dandelions. I imagine it must have irked them that someone so ordinary, just like them, would be talking about things they could not see, and had not experienced. Beliefs are comfortable borders. Many of mine were knocked down as easily as toothpick fences.

But looking back, I question whether or not I was directly and physically participating in the common story of abduction—greys and reptilians taking people, examining them, implanting devices, using them for the creation of hybrids, or training them as "Manchurian candidates" to spread alien gospels, with a purpose to conquer us, take us over. Were the aliens stuck, as we were, at the level of body consciousness? Like so many humans, did they see life as a contest to determine who had the strongest bodies, and most powerful brains and wills? Is this all this was? Just one more battle for supremacy based on bodies? If so, what could we learn from the drama? That life in outer space was as embattled as it is here? That even in outer space, the prime booty is bodies, or control over bodies? Cowboys and Indians, Germans and Jews, blacks and whites—now aliens and humans—battling it out, into the reaches of space and time beyond light.

But if bodies are containers for consciousness and soul, maybe human life is deemed to be precious, and coveted. Maybe through all our stumbles and shames, we have evolved the human body to a state wherein we can begin to realize a potential for creation never before experienced, except by a few, like Jesus Christ, who told his followers we would do greater things than he did while he was embodied like us. And if a consciousness described as "no more walls, but only windows" is the coming attraction of the big event we are preparing to meet, it may mean that we will literally see more than we could have imagined, which, without preparation, would shock us.

Quantum physicists have discovered that within dense forms are worlds without end. The quest for a singular basic building block of physical stuff has shifted to concentration on the nature of the energies and forces that create *appearances* of solidity. This is a troublesome proposition for body-centered consciousness. There are worlds without end *inside us?* Where is the mirror for *that?*

A prevalent belief today still insists on divisions, as if we were made like Tinkertoys. It is difficult to study us as whole beings, especially considering attitudes about the soul, or Spirit. The concept is often attacked or dismissed. I suspect this reflects a need to dethrone religion. I agree that we needed to advance beyond dictatorial religions as governing forces, but perhaps the science that wants to make of all a mechanized, spiritually defunct system is but a baby step in an evolution of awareness that will free our thoughts to discover and explore more in the direction of interconnectedness, wholeness, and harmony.

While some of us are doing womb work in preparation for the big mysterious event, others are gearing up to reap benefits, they think, of the 3 percent knowledge about DNA. From this limited knowledge, clones of animals (and possibly humans) have been "created." But is it creation? Or is it manipulation of already created materials? Do aliens "create" hybrids? Or are they "mimicking" what man is doing, projecting back to us in virtual consciousness?

In the mechanistic, "body-is-all" view of the human being, the only way we can live on is through the passing on, or transfer, of genes into another body. If we believe that nothing lives on except by DNA passed into another body, clones might look like an opportunity for continuation. Our minds are powerful, whether or not considered to be linked with soul, Higher Mind, or Spirit. We can close our minds off, as is illustrated in the story of the Hopi. A closed-door, body-centered mind might think: *Why not create a clone and transfer my brain into it? Voila*, man-made immortality (or so some may think).

During this transitory period, when the "veils are thin," and the "portals are open," when our minds and consciousnesses are quickly expanding, the expansion applies to everyone, no matter the spiritual links or ethical values. And no matter how many closed-door minds might be exploiting the increase in knowledge and awareness in violation of the laws of creation, there is a principle that prevents interference, and that is the Law of One, which protects the sanctity of individual will. As difficult as it is to watch the destructive energy at work, we of consciousness linked to Spirit are reminded to "respect all choices," and have faith in the natural checks and balances that insure that chaos will not overwhelm order.

You don't have to be religious or mystical to have such faith. For the science mind, there is the "Mandlebrot Set."

"These conceptual devices that we encountered on the 'order to chaos' side of the mirror are like x-rays, giving scientists the ability to glimpse the evolving skeleton of non-linear change."

This sentence begins a chapter, on page 83, that thoroughly discusses the Mandlebrot Set in *Turbulent Mirror: An Illustrated Guide to Chaos Theory and the Science of Wholeness*, by authors John Briggs and F. David Peat (1985).

In the first version of *Jonah*, by some foolish mistake I have forgotten, Jonah Mahoney is diverted into a secret military project where clones are being produced. (Like a segment of *X-Files*, but I wrote this before the show aired on television.) It took three months to finish that chapter. All the while, I was harassed by disturbing phenomena. Five times I rewrote the segment, wrestled with excising it, replacing it with a less troublesome scenario. But something in me said I was onto something that needed to be revealed. The harassment caused me to feel I *must* be onto something.

Fascination with clones seems a natural pull to learn more about the dynamics of bodies. But like the boy ignorant of the law of gravity, poised on the roof to leap like Superman, we do not yet comprehend that there are laws for dense creation. The ability to create computers and toy with artificial intelligence is not quite wisdom about the essence, intelligence, and evolution of sentient beings.

The following message, which I received, could be about where unenlightened clone-making could take us—or could it describe certain entities we call aliens? Were they once human? Did they go where no other human beings have gone—and wouldn't go if they knew the consequences? Or is this an "educational" message? Note that the transmitter does not tell me that this speaks of actual beings, or reality. The questions are for the mind that is free to consider them in the light of expanding consciousness.

February 24, 1996:

Hell is consciousness trapped in an immutable, indestructible body. How could this be, you say? If the aging and death stop-codes were removed from the DNA. But this is not to say that the body would not respond to conditions; say, the skin was to become tough like a lizard's hide, to withstand harsh conditions, or scales to appear over the eyes, scale-like lids that recede or cover the eyes, or small thin bodies with clawed appendages, and large heads to contain all of the added information that accumulates over the ages.

For these, would not death be release, to be born again as new informed expressions? Would these not seek to pirate bodies of those who still have the ability to lay down the body, to be born again?

Can they overcome by sheer focused concentration? Can they create a "force" that can propel consciousness, as if a rocket, into a desired receptacle, to fill it, to overwhelm the consciousness abiding there? And if the uninvited is forced to depart the host body, can it flee back to the body it escaped? Or will it instead be expunged to drift with no body reference—to lose, forever, consciousness, for does not consciousness speak to a point of reference? So shall these "particle-ized" consciousnesses return to be absorbed by wave consciousness, the particle aspect dissolving?

And so, if consciousness pertains to "containment," then must we not imagine an eternal form of containment, a transmigration into a new form to contain the (individualized) consciousness? Lest all that we know, and consider ourselves to be dissolve, at death, to rejoin the wave intelligence, the "all that is" intelligence?

So do you dream, your logic projecting continuation in some similar respect. Or is there evidence that your dreams speak of reality?

Soon after the appearances of implants in 1986, I was hot to study several subjects, among them genetics. And I did, just enough to arouse serious concern for Grand Plans and Projections based on knowledge of only 3 percent of the human genome, accompanied by an attitude that the unread 97 percent is junk to be ignored. Well . . . we're only using 10 percent of our gray matter; should I be surprised? And considering such grand plans in the dark of genius, should it surprise that the Something that *does* understand the 97 percent would intervene?

Clones or predatory minds were not the only thoughts to trouble this quester.

Journal notes, May 4, 1995: A bizarre thought . . . they are creating alternate bodies for us. These bodies are "copies," but don't look like us, because we need a new kind of body to withstand changes. These bodies are not fully energized/enlivened. We will enliven them, when the time is right. We are practicing "shifting," so that when the time comes, we will make a smooth final shift. Before now, when we died, we were in spirit until we were born again. Now we will shift into these bodies, because it is important that we are embodied this way to do the work after the "big shift" occurs. Many will die. And many will shift into these ready-made bodies. . . .

Eleven months later, April 19, 1996, from my journal:

Went to bed about 2:00 A.M. Before and after the dream-event, there were several loud noises, and I observed an intricate light funnel in the air, and felt tinglings all over my body. Finally went to sleep. Awoke to see a grid pattern of light, and found a little blood in my right nostril. Quickly I recorded what I could remember of a dream.

(The location reminds me of a previous dream, when I was in the company of "alien-aliens" and saw a mother ship.)

The place seems to be an X-ray room in a hospital. Three young men are paying attention to me in a very focused way. They have read my book (original *Jonah*), and know who I am. They seem like orderlies or technicians, but are not. (They remind me of the ones who implanted or activated me, the "widow-peaked" people I mentally associate with Sirius.)

I look in a mirror and panic. They changed me! I'm in a different body! Different face! Description: Long, reddish-blond hair; face, though attractive, has on the left side a reddish blotch—birth defect? Wide-set eyes, full lips, reminds me of actress Susannah York. The name of this "other body" is Roxanne.)

I say to the techs—"Look! I was taken, given another body!" They respond like, "Oh, who cares? . . ."

There's an order out to kill? One of the men tells me they should kill me because I'm Nordic. The edict/mandate is to kill all the whites. "But I'm also Celtic! Irish!" I protest (as if that's not white). I feel that this man, though he is very scary, and powerful, likes me, will spare me. But I am thinking I must have "Native" blood, or I wouldn't be spared. I'm thinking hard, looking back over past lives to find an "Indian in the woodpile" as an ancestral safeguard.

I know these "techs." Their manner is very businesslike, but you know they have humor. It's just that they are so highly intelligent, to them you are like a three-year-old. They are at once fond and annoyed with you, and just like them to do something radical like switch bodies without telling you!

In response to my thoughts about the possible creation of "alternate bodies," this was communicated: "A storehouse of thoughts, feelings, and pictures builds up in a lifetime, but does not cross over. All that is temporary imprints on the body, and in the DNA, and carries forth; at some point is the work of cleansing or deprogramming to 'clear' the design.

"Over the ages the work is to become aware, to wake up while 'in' physical form. Spirit marries matter to produce a wonder child. The wonder child has been developing over many ages, and is now ready to graduate, to begin to explore collective awareness, while maintaining individual awareness. . . ."

As usual, the question was not answered directly, but I was given more to ponder.

A message communicated in the fall of 1993 expands on the mystery. It makes clone production look like child's play, which maybe it is. Like most of the information communicated to me, it calls into question old ideas, both religious and scientific. It doesn't address mythical or historical stories, such as the "fall of mankind" due to poor choices in a pre-world paradise, or abuse of intelligence and technology in Atlantis; nor does it mention a breach in our evolution by aliens who "created" us in their image.

The message speaks to the indomitable human spirit. But read this information lightly, too. Whatever the source, it is just one way to look at what might be close to something true about our journey as human beings. We are each given clues, hints, or arrows that flutter in the waft of God's gentle laughter.

Was my bizarre thought and dream about alternate bodies a distortion about light bodies?

February 21, 1994:

> The building of a light body. The evolution of light bodies. Through love,[23] the material body evolves. The spirit, imprinted by its own experiences, is barred from entering a fetus that contains genes from a line that has not evolved itself through love. The spirit whose imprint lacks this history will gravitate toward a body that fits, that it can fit into.
>
> You do not like to hear that some are more evolved than others. You call this racism, but it cuts through and across races. Color is not a marker distinguishing spiritual evolvement. It is natural for the less evolved to point at such outward-most differences in an effort to conceal the missing links.
>
> When a line stops producing progeny, it is instinctual, as the baboon mother will bear no children in a drought. Families preparing to relocate preserve energy for the move. Many of the children coming in today are fit for the changes

---

[23] It would be interesting to learn that the golden rule—lived as love—imprints on the DNA.

occurring on this planet. Many are not. Many are too frail and sensitive to survive the changing molecular environment.

The light that radiates down is a cleansing agent, but it will not destroy what man has created. These measures are to forestall until all have come to a determination.

If you find these influences disorienting, be grateful you are aware. Outwardly there is drought, but inwardly you drink of living waters. Outwardly you cannot identify them. Some reside in mutated bodies, accepted for personal reasons. And many who seem to thrive strong and beautiful, are within dry vessels. You have always known this, but the forces of confusion darken memory.

You live by the hairs of intuition, the seat of instinct. You "feel in your guts" when someone is not trustworthy. And if you are attending to business, you are learning to trust more this sensitivity.

To answer the question about serial lives and deaths in relationship to the greater plan: Animals are governed by higher laws; they can commit no wrongs. Observing them you can see that all are not born equal. Some are orphaned, others are weak or diseased or handicapped. Because they are governed by higher laws, the strong, healthy lines survive, the weak ones die out.

Human beings are likewise governed by higher laws, with one more ingredient. They are endowed with will, in addition to instinct. The choices afforded them are myriad and none is greater than the choice to evolve the body—the serial of bodies to one that will survive death. This evolution transcends the limits set on the physical body that can result in the dying out of a certain line. The body that is being evolved by those who exercise their will, choosing this path, is a light body, and yes, its progression is imprintable on the DNA. With each death of the physical body, the DNA lives on to be reused in a continuous series of lives, in a continuous series of bodies.

While it may seem as if more violent and selfish aspects are thriving and the pure of heart are dying out, do not believe your eyes, except when they are turned inward. All will be sorted out. The harvest will occur. The farmers in the field will gather the crops, while those in another will help over stones and dry ground. And then the cycle will begin again.

Species proliferate and species die out. When the harvest occurs, there will be a separation of species. Some require a new environment. Others are equipped to remain and sow new seeds. As in all nature, there is an energetic spirit that burns, that life may survive. How it survives is determined by choice or instinct or both, and while accurate prediction of outcomes is possible, no one can see precisely how it will turn out in all cases. At each stage your "sight" becomes clearer, less hampered by illusions.

CHAPTER THIRTEEN:

Soul, Telepathy, Consciousness, and the Unthinkable Love Vibration

Soul and Immortality

According to the story in the Hebrew Bible, we were barred from the Tree of Life—immortality. A death code was written into the human DNA. This would allow for the proliferation of multitudes of human beings. Abraham knew the score. God told him (Genesis 15:5): *"Look up at the heavens and count the stars— if indeed you can count them." Then he said to him, "So shall your offspring be."* God did not say, "And you will live to see them all."

Imagine the population problems if all of the people who have ever been born on Earth were still alive today, in bodies. Like it or not, human beings are part of Earth's recycling program. And mostly we did not like it, hence the many legends about magic potions, elixirs, plants, or waters that were believed to grant unto the heroes and heroines of such stories, immortality. Some say that our claims to reincarnation are wishful thinking of achieving immortality, through a back door of sorts, as if to outwit the cherubim swinging the flaming swords at the entrance to the Tree of Life.

In a way I think this is right. "I," Dana Redfield, have never lived before and will never live again. But something of me is eternal. Beyond the Spirit that animates all life, am I a distinguished being—a soul? I think so, but my concept of soul is complex.

I envision soul like a chrysanthemum, stemmed by Spirit in the human garden. "I," this current embodied prototypical human being, daughter of carefully cultivated lineages, am like one petal on the chrysanthemum. The soul of which I am one petal is unfolding, petal by petal, and life by life.

As a "petal," I don't have full conscious awareness of my whole soul being. I am like "Eluxui" (chapter 7), a fragment, or fractal of a greater being. Also, the whole flower is one among many chrysanthemums in a garden of many varieties of flowers. A cluster of chrysanthemums in a particular garden could be a "soul complex," a higher order of being that exists on another plane.

I hope not to further complicate this, but this is my perception: I do not see soul evolution as a linear process; I believe in simultaneous and parallel lives, all lived as fragment consciousness of the soul, all like petals on the flower. Some of these lives may be on other planets or in other dimensions, and some people alive on Earth today may be a part of the same soul complex in which I am rooted.

All of the petals (or soul beings) benefit by the knowledge and experience of all other petals, so that all are changed and enhanced by the experience and learning of all; i.e., all of the petals, and the whole flower, are dynamic and ever-evolving. When full flowering happens, we/I, the soul, have completed our human journey on this third-dimensional plane. But full flowering also means seeds. From the seeds, new chrysanthemums root and begin the unfolding-to-full-flowering process. So, the chrysanthemum (or soul) that flowered and gave seed now informs or parents the new flowers rooting . . . in a long and complex chain of soul flowerings.

In other words, I am of a soul, and I am becoming a soul.

This may be a story about *some* of the beings identified as extraterrestrials. And some or all of us may be their seed, or off-spring. They may be "celestial gardeners." They may have been cultivating us to full flowering over a very long time, as we understand time. At this point, the words fall off the page. The mystery of the soul is in the whole of the belonging-gathering-becoming story.

The fact that we experience human life in separate bodies bur-dens the mind with a paradox impossible to resolve by the embod-ied. Body itself is a bridge, or door, between inner and outer realities. From this perspective, the belief that the mind is brain-generated may block consciousness of soul being and awareness of other dimensions of reality. I don't know that a body-centered conscious-ness can, of its own volition, awaken to awareness of the soul being. It may require agents of awakening. These may be entities, human or Divine or ET, or anything that jolts the daylight mind. For some it is the sighting of a UFO that begins the shift, or opens the chakra, activating inner vision. The agents are many and diverse, each just right for the one awakened. And then comes the natural tendency to worship the agent. Resist the temptation. All is passing. We are moving. Let go, clutch nothing, find the pace, ride the waves.

Reincarnation: Soul in Journey

Exploring past lives by hypnotic regression was part lark and part serious with me. The lark was in knowing it was a mys-tery I could not solve, so I was just having fun exploring; the serious part was knowing I was touching on something real, a valid piece of the puzzle.

All but one of my past life explorations were with Dr. Helen V. Walker, and always at the end, she asked, "What was the pur-pose of this lifetime?" And always, without hesitation, the answer was right there. If I struggled with details in the life sto-ries, always I was clear about the purpose, and always it could be stated in a short sentence.

From this and exposure to various metaphysical viewpoints evolved a vision of my soul in journey. Without such a vision, I don't know how I would have survived the UFO catalyst. I did not view myself as a human animal accosted by alien creatures. Awareness that I am more than a human animal was so deeply ingrained, I naturally responded from the center of my being, the source person, the intelligent presence that is more than this body and brain. While I balked at the idea of abduction, by the time these events were expressed on the physical level, I was already prepared in my mind to face the proposition that involvement with the UFO presence was on my soul's agenda. But to survive the catalyst, I would have to become more soul conscious, and nurture my bewildered human self along. I would have to become more truthful, and more courageous, to resolve the contradictions between old beliefs and what life was showing me.

I was never positive about reincarnation as a truth, despite several vivid recollections that felt real. Maybe I can't be sold on it because my sense of being a unique individual is so strong. If indeed I viewed actual human lives, all of those human beings were also unique beings. "Mikey," the Irishman, and I are not the same being. But both of us could be of the same soul. I viewed about twenty past lives, and feel there were more on Earth. I also viewed two that were not of this world (chapter 15).

Can you imagine the power of a being who is a composite of all of the lives lived on Earth and elsewhere? Can you imagine what it would be like to be conscious of hundreds, thousands of past lives? I can't remember what I did last Tuesday.

Perhaps human life is one stage in an evolution of becoming something we cannot imagine. Considering infinity, a million years on Earth is nothing, one spin on the Cosmic Clock. If the children of Abraham do equal the stars in numbers, maybe we will have to create new galaxies. In the meantime, there is a UFO mystery to pursue. . . .

Mirror Consciousness

Science teaches that self-awareness is recognizing ourselves in mirrors. At least on the science shows I have watched, always monkeys, chimps, children, and mirrors are trotted out to discuss self-awareness. Monkeys, we know, aren't self-aware because they turn the mirrors over, looking for the monkey in the glass. But chimps, apes, bonobos, dolphins, and humans recognize themselves. They know the body reflected in the glass is the same body from which their eyes are looking outward, although it is doubtful the child is thinking, "Oh, I get it; there is a relationship between the glass and my glass-like eyes—some force is shining my reflection back to me." The kid just smiles. And then we teach her who she is, by whatever beliefs the parents and the community possess.

Adam and Eve had two sons, Cain and Abel. Cain demonstrated a body-centered consciousness in the killing of Abel. In Cain's mind, Abel was not a person, or a soul; he was just a body in the way of Cain's ambition. God marked Cain then, not for killing, but for protection. And then Cain was sent into the world to evolve his consciousness. He found a wife in the Land of Nod. Adam and Eve, it is said, were the first human beings, and Cain and Abel were the third and fourth. Did Cain marry a good-looking chimp?

We are becoming, or coming to realize we are more than the selves we associate with the image in the mirror. If you want to meet yourself, look deep into your eyes in the mirror. Forget the character you think you are. Look past the silver at the back of the mirror. Maybe you will have a vision, as I did, of an elegant ET (chapter 14).

Meditation scares some people because, in the silence, the character we think we are dissolves. A quiet mind is foreign territory to a character, a vast terrain in which the person fears he or she will get lost or disappear. Ocean consciousness, some call it. If you remember that you are a human link in the belonging story, you won't drown. Connectedness and oceans are hard to equate. Oceans are not raindrops connected. Body-wise, we can hold hands or embrace another to feel our connectedness. If you know you are a person, a soul, know that when you meditate, you are connected. Expect to feel the connection. Your eyes may fill with tears, the ocean within spilling over.

Meditation helped to prepare me for the UFO drama. Through meditation, I knew I was more than a body. I knew I was connected to something higher, deeper, finer, something we cannot see in a mirror . . . unless the silver at the back dissolves. It will be interesting to see what science comes up with to establish soul awareness. I have no doubt that science will come to this, believing as I do that scientists are also ensouled beings.

From Body to Soul to ET

Freed from hive minds, in our seeking, some of us connect with "higher powers" not a part of any Earthly hive mind story, and then begins a new turmoil. From body to soul to ET . . . now we are really in trouble. Now there is no place for us in any earthly community. Now we are truly alone on Earth, it seems, for soon we discover that even among others aware of the ET presence, new hive minds are quickly forming to explain the new awareness in prosaic terms.

If we survive the journey through this catalyst, without succumbing to the comforts of a hive mind hastily constructed to accommodate the new awareness, we will become truly authentic individuals. At this level of individuality it seems that community is impossible. Maybe for awhile it is impossible. Maybe the test for such an individual is the waiting for others to awaken before the new community can happen. The gathering is subtle, maybe not visible, maybe happens in the fourth dimension, maybe is something like an invisible college.

For me, it is a time to mind links and connections, and while I mind them, to work on being a cooperative member of the old communities. Though I am no longer linked directly to them, the belonging story is still true and expansive. I am still in this world, and the more at ease I am with my "new mind," the easier it becomes to move in and out of the old communities and hive minds, without judgment or angst, or feeling alien. While others may seem to be "stuck" in hive minds, this does not mean they are inferior or dense. No one can see the soul of another, the path, the agenda, or the purpose of a given lifetime. We cannot even know the purpose of our own lives while we are embodied. Judging others as inferiors or "dense" is as ridiculous as judging one petal on a chrysanthemum as superior to another. Often we encounter angels unawares.

Telepathy

Thoughts are things, and we create with thoughts, so it is taught. Have you ever thought about a thought? Is the silent voice in your head a thought? Reading the stuff I write, people say to me, "You sure are a thinker." But writing isn't thinking, I tell them. When I write, I am not thinking, like I doubt a bird thinks about its wings when it flies. I think about what I write after it is written.

Writing is one expression of knowing-feeling. Or is it just that my thoughts are swift like the wind, transforming to words quicker than lightning? Ah ha. Thoughts are not words. Just as I thought. Words are a form we give to thoughts, a translation quicker than lightning. (like when we talk.)

So now we are one step closer to the mystery of how a thought creates. A thought is a conveyor of intelligent energy. Intelligence is what we know. Awareness and intelligence exist, whether or not we convert them into words. Blind, deaf, mute, Helen Keller was both aware and intelligent before she was introduced to language; we know this by all she produced afterward. Language is not the only distinguisher of awareness and intelligence. Letters are symbols, which the modern mind does not consciously read. The very shapes of the letters impressed the ancient mind with meanings filtered out by the modern mind. "Letter consciousness" was lost as knowledge became too complex to hold in consciousness. Now, many of us are moving beyond word consciousness. The next step is telepathy.

Telepathy is communication of intelligence and meaning in an energy wave, or ball, or packet form, and we translate it to words, like we translate intelligence-knowing to thoughts in our single minds. This is why alien intelligence or higher beings can communicate to us, no matter our diverse languages. Language is virtually by-passed. This is how a symbol, such as a crop circle, communicates to multiple minds, whatever the language. Science scoffs, but science is still impressed with thoughts. Thought gets in the way of telepathy. When I am recording telepathic conversations, I am not thinking. I am writing.

As the words flow on the page, they are not words to me. I am like an instrument through which intelligence flows out in the form of words. And yet I am conscious of the meaning of what I write in "wave consciousness." To write, tell your thinker to take a hike. Do I mean go into a trance, like a channeler, or "automatic writer"? No. Writing is an art beyond thought.

The word "channel" has been used to describe a form of communication between an embodied person on this plane and a being on another plane. Channel gives a picture, like a narrow rivulet inside the brain. Except, this is a channel of light, like a river of liquid light beaming off the head, beaming upwards in a loop from mind to mind. But in such words, I am restricting thoughts to the brain as the site of the mind, but I don't believe that. The brain is the reception-transmission tower. Electronic reception-transmission towers are not the intelligence received and transmitted. That which is communication is electric in nature. The intelligence is like the wind, and the brain is like a windmill directing. A generator uses the power of the wind to direct electricity to light up a house. Words are focus-directors for the energy of intelligence. Some words and sentences spoken are powerful. We more than hear them; we more than think them. We feel the vibration of the intelligence conveyed. We know more than the words say. Now we are closer to seeing how visualization and feelings enter into creation.

But how do you create something you have never seen, or thought about? How do you create something for which there are no words to host a thought? Do thoughts create? Or are thoughts the tools of creation? Do you need to know the words to think the thoughts to create?

We value "original art." A keen eye recognizes "original" from a variant of a formerly created art form. When art is *too* original, it may be many years before it is recognized. Original art is expression of intelligence that is not yet thought. By the time it is expressed in thought and words, by the time thought catches up to the art, the art is no longer original. By then other versions of the once original art have been expressed.

The same is true for visionary writing. "Original" writing is not understood until thoughts catch up to the vision expressed. Then people say the writer was a genius or a prophet. But while the writer was alive, he or she was a crackpot, a suspicious character.

The following came like a communication, but there was no feeling of telepathy. It was as if my soul began to write. . . .

The Unthinkable Love Vibration

Science is a way to think about reality. We have made of this thinking a great hive mind. We have made of this thinking a great school. We worship it for all that we understand and create from this mind. It has fed and clothed us, and made us affluent. So great is this school mind, we think it is the father-mother of thought and creation. We cannot imagine anything more or greater. Science thinks it knows the whole of the cosmos with only the details to discover. So great is our trust in science, it has become synonymous with truth. Reality is the word we use to describe the science of truth. If science does not pronounce it true, it is not real, and vice-versa; if not real by science, it is false, wrong, not true, not scientific.

We cannot build a rocket ship of religion, or, by religion we cannot convince Congress to appropriate funds to build our next ship. Science is now the way to Heaven. Cosmos is the new word for Heaven, and the rocket ship is the way to Heaven, not Jesus or Allah.

But Heaven is where it always was, not in the sky, but within us. Rocket ships are flying cathedrals with astronauts as the new high priests. We enter a cathedral and feel God's vibes. An astronaut inside his rocket ship as much feels the God vibration. God is not out there; we take God into cathedrals and into rocket ships. We feel God's presence, because God is present, everywhere, and in everyone.

Religion became like science is today, a great hive mind governing thoughts. The mind free of the hive sees the walls that enclose and direct the thoughts. When the walls fall and all is windows, there will be confusion and panic. See the hives, back away, see them. See the word constructs that direct your thinking. See the laws, see the commandments, etched in your brain as fixed as words carved on a stone tablet.

The way to prepare your mind for the moment the walls fall is to be aware that your mind is not your brain. How do you "be aware"? If you understand these words, you are aware. Now, do not make of these words a religion, or a science. Be aware. Be ready to see impossibilities.

If you have seen, close up, an alien spaceship, you have seen an impossibility, by the teachings of religion and science. If you have encountered an alien being, you have met someone who does not exist, by the teachings of religion and science. No one prepared you for this, admit it. But your heart prepared you, or you would not have survived to speak or write of it.

Heart is just a word for the closest vibration to Spirit/God within you. In you is an untapped source of creation, yet to manifest in ways recognizable by minds trained in hives. But the creative impulse was alive and active throughout all that you have created. You called it intelligence and assigned to it thoughts and words you came to think were the source of the intelligence. In the excitement of your discovery, feelings and knowings not easily put into words were pushed into unconscious realms. When they surfaced, they troubled you, and you pushed them down and away. Eventually you ceased to feel the vibration of the ineffable, which resulted in expansion and strengthening of the hive minds you created with thoughts and words.

But feelings and emotions did not disappear; they were suppressed as vague troubling things to ignore or to get under the control of thoughts. Feelings are the language of love. You know that love can sweep you off your feet and stop thought. When thought became your god, love became the demon that would unseat and unfeet you. In love, your thoughts are not king. The queen of love dethrones your thoughts. And you are in trouble.

A great trouble is coming. Long depressed under thoughts, love is a great wave, surging to overwhelm your kingdom. You will hear and feel it coming, for feelings speak below your thoughts, even as you have gone to great lengths to silence them. You let them speak in the arms of a lover, in the laughter of your children, in the eyes of your pets, in music, in art, in other modes clearly defined as not science. A bar across love marks the doors to your laboratories. Tempted by love, your science will be fouled. And yet, nothing you create in a laboratory is not love, for not a blade of grass, and not a human brain exists without love, for love is the essence of life.

Does love rise to shame thoughts? Love is above, below, in, out, all around, penetrating every thought construct. Nothing exists that is not love. To squelch the feelings that are the language of love is not to destroy anything. Everything that you make is love expressed. Do you not thrill in feelings of love when you admire the rocket ship you make? Apply this same love to your children. What are your rocket ships, if your children do not feel your love for them?

When the feeling vibration is restored, your thought forms will vibrate at a new strength. That which is not tightened and tuned will collapse, like a balloon deflating. This will be true for man-made structures, and to a degree true for all biological bodies, including human bodies. The human body will not shatter or deflate, but if energy centers for the new love vibration are not opened within you and tuned to the harmony, there will be trouble; for the thinking mind will have no words or understanding, and this will be cause for fear and panic.

You can imagine the chaos in the reactions of those not prepared. This is why we tell you to expand the love vibration while you can. It is not a time for ego to be jealous of more admired thought constructs. An ego so jealous will not vibrate with the feelings that inform the heart. This is not a time to compete for praise. This is a time to express the love vibration to the fullest you can, never mind the troubled mind when the feelings speak. If you do not know that the love vibration is the gathering force, your words will deflate like balloons with air escaping. Love is palpable. It is felt. It sings to the heart and tunes the strings of the brain harp.

Let love guide your thoughts and words, and the truth will be felt, and, eventually, known. But before the brain can recognize it, the heart must be touched with the vibration of love.

Let the conductor conduct. Let the music in your mind play upon the brain harp.

Consciousness on the Move

To speak of cosmic mind is to sound like I think I am cosmic-minded, one who has moved through all of the stages, and is now on the brink of graduation from this realm. Looking at my life, I can scarcely believe that. Definitely, I was making progress, extricating from hive minds, and questing on the path of individuality. Definitely I have a concept of global mind. As those in hive minds are simultaneously becoming individuals, those who are actively pursuing individuality are becoming global-minded, and becoming cosmic-minded. But I feel so awkward, so ordinary, so *young*. . . . If this is cosmic mind, I desperately need tutors. Fortunately, I seem to have them.

For all these ages, there have been models for every phase. The trouble now is that many are being nudged to leap ahead, or hurried, or quickened; and, in responding, we don't fit the familiar models. This is why many ordinary people are sounding like wise ones, and yet we do not fit the old models of wise ones. This is naturally resented by some. And naturally, many of us are confused, and many of us feel alien, or like "walk-ins."

I have described it all in terms of evolution moving in an ordered progression. But (I believe) evolution is no more fixed than the wind. It plays and blows where it will, driven by unseen dynamics. The old thought structures are breaking up, and this is good, a sign that we have shaped light with love to a point that global changes can happen. We have brought ourselves to a threshold of transformation—with a lot of help from guides and teachers abroad, and closer than our breaths. But we are not yet consciously "one-minded." We are still a mix of multiple hive minds. It is a very confusing time. It seems we are being rushed into a global mind before we are ready. Another way of viewing it is that "Christ consciousness" is becoming the vibration. Remember his words; he would come like a thief in the night; and when he returns, it will be like the lightning flashing across the sky—all will see. The man Jesus? The Son of God Jesus? The "I and the Father are one" Jesus? I cannot say. I can only mind his words in my heart and have faith that the mystery will continue to unfold. I was born into a Christian community, so this is what shaped the love vibration in me. But the religion was too narrow for me. I did not figure that out, did not think it over, and then make a decision to leave the church. It was as if I was expunged, as if I could not be contained in the hive anymore. But I had no understanding, and suffered the torments of feeling lost, rejected, and godless for a time. And then I was reconnected to Jesus, and he was like a door that opened to spiritual realities beyond anything I had learned in church. This marked the beginning of a quest into a labyrinth of experience that culminated in awakening to my involvement with those I call ETs.

I reviewed accounts and communications of other experiencers of the UFO presence, refamiliarizing myself with how different our stories are, and yet there are connecting links in all. It is as if consciousness is expanding so fast in multiple directions that there is no time to study and affirm what is true, as we could in slower-paced stages of development. It does seem as if the planet is being infused with a new vibration of light that is shaking the walls of our accumulated knowledge, erected to control information. This is something the "controllers" could have not have foreseen—light coming from an unidentifiable source, quickening consciousness beyond the rigidities that shaped the civilization.

Some of the accounts I reviewed tell frightening stories of powerful hierarchies composed of many kinds of extraterrestrials and other-dimensional beings who are messing with us, painting a picture of human beings caught in a cosmic drama that we are powerless to stop, even if we could agree upon what is happening. Now is a good time to test the substance of the faith vibration. I see it as a bridge across the chaos and confusion. It feels firm.

The UFO presence is not a cosmic trick, a sign that God does not exist or does not care what happens to human beings. Again I equate the UFO to a mirror. What we see in it, or think about it—whether disbelieving it exists, or insisting it does—reveals where we are in consciousness. This applies to all who are engaged in the phenomenon in the many roles, including messengers who speak for the UFO. By now it is plain that for every experiencer or contactee, there is a different story, a different perspective, a different angle, a different message.

The message that we are positioning at a threshold of transformation is a powerful and provocative one. But it will remain a "hidden message," for the lights and sounds of the world are glaring and loud, and outshine and outspeak it. We don't know how to "do" global or cosmic consciousness, all together. We have been so spellbound by hive minds, we think global mind is this on a grander scale. But you can see the problem: *Which* hive mind would rule? For ages, this seems to have been the all-encompassing question: Which race, tribe, religion, god, or nation would rule all? And even after countless destructions of civilizations, we have persisted, certain that soon a deity must come and elevate the chosen ones above all. In this perspective, some must be losers, damned, cast out, lost, doomed. In this story, free will is a whimper. It is a story that plays out in ET communications, too, making them seem the Divine Word, the way things are meant to be. Cultivated over the ages, the vibration of this story is so very strong in so many minds, it is hard to walk calmly across the bridge of faith.

Radical leaps and changes are occurring in consciousness. The confusion is great as hive minds become more insistent, bringing forth bigger and bigger guns, and making increasingly more complex laws to offset the feeling of chaos as the mindquakes increase in numbers and intensity. Walk the bridge. Try not to look down too often.

PART IV:
THE BECOMING STORY

Conversation with Rowah

Thinking about the vision of the "elegant ET" (chapter 14), my childhood companion Rowah came to mind. I felt the old yearning, and began to write. After I finished, I instantly began to analyze, questioning whether or not I was really in contact with Rowah. If I could answer that question definitively, I would be well on my way to solving the whole mystery that has engulfed me. It seems it does not much matter the name— Rowah, El, Clio—the essence is the same. The names are a kind of game, like the stories a child needs.

It is what happened in the conversation that caused me to include it in the book. As if tricking myself, some of my deepest feelings were exposed. The temptation is to explain what I, or Rowah, meant by certain statements, as if the intellect could improve on the voice of the feelings. I doubt that. So, I will let the conversation stand as is, as prelude to the remaining chapters. Think of it as a conversation between a student and a mentor. Here the student is human and the mentor is . . . I don't know; but definitely I am linked.

"Why didn't I know—why was I in the dark?"
Because this is how all roles unfold on the third dimension.

"But I thought we were supposed to be waking up, becoming more conscious."

Aren't you?

"Yeah . . . after I took the hits when I was still asleep."

Did not the hits work to help awaken you?

"But that seems so backward. Unfair or something. Before wisdom, ignorance and pride; before love, blame and resentment; before joy and freedom, pain."

You never did understand this plane.

"I remember. Everything here is contrast. But why would anyone go willingly into ignorance, resentment, and pain, even with the promise they would lead to love and freedom?"

You tell us, Little Sister.

"But I'm not there yet. I'm not free yet. Freer . . . but I'm not sure it can be accomplished. It's my Otherness. People feel it, and it makes them uncomfortable. I think they loved me more when I was lower on the chain in their minds, barely surviving, stumbling around, laughing through my sorrows. I was not exceeding their view of me; I was not crossing lines. Not exactly ignorance is bliss, but ignorance can be a shield."

And then you began to become wise.

"I started to wise up is the way we say it. But geez! It was like being churned up in a Cuisinart. They just thought I was crazy. But they could accept that. It was when I began speaking the wisdom, that's when the resentment showed."

Because they did not love themselves.

"You're right. I never did understand this plane. And my speaking 'alien wisdom' is supposed to help them? They didn't want to hear it. But I told them it wasn't me."

You lied. Maybe that is what they resented.

"I didn't lie! I didn't know!"

Then self-awareness and honesty is a step toward love and freedom, no?

"So now I'm supposed to tell them I'm ET?"

Only if you want to be free, Little Sister.

"But I don't know that!"

Is that not your work?

"To become aware I'm ET?"

To know yourself. How can you love others if you do not love yourself, and how can you love yourself, if you do not know yourself?

"Knowing I'm ET is supposed to get me there? They don't just fear that, they resent it."

Resentment is not fear?

"Yes, but I don't think most people realize that. No one likes to feel fear. Resentment feels powerful. How I know. I experienced it. I hated the fear myself. It made me feel so weak, so vulnerable, so childish, like a squalling kid."

So human.

"That's the secret, isn't it? A human is an ET becoming. But they either worship them like angels or gods, or they see them as demons, or loathsome creatures they would happily crush, like stepping on insects. Of course, it's all done with tremendous machine power. It's like they loathe anything that reminds them they are nature's children. I sometimes think they secretly wish they were robots. They wish they were rocket ships! With computer brains. They compare their brains to computers!"

Not you. You always welcomed the pain.

"Hmmm. That's what you mean about getting honest, knowing myself."

If you cannot move past the fear and resentment, how do you know and love yourself?

"That's where the pain comes in. But why does love hurt? That seems . . . wrong, just wrong. We have to know hate before we can know love?"

What is hate?

"Passion distorted to cover the fear?"

Fear of . . .

"Love."

Why do you fear love?

"It's the ultimate vulnerability. To love is to die, or so it feels."

Keep dying, Little Sister. It becomes you.

"That's one of those alien koans, isn't it?"

That is the question.

"Will I get past the pain and become free before I die?"

Will you?

"If I don't . . . another human life?"

Yes, unless you rewrite yourself.

"Wow. John was speaking the truth when he said the Word became flesh, wasn't he? You mean . . . I am my words?"

There are words, and there are words.

"I know. That's the problem. Is it like . . . when you wake up and get past the fear, and the loneliness, it is to know you are different; then you find the true words, the ones in your heart, the ones you knew before you came, the words you are?"

Then you are becoming.

"And becoming is as close as we can come, as humans, to what we are?"

Is this so hard?

"Not hard to grasp, but to live . . . very hard! You told me my life would be hard. You weren't just whistling Dixie."

Whistling Dixie?

"Never mind. I don't even know what it means myself. My head is full of words that aren't me. Why can't we just say 'I am' and be done with it?"

And miss the ignorance, resentment, and pain?

"I get it. To know our whole being, we have to experience it all. But, Rowah?"

I am here, Little Sister.

"How can I ever tell them? Even if I knew for sure I was ET, and felt it was safe to say so, they would construe it to mean like a *Star Trek* character, or one of those fetal geeks."

So human.

"You're laughing at me. I can feel it."

Just be your human-ET self, Little Sister. What more or less can you be?

"But neither is me. I'm becoming . . . we're becoming . . . No way can I see what we're becoming, but I'm supposed to write about it."

Once upon a time there was born on Earth a child fair and stalwart, a child of her ancestors, and the ones who made them all. For this story, we will call her Evangeline.

"Very funny. I remember when you gave me that. Evangeline means messenger. Those words were supposed to begin the novel . . . but J.Q. Mahoney took over."

Your love and admiration for men.

"They're all total trouble!"
> So you created one easy to love. A step in your own becoming.

"It's all about love, isn't it?"
> Is it?

"Yes. But nothing scares us so much."
> Maybe you can trick them.

"A trick is a lie."
> So, you choose. Do you try to trick them, or do you write from your heart?

"I can feel the knife now."
> Whether in joy or in pain . . .

"I remember. We don't care how you do it, just do. An arrow shot is better than not. You are ruthless. All of you."
> Should we be any less for love?

"Was this really the only way? Oh, never mind. I know what you'll say . . . we knew, we chose, we came . . ."
> To become.

"The mystery . . . we knew, but as humans we don't know."
> You cannot know something you do not yet know by way of experience.

"And that's the paradox. We knew, but it was abstract, just a concept, all in the mind. To really know, to realize it, we had to become flesh to experience the truth of our words. But until I know, until I become . . . all my words won't really tell it. But words are the only way to tell it. Paradox. But humans don't like paradoxes. This really is a crazy world, Rowah. What if we took on something . . . what if we blow it?"
> What if you are in over your head?

"Cute. You know that's where I'm stuck. Where is 'in'? Over the head doesn't translate as 'in,' here. Everything seems to be 'out here' or 'up there.' They don't really know in."

Are you ahead of yourself?

"That's code for I'm too much in my head again, isn't it?"

Would we double-talk?

"All the time—because we only become through experience, not through being told the secrets we seek to know."

What could you do with them, if you knew?

"We *think* knowing the secrets of life would empower us, get us what we want."

And what has getting what you wanted gotten you?

"I know! Supposedly the most affluent society on Earth . . . but what happened to all that leisure time we were going to realize from all the new inventions and technologies? That was the story in the fifties . . . before both husband and wife had to work to make ends meet, and we had time for more than e-mail friendships. And now the most popular show on TV is *Who Wants to Be a Millionaire?* Why can't they see the connection between affluence and consumption?"

You're asking us?

"I know. I'm supposed to tell you. When I figure it out, I will. What a weird life. I'm trying to explain ETs to them, and humans to you."

Your work is cut out.

"Thanks a lot."

We don't mind. We are mind.

"I think I better cut out those words. They won't get that. They'll say you are just in my mind, which means to them, you don't exist."

Maybe you will help them awaken to their own minds.

"Maybe I'll be driving a Rolls Royce next year."

Still stumbling around in your sorrows. Still lovable.

"You're going to make me cry."

God forbid.

"I love you, Rowah."

We love you, Little Sister.

"It's enough, isn't it?"

How will you know?

"Until I enter the vibration. . . . Okay, I'm ready to begin the becoming story now."

So brave.

"You know. Thank God, someone knows. Oh, if I could just help them know they are not alone. Never mind the becoming . . . if only they knew that all belonged. . . ."

And who can speak of it except one who knows she belongs?

"I guess I do know enough to begin. But it still takes courage."

The human story.

"You can say that again."

The human story.

"You're going to leave me again. I can feel it."

And you will forget again.

"No, I won't. I remembered the silver, didn't I? Rowah? . . ."

CHAPTER FOURTEEN:

Metafractals: The Elegant ET and the Seventh Jewel

Gnothi Seauton: "Know Thyself"

—Inscribed over the sanctuary of Apollo at Delphi

The question, "What is a human being" would be, for the child, like asking the reason for stars. The child is not thinking about reality. The child is living, experiencing, being. I cannot prove I was in the company of alien beings at the age of five. But I can fathom how I could have been, and blocked awareness of it. How does a child speak of realities for which there are no words? Perhaps without words to describe, the experience may seem like a dream. It would be tempting to dismiss it all as dreams, but the fact of the actual missing times stands in the way.

All who have been studying the UFO presence have questioned the contrariness of certain patterns. On one hand, the UFOs are stealthy, playing like cats with mice. On the other hand, they could be a lot more stealthy. Why would they involve a little girl in numerous missing daylight time events, when they could have as easily taken me secretly at night? The way it was, when my parents would demand to know where I had been, every time, I would say, "With friends!" As strange as these events is the fact that my parents did not investigate. Instead, they withdrew me from school. And later I remembered "sparky eyes" in the night, and feeling my hands swell large, while a pressure bore down on them. So maybe I was taken at night, as well as having the daytime encounters.

When UFO sightings were getting a lot of press in the 1980s, and the stories of abduction began to increase, I never once considered that the missing time events in childhood could be UFO-related, despite the signs of implants in my hands in 1986. Nor did it come to mind during the contact in 1993. The most unsettling thing after the breach was not the idea that maybe I was an abductee, but that, previously, I had been blind to the signs in my life. I thought I knew myself; I thought that if I were an abductee, there would be loud signals. There were, but I did not see them. It was like the door to that awareness was shut in my mind.

I have questions about my childhood experiences. First a comment about the "memories" viewed in hypnotic regression. All such are questionable without physical evidence to confirm the actuality of the events viewed. But at some point, sooner or later, an individual has to decide whether or not she or he believes the events viewed represent reality. I always hedge on the side of caution, for lack of proof. But essentially I believe that what I viewed happened. But on what level of reality? I know today that our dense reality is not the only reality. The spaceship could have been "transitionally real"; the beings, appearing to be as real as people in the third dimension. The poignancy of the event was in my response to the beings—my comfort in their presence. But I, the adult, was not comfortable with the idea of a lifetime of physical abductions of which I was not conscious. And yet, lightly hypnotized, I reported the childhood encounter with relative ease . . . this after failing to access the memory in two previous attempts; the taboo was strong. Some investigators would say that the absence of fear is a sign that either I was strongly programmed, or I did not get down to the awful truth. I try not to judge such experiences to be either positive or negative. I take my cue from my five-year-old self. As was reported, this was just life to me then, like the contact and phenomena became a part of my life in later years. Fear is present when we encounter something truly alien. I said I belonged with the Others, matter-of-factly. I knew they were different, but it didn't bother me, the child. This was hard for me, the adult, to accept. Could it be that the "monster" quality attached to "aliens" is not really the basis of the fear? Perhaps what we fear most is discovery that we are not the pinnacle of evolution, that the gods, angels, and demons of legends are real beings.

If the Others could have taken me secretly at night, as they do so many, why would they park a ship on the ground (if a transitory creation), and summon me so often that I would get in trouble with my parents? Maybe to leave a "metafractal" to trigger investigation later. The same question goes for the appearance of implants. If the Others are so advanced, couldn't they have put implants in us and erased the signs? In my case, it seems They meant that I would be aware They had been here. Though stealthy, they leave tracks and traces of their presence. I look to the result of my experiences for answers. The result has been an acceleration in consciousness, which was upsetting to my life because the society was not becoming aware in tandem. Society balked at our stories. This was as hard to accept as viewing myself at five years old, comfortable in the presence of the tall, spindly beings.

Why was it important that I know consciously that I was involved? I think it was important that I make a choice as to what I believed, and stand on it. There are many choices, many ways to view the UFO phenomenon, and our involvement. I had never been challenged to exercise my will in such extreme circumstances. I never imagined I would be so alone in my choices. I found out how much I had relied on others to guide my choices. I was engulfed in a very real and sometimes frightening situation, with which the people around me could not help me because, it seemed, they *couldn't* believe it was real. And this gave me a hard-won understanding of the dynamics of experience in the choice-to-reality equation. We create our own reality by our beliefs and choices? Sometimes reality doesn't wait for us to work out what we believe. Sometimes it leaps out of the future and rushes at us. And then a crisis. What to believe? What to do? There was no manual for this kind of experience, not even in the metaphysical library, with which I was familiar. In the metaphysical library, this could not have happened. The UFO presence broke the rules.

The question of an ET link may not come up with those who feel they were snatched up at random, trespassed, and/or abused. But signs of involvement at an early age calls into question history, plans, and purposes, especially when one feels a familiarity with the beings. When finally the signs were loud enough, I was moved to look at my whole life. That's where I found the links. I did not find them by concentrating on specific phenomenal events.

Nuts and bolts are something we ought to study, but a human being is more, so much more. I take issue with the judgment that UFO experiences are a "syndrome." People can frame it that way, it is their right; but for me to do that, I would have to call my whole life a syndrome.

Nor does "multiple personality" explain the calming of the human self during experiences and telepathic communications, and the ease with which I would shift into the feeling-recognizing-remembering state of being and mind. It was only in the writing of this book that I was able to look back curiously at the ease with which I conversed with Them, seldom asking the questions that were of most compelling interest to the human self who struggled to accommodate this emergent awareness. Certainly, I continually forgot to ask questions that were most compelling to investigators. The shifts were so slight, I never felt I was anyone but me. It was me, shifting back and forth in tiers of consciousness so seamlessly, my daylight mind was not overly suspicious. The disorientation and stress I associated with the difficulties these experiences imposed on my life among people who were naturally uncomfortable and sometimes disturbed with the changes in me. It was much easier to focus the angst out into society, at debunkers and faceless skeptics, than to face the pain that was in my personal relationships. There was simply no way to gracefully ease into the catalyst without exposing myself.

But my human self truly did not fathom what was happening. The daily journaling and the communications were a mediational bridge which kept me sane, and the fear at bay. I had a deep trust in the knowing-feeling inside. I look back now on the years of meditation as preparation for the experiences to come, though at every step, the "news" was increasingly unsettling to my psyche (ego); my foundation in spirit was firm. But it was never easy, and it still takes courage, though I am past the catalyst.

I was both baffled and troubled by the guidance to write about the ET link. Baffled because I didn't *know* I was ET, by soul or by bloodline, and troubled because I *knew* this was leaning too close to a truth wrapped in an old taboo.

But then I got a boost—a beautiful vision. And it was a gift and a blessing, too, because it would give me a way to sidestep the folly of creating an "ET persona," and reach for the becoming story. It is human nature, I suppose, to put ETs on a pedestal, to glorify them as the archetypical space brothers and sisters, inviting us to join the cosmic race. It is equally easy to see them as hideous monsters to knock out of the sky, flexing the muscles of our powerful machines. You have to be *brainy* to make and operate such machines, and this would be the message that had audiences howling with pride as we watched ourselves on the movie screen, demolishing a new enemy. I cannot tell you how sad this made me feel. Whatever I knew down deep, my daylight mind was beginning to know it too—we had come to anchor light in an ocean of sludge-like darkness.

When we answer the question, "What is a human being," we will have answered the question, "What is an alien?" So said Guidance. I don't want to try and create a new vision of who and what the ETs or aliens are, but to be honest, I must keep mentioning that I do not feel they are as we have colored them, after our science fiction stories and mythologies.

If you want to meet an alien, look in the mirror. Just for fun, consider, wonder for a moment, why nature would create a fragile, smooth-skinned being to live on a planet of such extreme conditions. Neither fur to keep us warm in cold climes, nor sun-sensitive skin to protect in hot climes; neither brawn to equal the ferocious animals of jungles and forests, nor size nor agility nor instincts to easily best predators. In place of all these, we were endowed with a special kind of brain and a peculiarity some call love, and others call humanity, a potential for stewardship of a wild, untamed planet. Ask yourself what nature had in mind, creating such a vulnerable animal, with a brain that is only an advantage if other beings of the same species carefully teach and educate it to take care of itself, and use its intelligence to create a safe environment, in which future generations can flourish. Consider the potential for using the intelligence to destroy rather than to create, to oppress, rather than to nurture. Consider the potential for this unusual intelligence to fight against nature itself, as if the life that sustained it were an obstacle to defeat; and then to blame nature for not cooperating with the aims of civilization, naming earthquakes, hurricanes, tidal waves, volcanoes, viruses, and every other uncontrollable force that interferes with the goals of the people, Acts of God, while denying the existence of such a deity. Considering all this, was nature insane to create a special brain in a species that would turn upon its own, creating never-ending wars to determine who among them would survive, the victors never getting the picture, teaching their children to repeat the cycles of violence and destruction, until finally, in order to salvage the planet, Nature would have to once again take out the dangerous species, and try again with a new model?

Are human beings just an evolutionary experiment gone haywire? Why do the most intelligent on the planet seem to be the most ignorant of the laws of life? That is what the "Elder Brothers" in Columbia want to know, and so do I. If I am alien, or hybrid, or infused with alien intelligence, or an alien soul, why do I relate more to Elder Brother than I do to "Younger Brother"?

Maybe to see and feel the same concern for the state of the planet as do the Elder Brothers is to feel alien among so many who seem either to not care, or to be asleep to the destruction taking place. But I think it is not an alien view to notice the insurgence of human beings who *do see*, and do care, and are committed to reversing the tides of destruction.

Nature is speaking in a proliferation of new healing gifts among the children of Earth. Not only healing gifts, but a multiple variety of gifts in vision and wisdom. The core vibration is shaking us, quickening consciousness, showing the way to heal and harmonize ourselves and the planet.

Before the breach, I was eager to keep it all in the realm of mystery, to write my novels, and call myself a visionary. Skip the implants, skip everything that demonstrated on the physical plane. I was a visionary, all right . . . I could see that an experiencer was marked for trials "beyond what should be expected of any human being," as was put to me with compassion in one conversation (included in *Summoned*). They were speaking of the "infusion" at birth, as if that put a dot on the "i" of the question.

Where did I get the idea as a three-year-old to draw paper dolls with bodies and dresses shaped like triangles? Were the triangles a mark left on a consciousness map to discover later? At a young age I showed a mind for symbols. In grade school, a teacher declared me an artist, but I never developed the talent, though I dreamt of becoming a fashion designer. The dream persisted until I learned I would have to become knowledgeable of fabrics, which did not interest me. Design interested, the lines and shapes, the colors, the endless possibilities. Something much more intriguing would capture my mind—words. But it would be many years before I became conscious of the provocative designs of the letters that compose words. At the table in 1993, schooled in letter-number designs, I would remember my grandmother teaching me the alphabet when I was two years old. The passion was seeded then, and at the age of forty-nine, it began to flower out of my soul.

And I remember listening to classical music when I was thirty-something, and drawing the shapes and colors of the music. It didn't seem odd to me that I could envision the shapes of sounds and catch their colors and designs on paper. It seemed odd that others could not see the same. But I had an excuse. I was artistic. Others had to take drugs to see such things. I had very little experience with drugs, other than uppers during the drinking days. I smoked marijuana with friends one night; we got in a car and traveled on a bridge over the train yards in Denver. The lighted windows high in the skyscrapers looked like portals to me. I thought we could just propel the car up through one of them and fly into another dimension. After that, I knew I was one who should not smoke pot, nor ever take LSD. But where, in the 1970s, did I get such ideas of flying up through windows in the sky?

Examining my childhood experiences, it was not a strain in the hypnotic regression to see the window at the back of the spacecraft as a portal to another dimension. Was it both a space and time portal? Through the window I saw a desert scene with big rocks and a pale red atmosphere. Forty-four years later, I moved to country that looked like that—red rock country with terrain often described as Martian in appearance. And this is where the fullness of my involvement would begin to open like a flower.

I call these things "metafractals"—when a metaphor combines with a real event at the physical level, and yet the meaning is cloaked in mystery, like another dimension bleeding through, like the fourth dimension impinging on the third. It is more difficult to see the metafractal, as a child in a spaceship, viewing alien babies in containers of fluid, and being told I would teach them when I was older, and connecting this to the multiple dreams in the 1980s of caring for intelligent babies with whom I conversed telepathically. It is more difficult because by the time I was hypnotized, I had heard stories about hybrid babies. You could say my consciousness was tainted by the stories I'd heard. The metafractal link is in the actuality of missing time events, and the actuality of such dreams that preceded public information. If I "confabulated" seeing babies in containers of fluid, still the missing time events are not explained, nor the countless dreams I had of "smart babies" in the 1980s before I was suspicious of direct involvement with ETs. That is the trouble with some skeptics; they ignore key parts of a story that do not fit their theories. But the purpose of the UFO presence is not to impress skeptics. It is for us to deal with, and make our hard choices.

I came to understand that you cannot teach a mystery to the intellect, like faith cannot be taught to those who must have proofs of spiritual realities. Mystery and faith are words that speak of experience and realities beyond the ken of the intellect; therefore, neither can be understood through reason, logic, or analysis; and yet, paradoxically, the only way to understand either is by expanding the mind. I'm not sure what the question is, but the answer is consciousness. When we understand that knowledge and consciousness are not necessarily the same thing, we are halfway to the right question.

I have a personal becoming story to tell in this chapter. (Or at least, it is prelude to a becoming story.) The first hint that I would write about the ET-human link came one night while I was washing dishes. I had just finished a session of title-making, which means I was blocked, having a difficult time finding the right focus. All I knew was, there were certain messages I felt I should share. So much had happened to me, I felt there was another book, but then this difficulty in seeing the focus.

So, I was washing dishes—water is a good medium for communication from within—and a thought-gram popped into my mind: "Scarlet Underwear." I burst out laughing. I knew what it meant. It was a suggestion for a book title. What Guidance really meant was "ET underwear." But I honestly thought they were kidding. Scarlet was a code for the embarrassment, and even the shame I felt at the notion of expounding on my feelings about an ET connection. *The Scarlet Letter* by Nathaniel Hawthorne stands out in memory as a novel I read while in high school. Though I was a very good Mormon girl, a virgin, somehow I understood in a deep way what the woman in the story felt, made to wear the scarlet letter. Her guilt was my own; we both had secrets. She was found out, something I feared at a depth below words, a secret I dared never even think aloud.

The thought-gram, "scarlet underwear" that had caused me to laugh, was not the end of it. I still felt I would have to camouflage the question, write it in code or invisible ink. I called a friend, Donna Kenworthy, who happens to be a psychic. (She's the author of *A 1-900 Psychic Speaks*.) Donna would be sympathetic to my plight. . . .

"That's exactly what you are to write about," she said. My guides had told her, she said. That required a leap. Why would my guides tell her what I should write? Maybe because I was so threatened by the idea, I was shutting out the subtle nudges? My guides seldom give me blunt instructions like this.

"But why should I write about that?" I asked. It seemed so wrong, so foolish.

"To give a voice to other ET-humans," Donna replied.

I swallowed the scoff in my throat. But below the torments of the dual identity question, my heartstrings were pulled. If I could help just one. . . . This was hard for me, a true dilemma. And honestly I was not certain I was ET; in fact, it turned me off when people declared themselves to be ET. Oh, sure, I would think, my cynicism flaring, your grandparents were praying mantises; I can see the resemblance! But the cynicism covered my fear . . . the old taboo.

I had my other side. At a UFO conference, a woman shared parts of her Ph.D. thesis with us, the audience. The thesis was on ET-human types. But I could not stay and watch all of her presentation, which included comparative histories of several human beings who claimed to remember lives on other planets. The statistics on the screen were all a blur. Tears filled my eyes. I felt so sad, but didn't know why. I was firmly against the idea of promoting "ET lineages." My daylight mind said I didn't believe it was true, and my shadow mind warned that this was dangerous terrain. I got up, left the room. After the presentation, I asked for time with the doctor, thinking that a talk with her would clear the confusion in my mind. She granted me the time; I fumbled and hem-hawed, trying to explain my problem. She never asked me the question dangling in the air—did I think I was ET-human? Instead her eyes reported impatience with me. I can't blame her.

I tried to talk about it with a few others at the conference, but still no satisfaction. The question of ET origins was not new, wasn't even exotic anymore. I used to joke about it, and I had thought about it seriously, and even written about it in *Summoned*. What was up? Why these feelings of sadness, depression, and almost panic? I had no answers.

And now this. Four months later, a trusted friend, a psychic, was telling me I was to write about the mystery . . . *to give other ET-humans a voice.*

Before hanging up, I told Donna about my vision of an elegant ET in my mind, and described him to her. "That's you," she said in that sure tone psychics use when they mean business. Sigh. I fussed and fretted for a few more days, wondering if I could bring anything new of substance to the subject. I wanted the way laid out for me, to see clearly how it would be done before I started. But that is not the way books like this happen. It's not like a novel, plotting the story first, seeing the beginning and the end with only the middle to fill with drama and adventure. Of course, characters have their own minds, so the story always veers in unexpected directions; but autobiography enjoys no such liberties. In this case, there was a mystery to solve, a question I needed to resolve, for the freedom I sought. As Rowah said . . . this was my work.

I don't know if the elegant ET wears underwear or not, but I saw him watching me through a glass. This was after seeing a ruby spinning inside my head. The vision relates to the story "Remember the Silver" in *Summoned*. A review: The story was an exploration of my connection to Rowah. My parents called him imaginary because they could not see him. Rowah did not appear to them as a physical being. If my parents saw such beings when they were children, they had long suppressed the memories.

In a hypnotic regression to find out what I could about Rowah, I saw him plainly, saw him down on a knee, his right hand at my back, his left pointing across "time and events." He told me my life would be hard, and to "remember the silver." The silver was something in the sky I could not describe. I felt strong emotions after this probe for buried memories.

After the hypnotic regression, my guides told me that the meeting with Rowah, when he told me to remember the silver, happened before I was born. This made sense to me. Pre-life, I would have known what the silver meant. But after we are born, our "soul minds" are veiled. The challenge for some of us seems to be work on "thinning the veils," to remember as much as we can!

In *Summoned*, I made a story about Rowah visiting my baby self. In the baby, I expressed the bewilderment a new prototypical human infant might feel in a tiny body it does not understand, and cannot operate. The infant perceives adults as giant aliens who speak "gobbledy-gook." Rowah explains that the baby is now "like the aliens," and they will program her mind. The infant is aghast. Not only is she trapped in a tiny body with useless appendages, her mind is not even her own, and others will program into her mind *their* agendas, and she will become spellbound—it is the nature of this world. *But*, Rowah tells her, *if* she is faithful, if she remembers the silver, later she can "forge a portal" of communication deep within her, which will reconnect her to him in consciousness. The purpose is transformation of consciousness. Born into a foreign world, each human infant will forget the past, will be programmed, will become spellbound, and will be challenged to remember the purpose for coming here. We are here to transform ourselves, transform consciousness. And the *prize*, Rowah tells her, is *compassion*, a word that puzzles the baby.

After Rowah fades, the baby thinks it all over, naming the "jewels" that she identifies as her senses: two for sight, two for hearing, one for smell, one for taste. . . . But what is the seventh jewel she knows is there?

Rowah sends a thought-gram: *You will see. . . .*

Because the story was the work of imagination, I didn't expect to see a "seventh jewel." But I don't know why it should surprise me; after all, the seventh jewel is symbolic of seeing. that is, seeing beyond the range of the physical outward-focused eyes—hidden vision.

One day in September 1999, soon after I had begun fiddling with starting this book, I was sitting on my bed and the vision came to mind. It is impossible to explain a vision. Suffice it to say, I envisioned a ruby spinning in the center of my head—envisioned as a large room in my mansion mind. (Please no jokes about me being big-headed.) Possibly the spinning ruby is a metaphor for the pineal gland, possibly a consciousness device representing the activation of the pineal gland. Along with the image was the *sensation* of something spinning in the center of my head.

Interesting, I thought of the ruby, then went about my business. Later that day, I was looking in the mirror, and realized I was looking at my reflection from the center of my head outward, and that before, I had always viewed the world from my eyeballs outward. It was as if there was now a new "mind's eye" behind my physical eyes.

A little history about the ruby symbol: During the days of working with letters and numbers, I went beyond words. Images began to appear in my mind that represented concepts too large for words. These developed into seven pictures that told a story. The fourth picture was titled, "Know Your Branches." There is a tree that represents the old human being, our evolution. High up, a limb has cracked, and sent flying, into the air, a child, a girl. On her shirt is the word "Ruby," her name. She looks totally bewildered, her little arms and legs flailing. The jolt off the broken limb caused her shoes to fly off—ruby shoes. Down below and to the right are seven women, our "mothers in Heaven," each representing seven creations of human beings. Their arms are stretched upward to catch the child. Around the women is water, and glistening in the water are . . . rubies. When I envisioned the ruby spinning in my head, I did not remember the picture, "Know Your Branches." But I did when I began to think about metafractals.

The next day, the vision expanded. I was not expecting it to expand; I had not expected the vision of the spinning ruby in the first place. Behind the ruby was a sheet of glass, and behind the glass, I could see an elegant ET, watching. And behind the ET, I saw the vast star-studded cosmos. It looked like the night sky. Sensing it to be the place I go when I "transfer" or travel, I dubbed it the inner cosmos. All this gave me much to ponder.

I could not have imagined the elegant ET. By this I mean, I could not have employed imagination to produce this image. When I employ imagination—and, as a novelist, I am very experienced at this—what I imagine always resembles something I have seen, such as a tree, a child, rubies, water, and seven women. I have never seen "raiments" (this word insists) such as this ET was wearing, and I don't even have words to describe the headgear. I couldn't even draw it; I tried. This is the difference between imagination and vision.

There is an aura of both youth and maturity. His garments are shiny satin, and gold, light green, and purple . . . I can't determine how the colors are distributed. An impression of a cape. The head cap is elaborate, has some sort of flaps, bringing to mind the wings of Mercury, a feeling of apprenticeship. Later Hermes Trismegistus came to mind. He is blond, I think, with a glowing countenance; tall, stately, elegant, shining. Is he the symbol of my becoming?

He seems to stand at the portal where I enter and depart this physical world through my body. Is it correct to locate the portal inside my head? Other images support the idea. Remember, in the vision, or memory, of receiving activators in my hands, aboard a dome-topped spaceship, my attention was riveted on a mercurial seam that arched across the ceiling of the dome. The seam was a portal, I "knew," through which the ship "enfolded" from one dimension to another. I have a vision of enfolding . . . I can see the ship changing in energy to reduce to a beam and spin into a dimension of another frequency. Can't explain it, but this belongs to "tetrahedron physics."

But I also equated the silver seam with the fold between left and right hemispheres in the brain. Expand the thinking, something is telling me . . . see that the mind is connected to another dimension of reality. See that the "silver cord" (an energy-light beam) is the connection between body, mind, and spirit. See the mind as a domain, an "inner cosmos," tucked within all that we observe and experience as "out here," and "up there." The mind domain or field is both outward and inward. The nature of the energy makes the difference. There are portals in the mind, "soft spots," where the vibrations are such that when one knows how to "touch" them in a certain way, the inner cosmos can be entered.

Our thinking mind cannot yet conceive it; how an inner cosmos could be tucked within the outer cosmos, hidden from human view. Everything we know seems to have a solid center; everything seems to be a closed system. But everything here, including our bodies, is outfolding from the inner cosmos—the creation realm. The Source of Creation, the Love-Life Vibration, is literally in everything. We will come to a new understanding of the word "in." I know we have a perception of "in," as relates to the cosmos, because we have the word "infinite"—that which is boundless and eternal. Outer external realities have borders. All is defined in outer reality. In the realm of mind, it is another matter . . . matter is of a different kind. All matter is first well defined by vibrations that are compatible with the frequencies of particular outer worlds. From the core vibration spring all vibrations, acting with intelligence, chemistries, and forces to produce the infinite expressions of creation. There are no limits on intelligent creation, except as are designed and imposed in relation to evolution, or readiness to expand the mind in a particular environment.

While working in a heightened state of consciousness in 1993, the rubies drawn were a metafractal to link with the vision, in 1999, of the ruby spinning inside my head. But no way did such a vision occur to me six years ago. It wasn't as if I consciously planted the image to enhance a future vision. These were consciousness events to discover and mark on the map of the new territory we are penetrating.

This is where my UFO-related experiences have taken me, to investigation of my own consciousness and being. I wanted to make a map of the links from childhood on, to show the pattern of events, metaphors, communications and physical phenomena, but it quickly became so complicated, it would take nearly another whole book to show and explain it.

The subject of this book is the ET-human link, and there is more to reveal. . . .

CHAPTER FIFTEEN:

Where Is Home?

At the presentation of the ET lineages at the UFO conference, I remember thinking . . . *this is the wrong direction*. Even if some, or all of us are of extraterrestrial origins, what could be gained by bragging up ET histories, like cosmic coats of arms? Weren't we supposed to be moving toward a global consciousness to realize that all together we are one human family, all related? These were the head thoughts, but the fear had a voice, too: *Would I be expected to reveal?* . . .

"You lied," Rowah said. "Maybe that is what they resented."

I didn't feel I lied, but here was the scarlet underwear, the sense of shame and discomfort at the prospect of submitting my own "ET resume" to the critical public eye. I have always prided myself on honesty, but inside I was harboring a secret. The frustration was, I couldn't articulate the secret to myself, much less to anyone else, except at certain times. When alone, I would "know" I was not only human, but "other."

What is the nature of the "otherness" is the question. Does the vision of the elegant ET resolve the question of the ET-human link? Can the question be satisfied with all I have written about the soul? Is the human being the child of a grand being we call a soul? Is Earth a school for evolving seed-souls to a state of maturity that calls for graduation to a higher dimension?

It took courage to disclose in a book that I was one who was experiencing "abduction." Even speculating an ET-human link made me feel far more uncomfortable. But there was no escape from putting to the test my belief that the truth sets us free. Not that I can know ultimate truth, but that my sense of freedom is based in living true to myself, and the choices and commitments made before I was born.

You would just like to be released from duty, for it is harder than you thought it would be . . . said the stern voice of the one who reminded me that I was a "human link."

And what is the nature of the duty I would like to dodge? To help quell fear as the "big event" draws near, as the confusion and chaos increases, as disinformation becomes increasingly more complex, as the "old order" braces for war, as the "Earth changes" continue to demonstrate, as the cries of the children ring louder in the ears of the soul . . . *save us, for we are the future of humankind.*

But how can a person help to quell fear in the community if he or she does not quiet the fear in his/her own heart? If I cannot achieve a sense of safety in this body and in this world, what is the meaning of my belief that I am at core an eternal soul? If I fear troubles, pain, disease, and death, what is the essence of my faith that I am more than human? Why do I strain to share visions and memories that challenge the "official stories," if I do not, myself, have the courage to believe what is in my own mind and heart?

The faith by which I live is not a theoretical belief system. Faith is a real vibration that informs the mind of the contents of the heart—metaphor for the closest portal to connection with the soul, or Spirit or God. The courage required to speak from the faith vibration is testament to the danger that is felt in a world of sleepwalkers who have not yet awakened to realization of their own spiritual natures. And that was the point, the tip of the arrow pointing at the choices I could make. I could let *Summoned* stand as enough, and try to fit myself back into the world as one who is engulfed in a mystery impossible to solve. Or I could go this extra mile. But going this way, would I succeed at anchoring a little more light, or would this effort to probe deeper into the mystery only add more confusion?

Living the faith vibration means acting without reassurance or guarantee of outcomes. Risk is inherent in all choices. The question was resolved in consideration of how I would feel about myself if I chose the "safer" path. *Summoned* was well received, and my novels were a safe way to present ideas that as non-fiction are subject to ridicule that carries the threat of ostracism. What is the reward for courage that challenges the core beliefs on which most stake their lives? But my personal stakes were not that grand. I was blessed with the obscurity of being a "little nobody." There was little to lose in disclosing more of my visions and memories. The question became: Was I willing to risk further discomfort, or even danger if I were perceived to be more than a little nobody? The "conspiracy mind" is unpredictable, seeing shadows of the enemy behind every bush . . . or book.

As I wavered at this portal of choice, I thought about the regression to a former life in another world. It was done in 1995, and I had not reviewed it since. All I had was a long paragraph summarizing it. I had tried to work the paragraph into the narrative, like a shrug. I had shrugged off the regression, like the evidences of implants in my hands, like not asking Dr. Walker to help me look for signs of ET interactions in this lifetime, like not connecting the missing times in childhood with later activities. Another missing link was chiming in my mind. . . .

The decision crept up in the form of a question: Why didn't I know the name of the other world place? This I remembered clearly . . . the lack of a name. If it was only imagination, wouldn't I have supplied a name for the "planet of origin"? If I wanted to believe I was ET, wouldn't I have enriched the account? Readers of my novels know that I do not lack for story-telling ability. But what I saw in trance was not much like my otherworldly imagination in my novel *Jonah*. It would be difficult to write a novel for the contemporary mind based on the world I had glimpsed while regressed. The reality is too different from this world. And I was reticent, a little afraid to look too closely. If it was a real memory, and I remembered too much, would it make life here more difficult? Would it evoke feelings of nostalgia for my "real home"? Would I care less about my life here, and this planet? That did not happen. Since the regression, I feel *more* attached to Mother Earth. And I care as much for human beings, and the future of this world.

I believed there was nothing of substance on the audio cassette tape; nonetheless, I went and found it to settle the niggling question of why I did not know the name of the other world I had viewed. Did Dr. Hover forget to ask for a name?

I had spent five days in Scottsdale, Arizona, in August, 1995, for the purpose of probing ET-related events. During the first two days, Dr. Ruth Hover thoroughly interviewed me to determine that I was sound of mind and not "fantasy prone." The main focus of the regressions was on events that I could remember a little about and wanted to probe; but, at the last, I wanted to explore the cause of my strong feelings of dual identity. Dr. Hover suggested I look at the lifetime preceding my birth as Dana Moore. (Incidentally, this regression conflicts with what I had supposed from a previous regression to be my most recent lifetime. But "Home" could be in another space-time frequency, where conceivably three hundred years might equate to six months, Earth-time. Conceivably, I could live an eon at "Home" between lives on Earth.)

Five years after the regression, I transcribed the contents of the tape. And the ET-human link clinked into place. What I heard on the tape did not prove anything, was not a solution of the great mystery; but after listening to it, something inside me was settled.

Something similar happened in the late 1980s when I met my birth father for the first time. I was forty-seven years old and he was in his mid-seventies. The effect of meeting him was like seeing my whole face for the first time. A missing element was slipped into place, the subtle Scots-Irish look now visible in my face alongside the prevalent Danish features.

Listening to the cassette tape, something comparable happened to my inner image. Oddly, it clicked into place at something I had seen in a part of my consciousness that was veiled from mental image (details later). But it was the question of location that had compelled me to find the cassette tape and transcribe it. I listened to myself evade Dr. Hover's question about the name of the other world place three times. The last evasion sounded like a blatant maneuver to sidestep the question. Instead of answering her, I began to speak of seeing *her* in a past life on Earth!

Why did I wait five years before transcribing the tape? The glimpse into a lifetime on another world was of no help to me in 1995. The most active year of the catalyst was 1996, the hardest time. The "memory" seemed irrelevant to the challenge in my very real and present life. I felt no secret security in former world experience or alliances. Should I even believe the inner visions were really memories? The fact that I did not discuss them with friends or family, or even think about them afterward, looks suspicious now. I asked, I probed, I found . . . and I hid it away, like the hidden message in chapter 7. It was not time to focus on the ET link. First I needed to survive the catalyst on my feet, with mind, body, and soul in balance. I needed to understand that this body was the outward portal of the person who emerges in this sphere on a vibration through an organic womb gate. I needed a picture of the birth dynamic as it occurs before the signs of the living embryo are recorded. "Conveniently," I was given information about the birth dynamic of transformation in September

1999 (chapter 16), which helped me consider the former life on another world, not as a "new frill" on my self-identity, but in the light of the transfers or migrations of the evolving soul.

Would examination of the regression material about the former life help shed light on coming events? The main impact of the UFO presence seems to be to awaken social consciousness of the existence of Others, our multi-faceted nature, and the multi-dimensional nature of the cosmos. The fact that not all people have seen UFOs is not a criterion for their non-existence. You know, or you don't know. If you do know, chances are you are in some way involved in the phenomenon. The stern voice comes to mind again: *Yes, there are many who have opted out. They do not want to participate in manifestation. . . . Respect all choices!*

Manifestation of *what*? The coming event may not be as we think of events. It may not be definable by a beginning or end. It may be a change so subtle, it slips in seamlessly, and we may think—this is how it has always been. If so, what of all the fanfare around "preparation"? For some it may be a seamless event, but for others it may be as fantastic as crossing into a new world. In that scenario, maybe it does help to share our other-worldly memories, and our stories about the becoming.

I couldn't always hear Dr. Hover's questions clearly on the tape. I was wearing a lapel mike, so my voice is strong and clear. But I caught enough of her questions to capture the essence.

Dr. Hover regressed me to early childhood, then as an infant in the crib. The crib slats looked like tall pillars. . . .

Hover: Going younger and younger . . . just being born . . .
Redfield: Shocking. I feel so light. I'm screaming. Feel rigid.
　　　　Warm blanket. Sensations . . . oil on body . . . rocking.
Hover: Before she was born . . . is it dark?
Redfield: Don't know dark from light. Slumber is the word.
Hover: Back further, before consciousness joined the tiny baby,
　　　　floating free . . . aware . . . tell me. . . .

Redfield: I'm seeing one of the ancients.

Hover: Are you one of them or just—?

Redfield: Seems I'm overseeing my own birth . . . confusing. I see this curious, very intensely interested tilt of the head. It (*the soul*) goes in on a (*pencil-thin*) light beam, into the womb.

Hover: [*Does the soul*] carry instructions?

Redfield: I don't know if that's the right question.

Hover: A question about awareness . . .

Redfield: I see this entity. Something to do with the birth process, but I'm not able to get the picture. But this entity looks very interested, very involved. Much closer up than on the ship. Right next to her. I don't think I ever looked like that. Maybe. I don't know. (*I sound slightly shocked . . . oh, my gosh, did I look like that? I could not bring the image into pictorial consciousness, but to make that statement, some part of my mind could see the entity I named as "one of the ancients." The surprise in my voice is genuine. The entity was not human.*)

Hover: The entity is helping the consciousness go to the baby?

Redfield: Wish I could see more . . .

Hover: Go back in time . . . before the process starts. . . .

Redfield: I see a bunch of them in robes—gowns. Tall, very tall. I want to say around a table, but I don't think it's a table. Shaped like a spiral table, but probably not what it is. This is a meeting of the council. Seems pretty happy. They don't meet together like we do. They don't do things like we do. There is such an instantaneous communication between them. This is a complex (*soul complex*). I can look at them as separate entities, but their true relationship would be like light globes arranged like a cluster of grapes. It's more how they operate. When I see them conferring as a council, I have to make this picture to comprehend it. They are somehow part of one energy pattern, and they appear as separate entities in order to communicate, because if they were communicating as a complex, it would be way, way, way too fast for us to begin to understand, so they separate out. . . .

Hover: Do you come from . . .

Redfield: I think this is what I aspire to be. I'm not them yet. But I may be a little pet project or something. A child in training. They have many, many children in many ways, so that the entity that aspires to be a part of them must go through the same schools, so to speak, to become that.

Hover: Can you see where you come from?

Redfield: I look like someone . . . like a young man who might be wandering around the Sinai Desert or something. A robe, a male. . . . Where do I come from . . . hmmm. Well, you know, we name all these planets and we think (*chuckle*) that's what they are called (*chuckle*). There's . . . hmmm. There's a place where there are very tall cathedral-like crystal structures. They are like free-standing spires, very tall. (*Resemble upside-down stalagmites.*) This has to do with energy systems. I see like stone palettes or stages. (*The shape of the stones is like an artist's palette, but much larger; the stones seem of a marble quality. Set in the ground, they angle upwards.*) All looks like energy systems. It's very strange, different.

Hover: Is it light?

Redfield: Lots of reds, but that's kind of a background feel to it. Like a dusty red. Crystal structures are filled with like ocean water, bluish. The ground itself is patterned after the waves of the ocean, and the stone part . . . they are like stone palettes, polished, and arranged to look like tops of waves. (*I was moving my arms around to describe.*)

Hover: Are there any beings around?

Redfield: People are sitting on some of the palettes. They're wearing tunics, like an Itzlantia[24] place. This energy system . . . grass is so beautiful. Don't have to mow it. We know how to tell it to grow this way. It's all in cooperation.

---

[24] Itzalantia, a play on the name Atlantis, was an "other world" described in the first version of *Jonah*; the people envisioned here in tunics resembled Rowah.

Hover: Do you feel joy about being born somewhere else?

Redfield: Apprehension! I was a student for too long. I can only grow by entering into the fray.

Hover: Do you have a purpose for coming down? . . .

Redfield: Just further growth. If you want more, you have to go for more. But we don't have goals like we have down on Earth because we know that we don't know where it's going to lead us. To set a goal is to be arrogant. You think you know where you are going . . . the whole purpose is to grow and expand. (*This does not match my feeling of mission; and the UFO presence seems highly goal-oriented.*)

Hover: (*Inaudible question.*)

Redfield: You can decide not to advance. Just be a servant, if that makes you happy. If you aspire to become like the old ones, you have to follow in their foot tracks. So that is the only goal, to become like them. Other than this, you can't plan because you don't know what to expect.

Hover: Do you carry memories from having done this before? (*Having come to Earth before.*)

Redfield: I don't . . . know. . . . (*Conflicts with other regressions to past lives on Earth.*)

Hover: Perhaps they promise you assistance if you go do this process?

Redfield: Oh, yes. But your awareness of the assistance depends. There's always assistance.

Hover: It will be a great adventure. . . . (*Speaking of a life on Earth.*)

Redfield: Yes, but you can get in trouble. It seems necessary that I do this. There are ones down there who are lost. (*Down on Earth.*)

Hover: They don't know why they are doing it. . . .

Redfield: They've forgotten. A lot of us are going down.

Hover: Many?

Redfield: Many, many, many.

Hover: As you go, are you carrying advice or wisdom? . . .

Redfield: You have the wisdom, but can you translate it on the other level?

Hover: So it's not like a solitary thing.

Redfield: Not unless you make it that way. (*If you tune out the assistance.*)

Hover: As you go down the beam of light and enter the fetus in the womb, are there sensations that come to you?

Redfield: (*I laugh.*) My feet just started tingling like crazy. Maybe I'm trying to be born feet first. It's so noisy. Oh, wow, so bright, noisy, chaotic! (*I've been saying that all my life.*)

Hover: Does the consciousness of the infant have any knowledge of—?

Redfield: It is not like in language. It is like on a sensational level. It's . . . the baby knows. The level of knowing is in a deep kind of way that allows for the child to adapt. If the consciousness had . . . if it is a totally foreign experience, the child will have difficulty developing. It brings with it a basic consciousness of life on this level. This is script in the DNA that we speak of. It is akin to the instinct that animals have. They know to suckle. They know to cry for food. This is just inherent knowledge. The child has such inherent knowledge, but he is not thinking like he will learn to think when he learns to process the language. But in the processing of the language, some of the basic information will be covered up to be rediscovered later, and that is that deep knowing of our connection.

Hover: Will this entity who comes down carry a memory or soul or heart recognition when she meets others of her kind?

Redfield: If she does her homework, oh, yes.

Hover: Let your consciousness ask to see if you can determine where you are from. Do you recognize—?
(*Here I shift completely away from the question of location, seeming a blatant maneuver. Possibly I had "assistance."*)

Redfield: Hmmm. . . . I see a band around your head. Hmmm . . .

I see you have on a white gown with gold striping around the midriff, and the pants are kind of . . . more like a toga. Blouses around the legs and comes up . . . crisscrosses on the feet. The band . . . diamond shaped . . . gold around here. (*I was gesturing.*) I'm seeing this in Egypt, but we didn't call it Egypt back then. It's back in that area.

Hover: Were we friends?

Redfield: I'm watching you walk very swiftly through this stone structure. I think you are male in that one.

Hover: Where are we?

Redfield: Structure like a palace. A living place. Definitely elite.

Hover: You were there too? Try to get a fix on it.

Redfield: I feel like I'm an older woman with gray hair. Hmmm. I feel like this is my son. Impetuous!

Hover: You're the mother?

Redfield: I think so. Very old. It's all I see.

(*Dr. Hover suggested next that we look at a possible life that has bearing on the current UFO activity.*)

Redfield: Whoa! I have on a skullcap with a widow peak, and I'm in a vehicle, just spinning! You put your legs around this instrument, hold on, and you just go with this machine. (*The instrument is like a lever that extends up from the floor. The vehicle is not much larger than I am; it seems mostly glass, and is egg-shaped. I see myself as a fully grown male with dark widow-peaked hair, and wearing a skin-tight body suit.*)

Hover: Are you traveling fast?

Redfield: Yeah, just spinning! Spin down this tunnel. It's an energy tunnel. You can't see it. Visually it would look like you disappeared.

Hover: You're off in this energy tunnel . . .

Redfield: Man, it's fun! You can swing from one side to the other—it's incredible! Pilot . . . hmmm. This is a . . . I'm watching the air waves. Guardian of the air waves? Keeping an eye on things. Like a security guy. Watching actual portals and things. . . .

Hover: Pretty responsible job.

Redfield: (*Laugh.*) You like guard the gates. Not a real high . . .
this is more like true adventure.

Hover: A chance to see what passes through . . .

Redfield: Very important but not very high, just . . .

Hover: Can you observe? . . .

Redfield: Just saw a fleet of ships in formation. I must know the
laws. This is pretty otherworldly.

The land of crystal spires filled with blue ocean water feels
like home . . . a very old home. Although there is a deep sense
of connection, I feel no emotional pull to this world, except for
a longing to return to a "teaching temple." But no feelings of
urgency. Maybe emotions as we experience them are a peculiarity of humankind. Another viewpoint is that we are both the
ancient ones and the children of Earth, always making ourselves
new. Think about it. What do immortals do for eternity?

But I did feel fully "present" in the glass-like vehicle, swinging across the air waves, watching the portals, zipping down
energy tunnels. I was laughing, feeling the joy. True memory?
Imagination? Where do we draw the line? The body is the line.
Here I am down on Earth.

Most outstanding was the look at the "tilted head" of the
entity, which I could not "show" to my daylight mind. For days
after listening to the tape and remembering what I had viewed,
I was fascinated by the image of what I could not see. This
sounds like a contradiction, but it is not. In *some* part of my
mind, the picture of the entity who helped in the birth event is
registered. Perhaps in a deeper trance state I could bring up the
image, but I don't feel it's important that I do. Always I have felt
that I should use hypnotic regressing sparingly in the investigation of my experiences. I am about the business of expanding
consciousness. Delving into the sub- or super-conscious may
help or hinder. My guiding principle is that my mind is my own
responsibility. The fewer professionals in the process, the better

for me, the more authentic my discoveries, the more *mine*. But I do much appreciate the help and support I have been given. Together we explore. . . .

The question looms: Why did I evade Dr. Hover's question about the location of this world? I chuckled about our names for planets, evading the question three times.

I see the cosmos, inner and outer, like a spiral in flux. This is an abstract concept to describe my vision. Each world is on a particular loop in the in-out fluxing spiral, and on some of the loops are worlds like Earth. At different stages of evolution, souls migrate across the spiral, in and out of worlds. The migrations are across such space and time designations as are constructed for each world to be "self-sustaining," as we are embodied individually on this planet. All of the principles of creation are embodied in each being, for each to evolve and discover, for each to become a creator, after the likeness of that which creates, and is Creation.

I'm not sure why I evaded naming the world I viewed. Definitely I feel it is not a world we could travel to in a mechanical ship. If space-time continuums are loops, does reincarnation happen both ways? Did I reincarnate from a future Earth? Is this the secret I guard? And still I want to connect this world viewed with Atlantis. . . .

But something is settled in me. Roll of drums, sound of trumpets. There is something ET about me. But I am nonplussed, gazing again at my human face in the mirror. So what if I'm ET? If I am, it must be true for all humans, because I am as human as anyone. But why the deep taboo against knowing the ET link? From all the various communications, I suspect there is a battle royal in hidden realms over the children of Earth. Some don't want a new tree. Or for us to see. . . .

Fascination with ET roots is natural but may distract from anchoring light on this, our real and present world. The question remains: What is a human being?

Where is home? I feel at home among these clunky red rock mountains surrounded by desert, and more at home high in the forested Rocky Mountains. There is a favorite memory perhaps, a cold place with white mists so crisp they almost talk, parting to announce naked mountain peaks striped with snow . . . a glimpse of a monastery. Beyond, the ocean is spread out forever like a vast dark blue satin cape, so calm, so cold, so old in my mind. There are many memories like this, Earth ports, I think, revisited by my soul, like curling up with a fine old book filled with living pictures inside the pages like secret windows.

My body feels these memories like gentle fingers stroking my skin. In my mind and heart, the land and the people are merged in a mystical blend. We live in Mother's energy fields, pulled and prodded by her light fiber fingers, like living puppets dancing across her body.

Souls . . . ETs . . . humans . . . together we are dancing on the becoming edge.

CHAPTER SIXTEEN:

Golden Children—or
Becoming Buck Rogers?

Metaphors do not walk on Earth, but thoughts create reality, students in the nursery school of Infinite Wisdom remind us. Yes, thoughts create; but what is the quality of the matter thoughts create? Do the thoughts of human beings create mansions more substantial than the House in which the Spirit dwells? What happens when light of a more powerful vibration penetrates these thought constructs?

It is nearly devastating to wake up with a mind of your own, with eyes that see the charades, with ears that can hear the false notes in the "official stories," while voices like harp strings strum from the deep, speaking Other Wisdom in a language only the soul understands. Whom shall I listen to, the human voices of authority and all their minions, or shall I heed the voices from the deep?

What is a human being? Clad in its flesh-and-bone costume, the body moves on the land, the eyes of the soul ever glancing skyward, as if beckoned by Sun, Moon, planets, and stars to lift off, come home, end your life as an animal bound by gravity, and addicted to sensory pleasure. Children of the stars, remember your home and why you came here—to indulge in the pleasure and beauty of this world? Or was your mission grander than the lure of showing off your creative genius to build up one more empire only to destroy it again because your spirit cannot abide? Children of the stars, it is time to remember your choice.

In our very minds is a doorway that in some is only a slender beam of light, while in others is closed so tightly, darkness is all they know beyond the flame of fire and the electric lights on the material plane. But in many, many, many, the doorway is expanded—light out to the arms outstretched and beyond—light fibers pulsating from hands connecting with other human links. The Light Tree is complete and cannot be broken. But when will all see it? When we are done playing King of the Mountain? When the Isle of Forgetfulness collapses into the sea and the dragon is set free?

I am writing this book to give a voice to other ET-humans. To let you know you are not the only one who suspects that you are more than human—not of this world. That phrase—not of this world—first chimed from the Bible as the words of Jesus Christ. But did he mean not of this Earth? Or not of this foreign world created by the spellbound and ruled by the archons of Gnostic legends? Stories, stories . . . but why do we think our current stories are truer than the ancient ones? Is there a sign that the human being has evolved, has made leaps in wisdom, now sees reality through the dark glass of illusion? Now are we waking from the dream, seeing in every human being the face of the Divine? Are we there-here-now; do we finally see that our souls are linked in the Light Tree? Is the "World of Illumination" merely a fancy of the Native or new ager trying to make sense of a reality so quickly changing we hardly have time to glance in the mirror, much less contemplate who might be watching from behind the silver?

The wonder child wishes to speak, to show herself. If you show me yours, I will show you mine. Remember the antics of the human child discovering the awesome secret between the legs? But now we are spiritual adults. Or so was the plan. The energy between the legs was to have moved up through the body to burst in a light flower in the crown. Now just looking at our magnificent opposite—male or female—we feel the love vibration pulsating through the whole body. But who taught us of our source energy, much less what we were supposed to do with it? There have been teachers—are teachers—silenced by a religious majority who knew better, or the scientific minds who couldn't care less. There is too much to explore in the external world, no time for the internal. Out—out is where *it* is thought to be—whatever it is they seek; it must be grasped by the hands, poked, thoroughly examined, proved to be real.

In this chapter are some "far out" ideas and images I have done my best to clarify. But still the words are densely packed in places; maybe work for minds trained to flit at the speeding, fleeting words on the mechanical screens, images screaming, voices soothing or commanding, telling us where to put our money. The wonder child scribbles with Crayola while the Goliaths of business hurl lightning rod words at the audiences planted before metal-enclosed glass screens, glaring, blaring, windows on the real world. Or so it is claimed.

Reality check: Do not underestimate the power of anchoring even a tiny beam of light. Every soul link shines a beacon from the lighthouse, showing the way for humans lost and tossed on the tumultuous waves in the upheaval of the castle collapsing. . . .

The story of *The Golden Scroll* that began this book is like the experience of some who encounter alien intelligences. We have profound experiences and are conduits for messages, but in the process of trying to fulfill our "missions," much is garbled in the translation.

Evangeline was shocked at the message the king read aloud: "Free my people." She remembered it as a prophecy about the birth of golden children. Everyone was invited to attend the birth of these children, even peasants. Of course, the king and queen would be invited, which in Evangeline's mind explained the reason for the golden scroll and the angel's instruction for her to deliver it to them. But, not only were the words different from what the angel had voiced, they were written on common paper, not a golden scroll.

Lost on both Evangeline and Terrence was the metaphor of the governing force in the world, the Isle of Forgetfulness, which was guarded by a dragon in the Moat of Memory surrounding the island. But Terrence perceived something of it in his comment about the king and queen forgetting the golden rule—do unto others as you would have them do unto you. While he could not articulate the link between the golden rule and the golden children, Terrence intuitively sensed the underlying meaning: "Don't you see? The world is a mix of royals and paupers, and those that lust for the one, and not the other . . . never seeing the wonders that be, the very golden faces shining everywhere with the secret that will not keep. . . . Ah it was a merry tinkering, inviting the royals to remember that people *are* free!"

Later Evangeline would envision the Isle of Forgetfulness collapsing into the sea, which she associated with the eventual births of the golden children. But it was hard for her to consider that maybe the golden children would be born in a prosaic time-unfolding way. It was Terrence who saw the magic in stories imbued with power by the profound events surrounding them.

Every "metafractal" in my own experience worked to encourage me to tell my story, even if the messages conveyed are so distorted in the communication transfer that they seem as glitterless as the paper inside the sheath Evangeline carried to the castle in the faith that she was chosen as an emissary.

The message about the golden children in this chapter may be as lost on the "rulers" of our current time, as was the blunt instruction to the king and queen: "Free my people." Let go of your rulership to make way for the birth of the golden children. Explicit in the story is the truth that people are free in the deepest reality of our being. Bold spirits who dare enter the Moat of Memory discover the great secret: The true gold is *in us*.

Long have we been Evangelines and Terrences, minding stories of seizing sovereignty from controlling powers by castles collapsing into seas; or by wars, after which the victors assume the royal robes, perpetuating the cycles of freedom, chasing control forever like a dog running in circles trying to swallow its tail.

The information about the golden children came at the end of a conversation that began with me asking Guidance one of those "why" questions that evoked a complex response. I will spare you the lengthy discussion that led to a prophecy so outlandish it caused me to probe deeper on another day, trying to get clarity on the fantastic statements about us and the golden soul children.

First the prophecy, then the results of the probe to clarify:

> As always, as a species, you are working to master certain principles and develop certain endowments. Now is a "time" when you are challenged to bring to awareness your powers of will. Naturally you see behavior at extreme poles of conflict, as human beings experiment with choices. Now is a time for the exercising of patience, tolerance, and compassion by long-experienced souls, as you watch less-evolved souls experiment with the poles of choices and their consequences.
>
> Now is the time to anchor yourselves in the time-tested principles you know work for balance and harmony in cooperation with the laws of nature. For in this seeming frenzy of competition for supremacy, the Earth doth seem to rock and heave, as if to shake loose of her moorings.
>
> See it as a woman in the throes of labor as she strains to give birth to a child. For indeed you are experiencing birth pangs, as you strain in faith to bring forth the golden children who are the souls you have labored to create. But it is not by faith alone that a birth occurs. And it is not by exertion alone that the child emerges.

The miracle happens through a synthesis of exertion and faith in time-tested principles, such as loving thy neighbor as yourselves.

You shall know them by their fruits.

(Me: And what of those who are still spellbound?)

A test of your maturity is your patience, tolerance, and compassion, and the exercising of your will to serve the cause of development of all souls to maturity.

To develop your wills in concert, it will be necessary to bring your awareness up out of the shadows cast over your minds by long development in conditions of spellboundedness.

Yes, there will be conflicts as you join to develop the endowments of will, through the expanding of your awareness.

Yes, you will be challenged and tested as to your readiness to become the stewards of Earth.

Yes, there are battles to come, as you labor to bring forth this child of the new consciousness.

Yes, this is a prophecy that speaks to the establishment of the Kingdom of God on Earth, whose constituents are the souls you have labored to develop and give birth to on this plane.

Yes, the Earth is your home, the place you chose as choice for the birth of the golden children, your souls matured, ready to begin a new epoch of experience.

(Me: Are the golden children perfected souls?)

Perfection is an ever-changing ideal, as life is ever-evolving, and ever-reaching for new heights of experience and creation.

It will be devastating for some to learn that ye are gods come down to this Earth to evolve through human beingness to become stewards of this paradise of creation.

Go ahead, let yourselves be devastated. Such devastations are the beginning of understanding.

Rejoice. Ye were created in love, ye live by love, and so it shall be forevermore. Awaken so that ye may know and experience the depth and breadth of your minds and souls.

Quicken ye together to form the councils of will, that ye may begin the work of harmonization and restoration.

Prepare ye the way for the golden children to be born to the paradise ye will all together create. For that is your legacy—to create a home for your souls, and all the living creatures born to your care.

Awaken, quicken, hasten, for the Great Mystery will soon burst from the shell to reveal the golden child—when the becoming meets the now in a convulsion of ecstasy.

Adonai, we are El, faithful to the Law of One.

The second probe was a reach to a tier of mind where I had to stretch and massage words to shape them into pictures that would reveal something beyond the limits of definition. My notes were clumsy and searching, until I tuned in and the El clarified. Or is it clarity? Maybe it compounds the mystery. For me it provided a picture of sorts of the birth dynamic.

Birth of the Golden Children

Notes: We begin as seeds. . . . Plants come up out of soil, and are sustenance. . . . The leap in evolution was a leap from the water to the surface ground. The essence was freedom from attachment to womb Earth, like walls of the womb flipping inside-out. Seed grows attached to a wall by the umbilical cord. Then we surge out of the womb to move freely in space. Beyond the second sphere (mother's womb), the force of gravity defines our boundaries. Free from confinement of mother's womb, we walk upon the source womb (Earth), or we construct vehicles to transport us beyond the pull of gravity.

The human mother's womb is a strange new environment, but designed for comfort. The fetus has no concept of a world beyond until it is expelled into this sphere of wonder and magnitude. The newborn baby must be nurtured slowly to adapt to this environment.

We now have mobilization in the third sphere (on the surface of Earth bounded by gravity), but we are still dependent on the source womb for sustenance. We must eat of the source womb, suckle Mother Earth's breast, while we are experiencing mobilization in the third sphere.

This sphere we call "on Mother Earth," and beyond we call "Outer Space." Beyond Mother are infinite spheres in gradations bounded by forces like the force of gravity. To go beyond, we depend on sophisticated machines, fueled by manipulations of Mother's chemical resources.

The symbol of the free-floating flower represents our next birth into the fifth dimension, which is accessed in the fourth dimension, as it was true that we had to enter an interim sphere (human mother's womb), before we could be born in the third sphere.

In other words, exploration of outer space is exploration of the fourth dimension. (This statement strains the metaphysical notion of the fourth dimension being an "astral plane." Perhaps the astral is one dynamic of the dimension named as the fourth here.)

(Below, the telepathic connection sharpens.)

Though we travel in the fourth sphere by means of rocket ships, our base is not the ship. We are Earth's organic creatures, entering homemade flying wombs to protect us in the environment beyond. In this way, we are now exploring the womb that is the fourth sphere, erroneously thinking this sphere is all that is, extending outward away from the Earth into the reaches of "space."

But the fourth sphere "curls" round to form a sphere unseen by human eyes, which are made to focus on the Earth sphere, and the surrounding fourth sphere that we call outer space or the heavens.

As your most advanced minds know, the force that must be mastered is that of anti-gravity in order to burst the boundaries of the fourth sphere or dimension. This writer does not have the language of how this is accomplished in scientific terms. Our scientific knowledge is bounded by our understanding of the laws of the third and fourth spheres. Access to the fifth sphere requires new understanding, new language. Metaphor or symbol is the mediative language between these spheres as our consciousness expands.

This is the correct track: To comprehend that our next birth and migration is by way of our minds. Now, our minds will be as our bodies were in the third and fourth spheres. Our self-awareness is now as attached to our bodies as we are to the Earth by the force of gravity. Just as we must create vehicles to launch ourselves into mobility in the fourth sphere, we must create vehicles in the mind to access the fifth sphere to explore the world into which we will be born next.

In this way, the "alien spaceships" in your skies are both symbolic of what many of you are doing in the realm of mind—monitoring, penetrating, interacting—and also they are emissaries from the fifth realm, midwives preparing you for birth.

The difficulty in comprehending them as both reflections of you, and midwives for your birth, equates to the confusion and disorientation of the fetus that is expelled from the womb. Inside the womb, the (human) fetus knows its mother in one way. Outside (after birth), the baby is wonderstruck—has no comprehension yet of its relationship to Mother; is not aware that the breast it suckles is of the same mother it knew in the womb.

From our perspective, the baby moves from an internal to an external world. From the baby's perspective, it moved from its source world to "outer space," where it encounters an alien being, the mother, who has complete control over it.

The womb being prepared is in the mental sphere, which we do not see with our outward focused eyes. Metaphor is the only language to approach description. But as the baby in the mother's womb is "hard-wired" with language that it will master after born, so our minds contain the means to communicate and understand life in the fifth sphere.

Metaphor and imagination—the ability to observe images in the mind—constitute an interim mode of communication. As you are being prepared now to enter the new sphere of existence, so the baby was prepared in the womb of its mother. You lack no fewer resources for preparation. But you will not be able to fully comprehend the fifth sphere until you are born into it, and are nurtured and guided as the baby experiences birth and childhood here.

The metaphor that represents the newborns into the fifth realm is "golden children." Your closest comprehension is the soul. Long nurtured in the womb of the third realm, now your "souls" are experiencing transition into the fourth realm, in preparation for birth into the fifth—a totally alien environment, from your current position and perception.

The purpose of this book is to provide a metaphorical bridge from third sphere concepts, across the fourth gulf to the glass-like veil, or door between spheres. You cannot yet cross the threshold in body, but you can imagine—picture the world beyond—and you can listen to those who have voyaged there in transitory forms.

Birth into the next sphere is not an achievement you can accomplish by will and exertion. As the baby in the mother's womb, you are being prepared. Some are actively participating in the preparation, some are aware that a preparation is in progress, but many are not aware. Not all will be born into the fifth sphere at the approaching birth juncture. Some will repeat cycle(s) in the third sphere.

Readiness for migration is determined by factors of which you are not aware in your current sphere of existence, though you understand some of the factors in metaphorical equivalence, such as the instruction to love one another as you love yourselves. Love is a mystery you have aspired to understand in body and mind. The soul that will be born understands in the language of the fifth sphere, for here is another mystery, a paradox: While as human beings you are foreigners to the fifth sphere, it is the very home from which you migrated to Earth, and will return. The mystery is one of the soul acquiring the raiment of immortality through experience in the third and fourth realms.

In your linear thinking, a journey from fifth to fourth to third is backwards, or devolution, or a "fall." But reality is like the figure eight, cross-looped, with no real separation between loops, only crosspoints. The symbol of the ankh represents awareness of the "spiritual realm," while you are "stemmed" on Earth. The line at the top of the stem of the ankh is the threshold between spheres of existence.

Another mystery: The outer space you aspire to explore, the planets you see, are like shells of the worlds they really are. Exploration of these worlds and interactions with their inhabitants can only occur in reality from the fifth realm, into which many of you are preparing to migrate in a birthing event.

Adonai, Adonai, we are El, emissaries and midwives, servants of the Law of ONE.

Or Buck Rogers Becoming?

My novel *Jonah* is a modern-day hero's journey. But instead of acquiring a Holy Grail or some other material prize, the test for Jonah is to bring back *himself*. After his unusual abduction, and adventure on another world, Jonah experiences an existential crisis at the portal of return, a novelistic approach to the question: What is a human being? Jonah must cross a threshold between spirit and matter to walk again as a man on Earth. Paradoxically, as a man at the portal in the "Land of Doubles," he cannot cross alone. A "midwife" (his soul counterpart) appears to transport him across the chasm.

I believe the alien abduction phenomenon is a forerunner to a mass event of a kind that will radically change our concept of ourselves—a kind of birth event. The task of the messenger is to help shift the mind away from the "womb body" to lessen the shock it will be to meet our "Other." The human becoming is both midwife and golden child, say the El, a mystery impossible to fully grasp until we experience crossing the threshold.

I feel the vision of the "elegant ET" is part of my preparation to meet my "other" at the portal of transformation when the wonder child will emerge from the spiritual alchemy of the human dissolving into the soul. Sounds like death? This time we are supposed to cross with the body, perhaps in a new vehicle we have been gestating in the dimension of mind.

While embodied as men and women, most of us have been virtually asleep to our soul link to the Creator. Deep, deep into the human journey, we are being called to remember our soul link, and to prepare to meet Ourselves in the Other. Without preparation, such a meeting can be terrifying—like abduction by an alien.

Or are the skeptics right?

The champions of external creation, so proud of the rocket ship, scoff at us who claim astral travel. It's "all in your minds," they say. And they put a man or a woman in a man-made simulated rocket ship seat, and they push buttons to simulate physical flight, and this is supposed to fool the man or the woman into thinking that he or she is experiencing actual flight. This experiment was aired on TV to show that pilots also experience the delusion of leaving their bodies; and, while in simulated flight, they hallucinate "aliens." These demonstrations are used to dismiss near-death experiences, as well as reports of ET encounters as "all in the mind." The demonstrators apparently think the mind is all in the head. When they say mind, they mean the brain inside the skull. The rocket ships they make are like flying skulls. The makers seem unable to conceive of flight out of the body; nonetheless the dream of ascending is in them, too, so they create replicas of the body, like sleek metal birds. They call it technology.

How awestruck we all were, October 4, 1957, when *Sputnik I* was launched and the space age officially began. Billions of heads cocked up, eyes gazing at a human miracle orbiting the Earth in Heaven's dimension. The dream was contagious—man becoming Buck Rogers. (Or was that man becoming Orson

Welles?) In any event, it was a twist on the wisdom of Hermes—as above, so below. It seems we are out to prove the opposite is true. We seem hell-bent to traject the below to the above. From ground up, we mean to create our own heavenly abodes, to hell with the old mystical dreams of Heaven floating down as a golden city to settle atop our toxic heaps. To hell with the gods of old. Now we see the dream—man becoming God. From our flying dream machines, it was a logical leap, for who created these technological marvels? Consulting Einstein's brain in a jar, *Homo sapiens* can reach Heaven. All eyes on Mars now, the face of Man staring back. Quick, erase that, can't be, that's backwards. The dream is man becoming the Martian, not the reverse. It was a trick of the light, we were told. There can be no old crumbled pyramids on Mars, for we did not construct them. Man is becoming God, not the reverse . . . *man discovering he is God*. That is problematic for the technical mind confined to a brain. What god would choose to occupy a body that dies in Nature's season, dust to dust?

The vision tinkers. To become the god of modern man's dream, bodies are required—a perpetual succession of bodies emergent from organic wombs, human links on a chain gang imprisoned on the ground. Linked to Infinite Mind, the human mind has no limits, except the beliefs that clip the wings of the bird of creation. Where there is a will, there is a way. In the brain-mind of modern man, there must be a body to become the god of the Great Dream. Human wombs are fast becoming endangered. Petri dishes emerge in sync with knowledge gained about the secrets of DNA. Minds twist in brains to focus on the vision: clones, robots, biomachine man to pilot the cosmic metal egg enclosing the god becoming. Now the mystical dream of bringing Heaven down to Earth is all but sugar plums dancing in the heads of peasants. Hermes be damned. We have seen the light—ET becoming. Prometheus, choke on your fire.

Not so fast, human. Slow down, Buck. Before we make of this world a junkyard to fulfill our dream of god becoming to conquer and trash another planet, ought not we to know ourselves as we are? Did Nature create the modern brain to discover the way to escape the very garden from which the human has barely found his legs out of the water? Did Nature create the billions of intricate life forms that compose the garden just as food and resource for the human being to consume and exploit to escape this world to build another, from the ground up, to the next Heaven beckoning?

Man dreams and creates forms to match the visions in his mind. But Buck Rogers never dreamed beyond a brain in half darkness. Buck was a virtual stranger to his mirror opposite, woman, the feminine principle. Buck knew not woman, except as handmaiden to his voyage to become God. A beard was on the old god; the new one is bald, with a head large enough to contain Einstein's brain and then some. We seem unable to dream a god except that he is the image of Man. Enlarging the eyes would surely expand the vision. But what is this story of large almond eyes staring a captive human down to his soul? Who scripted this distortion in the dream sky god that he would look *into* us?

What are these emotions, this fear, this quaking, this awe that grips the heart when the alien eyes stare? What in our minds did we create? Did we not kill the old gods good enough to escape this ET ogre who gazes down on us paralyzed on a table? Thou preparest a table for me in the midst of mine enemies? Out of the Bible into our heads, minds turned inside-out to meet our makers in the images of robotic fetuses on feet? Some with cloven hooves—that's a nice touch.

Are the skeptics right? All in my mind? My mind flew the coop of the brain. The door was opened, and I flew, soul soaring free of the bones. But though I fly in memory's chamber, enfolding in the silver seam to glimpse Home away from home, I am still daughter of Earth by some mad design. They summoned, They whisked me up, They made their marks on my hands, triangles cut into my skin to show me the body is a divine link, a temporal home away from Home for my soul who remembers what I the human have forgotten, except as I can translate the signs.

Living double is to see the double exposure, the body reflecting the soul in a world above manifesting below. If you want to go out, go in. But remember—no one goes in except by way of the heart. The way is not up from the genitals to the head in bypass of the heart to reign in the lofts of the brain. By what genius would we be visited by beings who resemble fetuses grotesquely larger than any human woman could contain in her belly? Could these be astral tricksters mirroring our mental leap ahead of ourselves? Or a space age distortion of the Holy Birth story? What are these frail and hideous hybrids . . . breed of men and women copulating in the head to birth the dream of man conquering space? Can the mind nurtured by love do better? Light is the stuff of which our souls are made, Love vibrating to make the Tree of Life.

Light workers do not seek escape from home. We make home.

Dancing on the Becoming Edge

As I was finishing this book, two seasoned UFO investigators came to visit . . . new friends. I was updated on the continuing down-to-Earth saga of UFO sightings, multiple abductions, cattle mutilations, crop circles, conspiracy intrigues, secret projects to penetrate "stargates," advances in the back-engineering of alien spaceships to build anti-gravity vehicles (if true). . . .

After a late dinner, as we left a restaurant, pausing to gaze up at the symphony of stars, Ryan said, "By the way, we're government agents."

"Yeah, sure," I quipped. "I'm sure the government is very interested in a woman out on a remote desert, writing about the love vibration."

"Love . . . that's what it's all about, isn't it?" Ryan said, stopping me in my tracks. *Did he "tap" my conversation with Rowah?* Ridiculous. No, it was just the latest synchronicity, a sign I was in good company.

Drawn by the turn in conversation, Steve stepped closer. Now we were talking. Both men confessed to have been driven to pursue the UFO mystery since they were kids. What drives us? Can't remember who said it, but we all agreed: We do the work and take the risks for the love of humanity.

Lots of excellent company these days. Old relationships mended and strengthened, new friends all over the States and abroad. I am in correspondence with researcher/investigator/ amateur astronomer Gary Anthony in England, who is gathering symbols and other communication devices, possibly languages, reported by ET-UFO experiencers for a database. (If you have symbols and related information you are willing to share, contact him. E-mail: garyant@mithrand.karoo.co.uk, or write to Gary Anthony, 39 Barnetby Road, First Lane, Hessle, East Yorkshire, England, HU13 9HE.)

Anthony put me in touch with Mary Rodwell of Perth, Australia. She is an R.N., therapist, researcher, and principal of ACERN (Australian Close Encounter Resource Network—e-mail: starline@iinet.net.au). Mary is a pioneer heart, actively helping a group of abductees and "star children" to find their feet on the becoming vibration. These people are doing work similar to what I did with letters and numbers, but they have taken it much further. With Rodwell as director, Bradley DeNise as producer, and musical director/composer, David Sandercock, the artists and experiencers made a video called *Expressions of ET Contact, a Visual Blueprint?* I was stunned not only by the art, but by certain pictures of ETs that were like drawings I had made. More links connecting in the spirit of "we are the message."

The video helped in a special way. Feeling that my mother would enjoy the art, I invited her to watch *Expressions* with me. She saw my tears when the image of a particular lion man (drawn by Jane) came on the screen, and as the art began showing, I reached into a box and brought up art I had done to show Mother the similarity. And she saw, she really saw; finally she *got it.* Got that the UFO presence is real? She got that something inexplicable is happening in consciousness. She knew I had not been in contact with the Australian experiencers seven years ago when I produced similar artwork. This was evidence for Mother that this business was not all in my mind—the way we have thought about mind. We are coming to see that mind is not the brain, but is a domain—a dimension that contains the body vessel and the brain control tower. . . .

Mystery and Paradox dance the Eternal Jig on the becoming edge.

Jesus said we must be as children to enter the kingdom of God. With so many still asleep in the womb of forgetfulness, the world can seem a foreign place to a child of new consciousness.

Are we ET-humans? Or humans, awakening?

Child of the Womb of Forgetfulness
Born of
Father Genius and
Mother Love,
Wisdom shall be your
First name acquired by the
Trials of Experience
Made by the Will and
Honed on the stones of
Desire.
Child born of the Womb of Forgetfulness,
Memory is your middle name.
By genius your father guides you,
By love your mother nurtures you
That you shall know your Face
In the mirror
Handcrafted by your soul.
It was the plan
That you would live many lives
In mystery, and yes,
In sorrow and pain,
That your last name would be
Compassion.
When the bough breaks
And you fall,
Get up and walk,

And never forget
You may lie down in
Green pastures,
And beside still waters,
To remember that
We are with you
For all the days of your
Lives.
Adonai. We are El.

For last, a response to a question I have posed many times:

"You asked, 'What are the stakes?' In any event, physical or metaphysical, the stakes are the same. The soul is in journey, and throughout there are multiple 'dramas' and schemes and intents of will; and your insurance against *real* manipulation is to seek to live by the signals from the 'heart.' This is your closest connection to that which is love—or God, or Great Spirit—your highest concept of goodness, mercy, truth, justice, joy, freedom, beauty, and well-being. The way to these qualities is always open to all who seek them. Seeking any or all of them, you cannot go wrong."

Thank you Jesus, Rowah, El, readers, and all souls who helped make this book a reality. Together, we create!

Selected References

Armstrong, Karen. 2000. *The Battle for God*, New York, Alfred A. Knopf, Random House.

Briggs, John and F. David Peat. 1985. *Turbulent Mirror: An Illustrated Guide to Chaos Theory and the Science of Wholeness*. New York: Harper and Row.

Campbell, Joseph. 1972. *The Hero's Journey*. Princeton, NJ: Princeton University Press.

Capra, Fritjof. 2000. *The Tao of Physics*. 4th ed. Boston: Shambhala.

DeVoto, Bernard. 1997. *Mark Twain's America*. Bison Books Edition, Lincoln, NE: University of Nebraska Press.

Elkins, Don. 1991. *The Law of One*. Atglen, PA: Schiffer Publishing, Ltd.

Ereira, Alan. 1993. *The Elder Brothers*. New York: Vantage Books.

Expressions of ET Contact, a Visual Blueprint? ACERN Video. Director: Mary Rodwell.

Flem-Ath, Rand and Rose. 1995. *When the Sky Fell: In Search of Atlantis*. New York: St. Martin's Press.

Lilly, John C. 1972. *The Center of the Cyclone: An Autobiography of Inner Space*. New York: Julian Press

Mack, John E. 1995. *Abduction: Human Encounters with Aliens*. New York: Ballantine Books.

———. 1999. *Passport to the Cosmos: Human Transformation and Alien Encounters.* New York: Crown Publishers.

Narby, Jeremy. 1998. *The Cosmic Serpent: DNA and the Origins of Knowledge.* New York: Jeremy P. Tarcher/Putnam.

Ra (spirit), J.A. McCarty, J. Allen, D. Elkins, and C. Reuckert. 1984. *The Ra Material.* Atglen, PA: Schiffer Publishing, Ltd.

Robinson, James M., ed. 1990. *The Nag Hammadi Library.* San Francisco: Harper.

Ross, A.C. 1997. *Mitakuye Oyasin "We are All Related."* Denver, CO: Wicóne Wasté.

Sams, Jamie. 1991. *Other Council Fires Were Here Before Ours.* San Francisco: HarperSanFrancisco.

Sheldrake, Rupert. 1994. *The Rebirth of Nature: The Greening of Science and God.* Rochester, VT: Park Street Press.

Sitchin, Zecharia. 1990. *Genesis Revisited.* Santa Fe, NM: Bear and Company.

———. 1991. *The 12th Planet.* Santa Fe, NM: Bear and Company.

Strieber, Whitley. 1988. *Communion.* Boston: G.K. Hall.

Swartz, Gary and Linda Russek. 1999. *The Living Energy Universe.* Charlottesville, VA: Hampton Roads Publishing Company, Inc

Turner, Karla. 1994. *Taken: Inside the Alien-Human Abduction Agenda.* Roland, AR: Kelt Works.

———. 1992. *Into the Fringe.* N.p. Berkely Pub Group.

Vallee, Jacques. 1991. *Revelations: Alien Contact and Human Deception.* New York: Ballantine Books.

Waters, Frank. 1977. *Book of the Hopi.* New York: Penguin Group.

Watson, Lyall. 1991. *Gifts of Unknown Things: A True Story of Nature, Healing, and Initiation from Indonesia's "Dancing Island."* Rochester, VT: Destiny Books.

About the Author

Dana Redfield was born in California and raised in Utah, Wyoming, Texas, and Oklahoma. She attended Northeastern State College in Oklahoma, and Brigham Young University in Utah.

Redfield lives and writes in southeastern Utah. She is an accomplished novelist and *The ET-Human Link* is her second published work of nonfiction.

Hampton Roads Publishing Company

. . . for the evolving human spirit

Hampton Roads Publishing Company
publishes books on a variety of subjects,
including metaphysics, health, integrative medicine,
visionary fiction, and other related topics.

For a copy of our latest catalog, call toll-free
(800) 766-8009, or send your name and address to:

Hampton Roads Publishing Company, Inc.
1125 Stoney Ridge Road
Charlottesville, VA 22902

e-mail: hrpc@hrpub.com
www.hrpub.com